ADVANCES IN LIBRARY ADMINISTRATION AND ORGANIZATION

ADVANCES IN LIBRARY ADMINISTRATION AND ORGANIZATION

Series Editors: James M. Nyce, Janine Golden and
Delmus E. Williams

Recent Volumes:

ADVANCES IN LIBRARY ADMINISTRATION AND
ORGANIZATION VOLUME 27

ADVANCES IN LIBRARY ADMINISTRATION AND ORGANIZATION

EDITED BY

WILLIAM GRAVES III
Bryant University, Smithfield, RI, USA

JAMES M. NYCE
Ball State University, Muncie, IN, USA

JANINE GOLDEN
Texas Woman's University, Denton, Texas, USA

DELMUS E. WILLIAMS
University of Akron, Akron, Ohio, USA

Emerald

JAI

United Kingdom – North America – Japan
India – Malaysia – China

JAI Press is an imprint of Emerald Group Publishing Limited
Howard House, Wagon Lane, Bingley BD16 1WA, UK

First edition 2009

Copyright © 2009 Emerald Group Publishing Limited

Reprints and permission service
Contact: booksandseries@emeraldinsight.com

British Library Cataloguing in Publication Data
A catalogue record for this book is available from the British Library

ISBN: 978-1-84855-710-9
ISSN: 0732-0671 (Series)

Awarded in recognition of
Emerald's production
department's adherence to
quality systems and processes
when preparing scholarly
journals for print

INVESTOR IN PEOPLE

CONTENTS

LIST OF CONTRIBUTORS

Hermina G.B. Anghelescu	School of Library and Information Science, Wayne State University, Detroit, MI, USA
Aleksei S. Asvaturov	Department of National Literatures (Non-Slavic Literatures) of the Russian National Library, St. Petersburg, Russia
Svetlana Breca	Information Resource Center, US Embassy Pristina, Kosovo
Catherine Closet-Crane	School of Library and Information Management, Emporia State University, Emporia, Kansas, USA
Susan Dopp	School of Library and Information Management, Emporia State University, Emporia, Kansas, USA
Miroslaw Gorny	Department of Information Systems, Institute of Linguistics, Adam Mickiewicz University of Poznan, Poznan, Poland
Maria Haigh	School of Information Studies, University of Wisconsin-Milwaukee, Milwaukee, WI, USA
Stanley Kalkus	Institute of Information Studies and Librarianship, Faculty of Philosophy, Charles University, Praha, Czech Republic
Ellen M. Knutson	Charles F. Kettering Foundation, Dayton Ohio Office, Dayton, OH, USA

Dmitry K. Ravinskiy	Department of National Literatures (Non-Slavic Literatures) of the Russian National Library, St. Petersburg, Russia
James Lukenbill	Ingenix, Austin, TX, USA
W. Bernard Lukenbill	School of Information, University of Texas at Austin, Austin, TX, USA
Tatiana Nikolova-Houston	2100 Rio Grande, Austin, TX, USA
James M. Nyce	Department of Anthropology, Ball State University, Muncie, IN, USA
Irene Owens	School of Library and Information Sciences at North Carolina Central University, Durham, NC, USA
Mark Skogen	Internet Access and Training Program, International Research and Exchanges Board (IREX), Tbilisi, Georgia
Myles G. Smith	Internet Access and Training Program, International Research and Exchanges Board (IREX), Ashgabat, Turkmenistan
Jacqueline Solis	University of North Carolina at Chapel Hill, Chapel Hill, NC, USA
Zsuzsanna Toszegi	Department of Social, Library and Information Science, University of Kaposvar, Kaposvar, Hungary

PREFACE

This is ALAO's second international volume. It represents the editors' commitment to internationalize the journal's contents and interests. The volume of this sort within ALAO, published in 2007, as Volume 25, outlines the history of Library and Information Science in Finland and reviews the scholarly achievements of Finnish scholars working within this discipline.

This second international volume in the series, now published by Emerald, provides the reader with a number of different perspectives on and from various former Soviet bloc libraries and information institutions. Included in this volume are contributions from Russia, Ukraine, Poland, Czech Republic, Hungary, Bulgaria, Romania, the New Republic of Kosovo, and the post-Soviet successor states of Eurasia. This areal volume also provides value because it not only highlights the diversity of interests, backgrounds, and perspectives on LIS in these countries, but also gives the reader a glimpse of the history and ongoing political, economic, social and cultural change there.

We believe this book serves both LIS scholars and everyday practitioners. For scholars, the volume's authors have provided an historical view of library and information science education and practice that focuses on organizational changes that have taken place in former Soviet bloc libraries. As such, the volume offers practitioners an opportunity to compare and contrast library administration, library services, service quality, and library users in former Soviet bloc libraries to those in their own country. This will help LIS professionals examine more critically what we do in our own institutions. The volume's contributors, we also believe, provide some best of practice ideas that others may wish to adopt as well.

We would like to thank William Graves III and James M. Nyce for the work that they have done on this volume. Graves deserves special thanks for his translation and close editing of the several of the chapters. In addition, we would like also thank the contributing authors who have helped to make this volume another landmark in the history of this series.

As a final note, we would like to mention that ALAO is now accessible online to subscribers. This title is available as part of Emerald's e-book collection and is cross-indexed with their journals.

Delmus E. Williams
Janine Golden

INTRODUCTION

This volume brings together a range of reflective essays and empirical analyses of the changing character of the library world in what is sometimes called, "post-Soviet space." Specifically, individual contributions from Russia, Ukraine, Poland, Czech Republic, Hungary, Bulgaria, Romania, the New Republic of Kosovo, and the post-Soviet successor states of Eurasia all provide different perspectives on Library and Information Sciences within the former Soviet Union and "Eastern Bloc" in terms of national and cultural identity and diverse institutional contexts. Thus, the included chapters range in focus from broad transformations in National Libraries and national library systems to the more specific problems facing municipal and local public libraries and information institutions within decentralized and, in some cases, privatized post-Soviet environments.

These chapters also represent an interesting collection of quite different vantage points on LIS and the library world from within post-Soviet space. Among the contributors, the reader will find senior administrators of National Libraries and professional librarians with experience spanning the Soviet/post-Soviet divide, younger, American-trained LIS professionals conducting research in specific information institutions, and Information and Technology and information management specialists working in different institutional contexts in post-Soviet space. This volume testifies to what we see as characteristic of the diversity of interests, backgrounds, and perspectives on LIS in contexts of ongoing political, economic, social, and cultural change within post-Soviet space.

Although all 11 chapters testify to various perspectives, interests, and commitments, a common concern unite them. How does the demise of the Soviet system help us to understand the character of library and information institutions and practices within post-Soviet space today?

Four of the chapters chart the importance of attitudes toward nation building and the role libraries and librarianship may play in this process. Maria Haigh's analysis of changes in librarianship and library education in the context of post-Soviet Ukrainian nation building points to an essential tension between expressions of interest in reforming library education and practice through the adoption of open access mechanisms, patron-centered practices and Internet resources, and the de facto preservation of Soviet-era library organization and practices that were designed to create and maintain stability, discipline, and order. Quite to the contrary, Asvaturov and Ravinskiy's discussion of the historical character and the present role of the Department of National Literatures of the Russian National Library argues that the traditional institutional focus on preservation, curatorship, and cultural education actually allows the Library to play a much greater role within the changing "information space" of St. Petersburg today in promoting a new national agenda of multicultural understanding in the service of developing a cosmopolitan citizenry.

Nikolova-Houston and Zsuzsanna Toszegi detail dramatic changes in libraries, librarianship, and LIS in post-Soviet Bulgaria and Hungary as they envision a quite different nation-building project, one that is predicated upon a total repudiation of the previous soviet system. The demise of the Soviet system provided Bulgaria with an historic opportunity to forge new international alliances and develop new forms of international cooperation. Nikolova-Houston documents the ways these alliances and partnerships are transforming the very nature of libraries, librarianship, and LIS education in Bulgaria. As she describes them, Bulgarian efforts to conform to EU principles of harmonization and standardization and to strengthen commitment to developing a national information order are being used to promote democratization.

Although it is apparent that Toszegi and Nikolova-Houston share much common ground and strategic vision, Toszegi's contribution reminds us that the economic consequences of the post-Soviet transition often have been painful for many even as some have directly and immediately benefited. As the higher educational system in Hungary responds to these circumstances by promoting a general mission of "knowledge, ethics, and responsibility," librarianship in the 21st century must face new challenges in defining the structures and functions of library resources and information institutions.

As most of the chapters in this volume make clear, the impact of post-Soviet decentralization and the decoupling of individual libraries and information institutions from national administrative and fiscal oversight has resulted in different definitions and functions for individual libraries and information institutions. Two of the chapters explicitly deal with the significance of these structural changes. Stanley Kalkus' reflective essay on changes in the Czech national library system since the Velvet Revolution concludes that the elimination of censorship combined with the decentralization of the former state system has broadened collections, motivated a renewed interest in improving the LIS educational system, and opened the door to the development and implementation of new online information systems. These developments also have led to the emergence of new special libraries in the private sector, creating demand for a new "information specialist" professional and developing for a younger generation of LIS professional positions they often find more attractive than work in traditional academic and public libraries.

Stanley Kalkus and Miroslaw Gorny both point to a growing recognition among librarians and information specialists that the nature of all of these post-Soviet developments demands the attention of stronger and more independent professional LIS organizations than currently exist. According to Gorny, fiscal and administrative decentralization resulted in the closing of libraries, a general reduction in holdings, and the elimination of library positions in Poland. At the same time, online information systems and Internet access, funded not by the State but by the international NGOs and private foundations, pressed academic libraries to expand service in their role as "public libraries." This has resulted over the years in the development of two national digital libraries under the direction of the Ministry of Culture and 15 regional digital libraries. Gorny describes these latter as "organizational-technical platforms" that academic libraries and organizations can use to make their collections available to the general public on demand. More serious consequences of these developments, according to Gorny, are the lack of qualified library staff to digitize holdings, the resistance of Polish academics to become actively involved in these initiatives, and the general public's rising expectations for online access.

One common and important theme found in all of the chapters is the negative impact on both the livelihood and the social status of librarians and information workers when post-Soviet governments assign low fiscal priorities to libraries, library work, and library education. These changes devalue libraries and library work in the eyes of the general public. Contributions to this volume by Breca and by Anghelescu et al. present stark portraits of the negative impact on library work, library organization, and library staff motivation that have developed as a result. Anghelescu et al.'s survey results indicate that Romanian librarians have not been motivated to explore the value of social marketing to promote changes in traditional Soviet-era attitudes and behaviors, primarily because they have seen no evidence that libraries are important institutions or that they have any substantive contribution to make to a democratic transition in post-Soviet Romania.

Similarly, in the post-Soviet, NATO-occupied city of Pristina, Kosovo Svetlana Breca, working as a consultant to the staff of the Pristina Regional

Public Library, discovered a host of lost development opportunities, a general lack of motivation to change, poor communication between staff and management, and a general lack of trust. Breca proposes a number of positive steps she believes library management and staff could quite easily have taken, but did not, to create a more user-friendly and resource-rich library environment.

In stark contrast to this, Ellen Knutson's extended case study of the Bryansk Regional Public Library in western Russia provides a clear example of just how much can be accomplished with very limited resources and support. The librarians in the Bryansk region found creative ways to respond to local user needs and, in so doing, transformed the role and functions of the regional public library system. In a region directly impacted by the environmental disaster at Chernobyl in 1986, the library staff of the Bryansk regional public library transformed local libraries into very powerful community information centers within a "regional ecological community" that included transnational linkages with Belarus and Ukraine.

Two of the factors that contributed to the success of the Bryansk librarians' initiative were Internet access and the attention and support of local government. The general significance of this is clear from Skogen and Smith's contribution to this volume. In their comparative study of rates of Internet penetration, distribution, and development of locally relevant web content in 10 post-Soviet successor states in Eurasia in 2008, Skogen and Smith claim that nearly every community across Eurasia has a local library, yet most libraries are struggling to demonstrate their relevance to community members. According to Skogen and Smith, one way of accomplishing this is to provide free Internet access. Those few that have managed to provide free Internet access are also those that have invested in adequate staffing, training, and improving services for users and, most importantly, have garnered the support of local government officials.

The final contribution to this volume by Closet-Crane et al. brings us back to the beginning of this post-Soviet project. Many of the contributors to this volume have started from the premise that the essential problem for libraries, librarianship, and library education under the traditional Soviet system was the centralized and hierarchical control of information and the institutional structures and practices that naturalized differential access to information, constructing what Michel Foucault referred to as "regimes of truth." Thus, the project of moving beyond the soviet system has been largely dedicated to transforming Soviet-era institutions and practices. Efforts to modernize, develop new programs and transition to LIS models more common outside of this region have constituted the fundamental goals. Echoing Zsuzsanna Toszegi's concerns about the economic consequences of post-Soviet change in Hungary, however, Closet-Crane et al.'s ethnographic study charts the ways differential access to information has permitted local elites today to appropriate and to profit directly from the commodification of the customs, traditions, and ways of life of non-elite rural communities. This should stand as a strong warning to all LIS professionals who assume that the end of the Soviet system and the "transition" somehow signify the end of structural inequalities and naturalized regimes of truth.

We express our gratitude to Delmus Williams and Janine Golden for unwavering support of this project and a great deal of hard work to help bring it to fruition. Our thanks.

William Graves III
James M. Nyce

TWO STEPS FORWARD, ONE STEP BACK: IDEOLOGICAL AND HISTORICAL ASPECTS OF LIBRARY AND INFORMATION SCIENCE EDUCATION IN INDEPENDENT UKRAINE

Maria Haigh

«Книга, могучее орудие общения, труда, борьбы. Она вооружает человека опытом жизни и борьбы человечества, раздвигает его горизонт, дает ему знания, при помощи которых он может заставить служить себе силы природы»

The book is a mighty instrument for communication, labor, struggle. It arms a person with life experiences and the toils of humanity. It expands his horizons and gives him knowledge to tame the forces of nature.

N.K. Krupskaya, wife of V.I. Lenin

ABSTRACT

This chapter examines historical developments and current trends in Ukrainian library education, based on a review of the Ukrainian literature, a survey of Library and Information (LIS) curricula, and

Advances in Library Administration and Organization, Volume 27, 1–24
Copyright © 2009 by Emerald Group Publishing Limited
ISSN: 0732-0671/doi:10.1108/S0732-0671(2009)0000027006

conversations with senior figures in Ukrainian LIS education. Ukraine became an independent state only in 1991 after the collapse of the Soviet Union. Prior to independence, Ukraine's LIS education was integrated within the Soviet system. After independence the system evolved slowly, but with the recent Orange Revolution, reform efforts have increased apace. Ukrainian LIS education remains more vocational than in the United States, with a two-year nondegree certificate as the most common training, and a four-year bachelor's degree offered by elite institutions. One emerging trend in LIS education there stresses the new opportunities for librarians and information professionals because of Internet techno-logies. Another trend is part of a more general shift, inspired by a new Ukrainian higher education law, stressing the country's independent culture and formalizing standards for different degrees. Although Ukrainian LIS leaders advocate adoption of open access mechanisms, customer friendly practices, and electronic resources, my own experiences as a library user suggest that Soviet-era habits continue to shape library practices. LIS education has now reached a turning point as reformers grapple with the limited resources, the power of inertia, and remnants of Soviet culture in their efforts to meet current challenges and prepare a new generation of information professionals.

INTRODUCTION

In 1904, frustrated by the chaotic state of the exiled Russian revolutionary community, Lenin published the book *One Step Forward, Two Steps Back (The Crisis in Our Party)*. Fundamental institutional change has never been a quick or easy process. More than 90 years after his eventual triumph in the October Revolution of 1917, Ukraine is now working to undo Lenin's legacy. Its progress has been similarly indirect, but one can at least be sufficiently confident about its direction (to reverse the directions involved): in recent years the country has been making at least two steps forward for each one back.

Within Ukraine's libraries, as in its other social institutions, attempts at bold reform and a decisive break with the Soviet past have struggled against the prevalent culture of passivity and corruption inherited from the Brezhnev era of the 1970s. Ukraine was one of the 15 Soviet republics and was fully integrated within the U.S.S.R until its collapse in 1991. Today, Ukraine struggles quite publicly with the legacy of its seven decades of Soviet misrule. Although the Soviet Union contained one of the world's best-developed library networks, its libraries were charged with a very different task from their counterparts in liberal democracies. The ideology of Marxism-Leninism was woven into every state institution and libraries played an important part in shoring up Lenin's legacy. Librarians were educated to ensure that reading and research was conducted according to socialist principles (Kimmage, 1992). Very often libraries were part of the communist-led cultural and entertainment clubs provided by the Ministry of the Interior for the use of members of different occupational groups.

Ukraine's history and geography present some particular challenges to librarians. The country has a culturally and historically diverse population, with several languages and national traditions. Today Ukraine has a population that has shrunk to 48 million, though it remains, the second biggest country in Europe (after Russia) in terms of land area. Ukraine borders Poland, Romania, and Moldova in the west, Belarus in the north, and Russia in the east. Until the borders of Europe were redrawn by the 1939 Molotov–Ribbentrop Pact (in which Poland was partitioned between Hitler and Stalin), most of present-day western Ukraine was Poland. In this region, Ukrainian (closely related to Russian but with many Polish elements) is widely spoken, and most citizens look toward the European Union for their political future. Eastern Ukraine was the traditional heartland of Ukrainian nationalism and Cossack traditions, but Stalin crushed most resistance through artificial famines, deportation, and the resettlement of ethnic Russians. And so, today, most in the region speak Russian and look toward ever closer ties with Moscow. The Crimean peninsula, in the south of the country, was only merged into Ukraine in a 1954 internal shifting of borders within the Soviet Union.

Since independence, the use of Ukrainian language has become a highly politicized issue dividing pro-Western politicians from their pro-Russian counterparts. Currently Ukrainian is the nation's only official language, but the vast bulk of existing library materials, and indeed library patrons, rely on Russian. One challenge facing library education is the promotion of Ukrainian language and culture within libraries, a task involving many practical and political difficulties.

BRIEF OVERVIEW OF LIBRARY AND REFERENCE EDUCATION IN THE SOVIET UNION

Vladimir Ilyich Lenin, like George W. Bush, married a woman with a keen personal interest in the promotion of libraries. Nadezhda Konstatinovna

Krupskaya was credited with defining the foundations of the content and methods of Soviet Library education (Karetzky, 2002). After the 1917 Bolshevik revolution, Krupskaya became the country's director of adult education and propaganda and Deputy Commissar of Education. Krupskaya borrowed the German model of multiple tiers in Library and Reference education. This system offered two-year non-degree programs to prepare junior and middle level library specialists and four and five-year higher degrees to prepare higher level specialists (Raymond, 1979).

Under Krupskaya's guidance, libraries were reborn as a crucial part of the ideological infrastructure of Soviet society. Krupskaya published a 1920 article in *Pravda*, the major newspaper of the new state, titled "Centralization of Librarianship." In this article, she outlined the new place of public libraries in the Soviet Union "In order to provide everybody with books, we need to increase book publication hundred- or thousand-fold. Currently, given the overall collapse of the economy, this is impossible to achieve. Therefore, we have only one solution: to move from individual book ownership to collective book usage. Collective use of books is possible only with the development of the wide network of libraries" (Krupskaya, 1934). Books, like agricultural land and industrial resources, were to pass into common ownership. Soon after Krupskaya's article appeared, the Bolshevik Commissariat issued a directive to confiscate and nationalize all private book collections with more than 500 books "belonging to the citizens whose professions do not require books as proletariat require their tools" (Verzhbizkiy, 1924). Confiscated books were supposed to be moved to the newly created libraries.

The collectivization of books within library collections also facilitated Communist party control over their contents. From the very beginning, Krupskaya stressed that only certain books should be made available to the masses. In 1924, she wrote that "There are books that organize and there are books that disorganize" (Likhtenshtein, 1978). As Lenin's wife, she put in place the practice of cleaning these "disorganizing" books from library collections (Verzhbizkiy, 1924) (Fig. 1). Throughout the Soviet period, librarians were responsible for maintaining up-to-date lists of forbidden works and removing them from public view. As Soviet rule spread to new states, librarians were trained in these techniques and were required to move unsuitable books into "special collections" (Abramov, 1974). Later in the Soviet period, some books purged from libraries would resurface illicitly as Samizdat, passed clandestinely between readers often as self-published copies in hand-written, manually typed, or carbon-copy form (Biriukov, 2000; Daniel, 2005).

Krupskaya initiated the founding of the first "Soviet Library Seminaria" (college), which opened in Moscow in 1918, just one year after the

Fig. 1. The Caption Reads "Read according to the system: The library will help you to compile your reading plan". Propaganda Poster, 1920s.

revolution and several years before the final victory of Red forces in the ensuing civil war. This was the first sustained attempt to offer library education within the former Russian Empire, despite sporadic earlier initiatives to create textbooks and offer instruction in librarianship (Choldin, 1976). Librarians were formerly drawn from a variety of educational backgrounds and were often trained as teachers (Abramov, 1980). Library education became a required subject in the humanities departments of many Russian institutions by the end of the 1920s. At the same time, more than 20 library departments opened in Russian Institutes of Political Education, Pedagogical Institutes, and Academies of Communist Education (Kazanzceva, 1958). From the beginning of the 1930s, the library education system started to develop in other republics of the Soviet Union. Library departments were transformed into specialist educational institutes. The first library institute in Ukraine opened in 1934 in Kharkiv (Kharkov in Russian) in Eastern Ukraine. Like other early Soviet library educational institutes it was rechartered as a library school after previously serving as a Political-Educational

Institute to provide specialist ideological education to new Communist party members (Kazanzceva, 1958; Sheyko & Kushnarenko, 2004).

In the postwar years, the number of library higher education institutes continued to grow. The network of library institutes spread not only across Soviet republics, but also to the other countries of the Soviet bloc. In 1964, Soviet library institutes went through another transition and were reborn as Institutes of Culture, positioning library education as the institutional peer of theater, dance, circus, and cinema education. This reflected the shared role of these professions in providing propaganda mixed with culture and entertainment. By 1970, the Soviet network of library higher education institutions consisted of 10 Institutes of Culture and more than 20 library faculties (departments) within universities (Grigoryev, 1975).

Here, as in its overall organization of library education, the Soviet Union followed the German system. Graduate study and the completion of a dissertation led to the Candidate of Sciences qualification ("Kandidat Nayk" – the equivalent of the American PhD). Studies for the Candidate of Sciences degree occurred in the consortia of universities belonging to the Academy of Sciences, where students took courses at a number of different institutions. Studies for the Candidate of Sciences degree in the humanities required courses in four areas: history, philosophy, foreign language, and profession. Librarianship was offered not as a self-contained discipline but as a specialized series of courses within the "profession" component of this broader educational program. People who studied librarianship as a professional specialization received the Candidate of Sciences degree either in history or philosophy, or pedagogy. From 1948–1956, Aspirantura (postgraduate study for Candidate of Science) took place at the Vernadsky National Library of Ukraine, the main information center of Ukraine. These studies ceased in 1956 after Soviet authorities accused this library of fostering nationalistic sentiment. After 1956, only the Moscow and Leningrad Institutes of Culture offered graduate research degrees with a librarianship component.

Subsequent completion of a second, larger, and more innovative dissertation, which is the equivalent of the German *Habilitationsschrift*, would grant the status of "Doctor." "Doctorants" required strong national and international reputations, and usually headed departments or institutions. Doctorants did not have advisors or take additional courses or examinations, since they themselves often served as advisors to the students studying for Candidate of Sciences degrees.

These specialist library schools offering instruction to candidates seeking higher degrees were merely the top tier of a much larger system of library education. This concept, too, can be traced back to Krupskaya. The tiered hierarchical system was adopted from the German model even though the content was changed. Within larger libraries, jobs were rigidly stratified according to the level of library education received. Vocational library education initially took place within the political–educational departments of Sovpartshkola (an abbreviation of "Soviet Party School"). Later, fully fledged library education departments opened within the political education faculties of vocational colleges which were two-year schools granting diplomas (Oleneva, 1961). From the beginning of 1929, separate vocational library education schools started to appear. By 1970, the Soviet Union reported a network of vocational library education institutions, which consisted of 12 separate vocational library education schools and more than 100 departments in vocational colleges. At that time, the total body of vocational library education students studying librarianship was said to be approximately 30,000 (Grigoryev, 1975). These vocational schools were educating far more librarians than their degree-granting counterparts. Soviet statistics reported that, in the 1968/1969 academic year, 4,000 librarians graduated with university degrees, and 11,0000 librarians graduated with diplomas from vocational schools (Grigoryev, 1975).

As one might expect, given the ideological weight accorded to libraries within the U.S.S.R., the curricula developed for library students stressed the role of the library in the long march toward the eventual realization of a utopian communist society. Librarians were being educated to play an active part in the dissemination of ideological propaganda. All courses had some Soviet ideological components with more than a third of them devoted exclusively to Marxist-Leninist ideology. The curricula of Soviet Library education included the following core components for librarians educated in the institutes of culture and universities:

- History of the Communist Party of the USSR.
- Marxist-Leninist Philosophy.
- Political Economy.
- Foundations of Scientific Communism.
- Foundations of Marxist-Leninist Ethics and Aesthetics.
- Foundations of Scientific Atheism.
- Foundations of Marxist-Leninist Theory of Culture.
- Pedagogy
- Psychology
- History of the U.S.S.R.
- History of Foreign Countries

- Russian Literature and Literature of the Soviet Republics
- Foreign Literature
- Foundations of Library Science
- History of Library Science
- Foundations of Librarianship and Reference
- Collection Management
- Cataloguing
- Working with Readers
- Soviet Library Organization
- History of Books
- Reference Librarianship
- Special Library Reference
- General Foreign Reference

Elite librarians being trained to work within special libraries received additional courses. These included history of the Soviet economy, history of technology, fundamentals of modern natural sciences, fundamentals of modern industrial production, and "technical propaganda and information" (Grigoryev, 1975).

LIBRARY AND REFERENCE EDUCATION IN UKRAINE AFTER THE COLLAPSE OF THE SOVIET UNION

Opportunities to create national schools in library science presented themselves only with Ukraine's independence, which took effect at the start of 1992. The new Ukrainian Constitution guaranteed the democratic principles of intellectual freedom and free and equal access to information. The new constitution had a positive influence on library democratization, expansion of professional contacts, and collaboration between librarians (Konyukova, 2002a, 2002b). Democratization of Ukraine became one of the driving forces in effecting changes in library science education. In 2002, a new law implementing new standards for higher education came into effect. This law established standard requirements for bachelor's, master's, and doctoral degrees. These replaced the old standards defined by the centralized system of the U.S.S.R.

With the collapse of the Soviet Union, the required courses in Marxist ideology rapidly vanished from Ukrainian degree programs. However, the creation of a modern and democratically inclined library culture required rather more than simply jettisoning the overtly ideological chunks of the old curriculum. Rapid change would have required a rapid and fundamental shift in educational personnel, teaching materials, learning styles, organizational culture, and professional identity. This was not possible. In fact, the immediate effect of independence was a sharp drop in available resources for both libraries and education as the Ukrainian economy imploded and centralized Soviet infrastructure networks unraveled. During the chaos of the early 1990s, universities struggled simply to pay instructors and to keep the lights on. As one Ukrainian library specialist summarized the era, "Economic crisis in Ukraine led to a sharp decline in library networks, student enrollment and graduation of new specialists" (Khlynova, 2001).

According to one Ukrainian observer, "Before [independence in] 1992 no periodical journal of librarianship existed [in Ukraine]" (Mozyrko, 2002). Scholarship in the field was centered in Russia. Soviet centralization left newly independent Ukraine without a single graduate library school (Mozyrko, 2000). As a result, the lack of library and information (LIS) science researchers with graduate research training focused on the discipline has been a particular challenge to the expansion of graduate education in the field. However, Ukraine inherited a reasonable complement of vocational and undergraduate library training programs.

The main structural difference between the Ukrainian and the American library education systems remains the multitiered hierarchical system of education in Ukraine, which contrasts dramatically with the American model in which the graduate MLIS degree is the main professional credential recognized by the field. Library and reference education in Ukraine still follows the German–Soviet model and consists of two tiers. The first tier prepares junior level library workers in vocational two-year schools. There are two levels of vocational schools. Vocational schools at the lower level (level I of accreditation) accept applicants at the age of 14–15. At graduation, students receive a vocational certificate and the equivalent of a high school diploma. Vocational schools at the second level (level II of accreditation) accept applicants at ages 17–18 from a variety of academic backgrounds. At the end of two years of studies, graduates receive a professional certificate for the middle level library worker (Golovko, 2003). There are many vocational schools in Ukraine to prepare junior and middle level library specialists. Programs are offered in different formats: day-study, evening-study, and correspondence classes (Demchyna, 2003; Golovko, 2003).

The second tier of Library and Reference education consists of four and five-year colleges and universities (III and IV levels of accreditation).

Library and Reference departments operate within a university, or Institute of Culture, or within degree-granting teacher training colleges ("Pedagogical Institutes"). After independence, many colleges that had previously been called institutes renamed themselves as universities. After completing these colleges, graduates receive the equivalent of a bachelor degree. Four Ukrainian schools grant bachelors' degrees in Library Science, covering the main geographical areas of the country:

- The Kyiv National University of Culture and Arts (Central Ukraine).
- The Kharkiv State Academy of Culture (Eastern Ukraine).
- The Rivne State University of Culture (Western Ukraine).
- The Mykolaiv branch of the Kyiv National University of Culture and Arts (Southern Ukraine).

During Soviet times, the place of natural science and engineering at the top of the academic status hierarchy was unquestioned. Their prestige was boosted both by the state's strategic commitment to science as a showpiece of Soviet accomplishment and to the relative lack of ideological distortion imposed on the work of researchers in these fields. Librarianship was grouped with other professional, artistic, and social science fields as part of "the humanities." Even within the humanities it suffered from an unusually low level of prestige. The ideological mission given to libraries during the Soviet era cost them much respect in the eyes of both library users and librarians. Because undergraduate library schools were located within Institutes of Culture and were responsible for the creation and dissemination of propagandistic entertainment, they enjoyed a lower status than other professional disciplines. This mitigated against the emergence of a strong culture of research in the field (Mozyrko, 2000). From the 1950s onward, leading library schools and ambitious researchers in the United States remade themselves as practitioners of "information science," embracing the mantle of science, the rigors of quantitative and experimental research, and the power of new electronic technologies in an attempt to legitimate the field as a modern and theoretically grounded endeavor. Information science eventually edged out librarianship as the dominant identity in the field. Library education in the Soviet Union, in contrast, remained closer to its vocational roots. Within the institutes of culture, it was institutionally allied more with the performing arts than with new ideas such as information retrieval or information theory that predominated elsewhere. Soviet library specialists do not seem to have enjoyed appreciable success in making a similar claim to scientific status for their field.

This situation has been slow to change. Today, Kyiv's (Kiev in Russian) only undergraduate library education program is at the Kyiv National University of Culture and Arts, a former Soviet institute of culture. This university offers education in singing, dancing, hairdressing, and the hotel industry as well as professional studies, such as law and business. Library education, formerly one of the three main divisions of the institute, has been demoted to a Department ("kafedra") of Information Resources and Services within the university's School ("institute") of Culture. Its peer departments within this school include the Department of Applied Cultural Studies offering degrees in stage training, fashion, tourism, and the rather cryptically titled "psycho-technology of the entertainment and recreation industry." The university heavily promotes its performing arts programs, as evidenced by the photograph below of its celebrity president Mykhajlo Poplavsky performing alongside students in a showcase review (Fig. 2).

Although explicitly ideological courses have been removed (to be replaced in a sense with proudly nationalistic courses on Ukrainian history, culture, and language), the curriculum is still skewed toward giving students a grounding in the content of different subject fields such as history, literature, and foreign languages rather than dealing in-depth with the specialist knowledge and skills required to function in a modern library. And, since

Fig. 2. The Kyiv National University of Arts and Culture's Singing President, M. Poplavsky. *Source:* http://www.knukim.edu.ua/rector.htm

the degrees are at the undergraduate level, students cannot necessarily be expected to have satisfied general education requirements and mastered at least one specialist area before entering library education as is the case for those entering an American MLIS program.

The field of study is known officially as "Spezcialnist 6.020100: Knyhoznastvo, Biblioteka, Bibliographia" which may be translated literally as "Bibliography, Librarianship and Reference" but which I shall refer to below simply as librarianship. At the universities granting bachelor's degrees, including the Kyiv National University of Arts and Culture, Ivan Franko Lviv National University, and Khrkiv National University, a Master's Degree in librarianship was introduced as an option for graduate studies. The Master's degree requires an additional two years of study after completing a four-year Bachelor's degree. The fifth year of study grants a "specialist level" qualification, and the Master's degree follows after a sixth year. These programs are aimed primarily at students who already hold, or are about to complete, a Bachelor's degree in librarianship (a contrast with the North American model). The specialist qualification serves in practice to add back the fifth year of study present in the Soviet undergraduate degree but removed during curricular reform postindependence. The specialist qualification is expected for department heads in larger libraries and for librarians working in specialized technical institutions. It includes a significant fieldwork component.

Master's degrees did not exist under the Soviet system, but have rapidly gained popularity in many fields as a new and Western-oriented qualification. They symbolize Ukraine's participation in the "Bologna Process," a major European initiative to restructure higher education, improve quality standards, and give greater international transferability of qualifications. The Master's degree in librarianship is intended to prepare students for management positions in libraries, scientific research positions, and educational roles. The Master's degrees include advanced courses on all aspects of librarianship, including theoretical areas, technological skills, and courses aimed at practical professional issues such as managing and marketing libraries.

Ukraine has retained its dual level German-inspired system, separating Candidate of Sciences from Doctor. Since its independence, several Ukrainian universities and institutions opened postgraduate studies for Candidate of Sciences and Doctoral degrees. A number of Aspiranturas (graduate studies programs) opened in independent Ukraine. As in Soviet times, graduate studies in librarianship exist as a specialized component within more general areas such as history, pedagogy, and technology. Since 1998, more than 70 students have received the Candidate of Sciences degree with specializations in librarianship. For instance, the Vernadsky National Library of Ukraine, its leading scientific library, reopened its Aspirantura in 1993. It offers such specialized courses for doctoral students in librarianship within two tracks: (1) Book, Librarianship, and Reference and (2) Automated Control Systems and Progressive Information Technologies. Students interested in the former would usually enroll for graduate degrees in history or pedagogy, perhaps at the Kyiv National University of Arts and Culture. The second stream is usually integrated with a graduate degree in Technical Sciences. The Kharkiv State Academy of Culture started offering a Candidate of Sciences degree program with a specialization in Librarianship and Bibliography in 1994 and a Doctor degree program in 1996 (Sheyko & Kushnarenko, 2004).

CURRENT SITUATION IN UKRAINIAN LIBRARY EDUCATION: TWO STEPS FORWARD

The development of modern library education in Ukraine remains very much a work in progress. But a new connection between libraries and information science is an example of the progressive thinking that is gradually spreading among Ukrainian colleges and universities. Despite this, Ukraine's librarians are not all well prepared for current and future demands. Most currently practicing librarians, particularly at senior levels, were trained under the Soviet system. Library work is not well paid, and the profession does not have a high profile among young people. Even those being educated today are largely studying under an educational system shaped by the Soviet experience.

Most of the existing libraries are specialized, whereas library education in the higher degree institutes is geared toward general public libraries. This has created a mismatch between existing demands from the job market and the preparation provided to the workforce. In many cases, the training and experience of a credentialed librarian does not correspond to the demands of the job. Library managers complain that recent graduates need a lengthy training period to prepare fully to meet their job responsibilities (Mozyrko, 2002).

To address these problems, library schools of all tiers started changing their curricula. Today, several universities offer a specialization in "Bibliography, Librarianship, and Reference" intended to prepare graduates for the following professions: "bibliographer, manager of information systems and technologies, international information manager, information manager, abstracting and indexing analyst, records management specialist, abstracting and indexing specialist of subject-based information services systems" (Kushnarenko & Solianyk, 2001; Zhuk, 2004). The Kyiv National University of Culture made its first steps in this direction during the 1991–1992 academic year when an archives specialty was added to the library degree. In 1993, a course on Foundations of Bibliographic Control was also added, and, in 1994, a new specialization in Documents and Information Services appeared (Konyukova, 2002a).

The Kharkiv State Academy of Culture provides another example of the conceptual restructuring of LIS education. In 1994, the Library Faculty at the Kharkiv State Academy of Culture was renamed the Faculty of Librarianship and Informatics. The faculty was reorganized to include the Department of Librarianship, the Department of Bibliography, the Department of Document Management, and the Department of Informatics, Information Systems, and Processes. In 1995, this school became the first in Ukraine to offer the new specialization of "Record Management and Information Services" (Sheyko & Kushnarenko, 2004). This attempt to link library education to management and information work outside traditional libraries is quite new for Ukraine and follows the model of Western education in LIS science.

Education in library science was traditionally focused on the humanities (history, literature, Marxist-Leninist philosophy). Library science education is gradually acquiring a new focus that reflects the conditions of the new information-oriented society. Information technology courses have been added to the core curricula at Ukraine's leading centers of library education (Matvienko, 2000). As in the rest of the world, libraries in Ukraine have been shifting their attention to electronic sources, audio recordings, and other media resources. This has been accompanied by a new focus on information technology in library education (Filipova, 2001; Shvakina, 2001).

Another important driving force is the inclusion of new technologies (computer and telecommunications) in the processing of documents, document preservation, information search, and information exchange by using new technologies. "Due to the new technologies, the library transforms itself from a book storage into a social institution that ensures accumulation and preservation of knowledge to be widely used" (Khlynova, 2001).

Meanwhile, the ideological Marxist courses in the curriculum have been replaced with a new focus on Ukraine, including such disciplines as Ukrainian history, Ukrainian literature, and the "Culture of the Ukrainian language." Under the Soviet system, Ukrainian culture was presented as a lesser derivative of Russian culture, and Ukrainian history was taught very selectively. Even the grammar of the Ukrainian language was modified to make it more similar to the Russian language (Bilaniuk, 2005). Ukrainian national sentiment was actively discouraged. Therefore, it is important in the new democratic Ukraine to prepare qualified professionals who both respect their profession and are proud of their heritage. "Reforms in the Library education happen when history of Ukraine, culture and literature of Ukraine, culture of Ukrainian language are taught; when previously banned pages of history of Ukrainian librarianship, book, and bibliography are told" (Mozyrko, 2002).

THE USER PERSPECTIVE: ONE STEP BACK

These shifts in the educational curricula have been accompanied by a more general shift in the role of the library within Ukrainian society. Whereas, in Soviet times, libraries were required to restrict and filter the flow of information, their stated mission is now to facilitate and expand information usage (Apshay, 2004). Librarians are beginning to see themselves as part of the cycle of information distribution from author to publisher to libraries and information centers, and, finally, to users (Kostenko & Soroka, 2002). Two specialists in the Vernadsky Library in Kyiv captured this new spirit when they wrote

> The Ukrainian Library System is a part of the world's information resources and cultural heritage ... Libraries must take responsibilities of collecting, organizing, and storing electronic information resources accessible to everyone ... Libraries must take it upon themselves to implement the digitization of the whole book heritage of the Ukrainian people. Providing access to these Ukrainian resources to all users, without restrictions on time or location, will ensure preservation and active use of these resources to solve scientific, educational, and cultural problems. (Kostenko & Soroka, 2002)

In practice, this fundamental shift in the culture of librarianship is taking place slowly. Despite the shifts in library rhetoric from information control to information access and a user focus, and despite the shifts in library education curricula to reflect that rhetoric, changes in personnel and leadership practices are very gradual. My personal experience as a library user during my Fulbright fellowship award in 2007 gave me an opportunity to compare rhetoric with reality. My decision to use a trip to the library as a tool to research the library itself as well as the topics I was reading about reflect a recent focus in the study of organizational information systems (Yates & Maanen, 2001), on the one hand, and science and technology studies (Oudshoorn & Pinch, 2003) on the other, on user experiences as a key means of analyzing socio-technical systems and a valuable corrective to traditional top-down methods of understanding.

Initially, I visited the Vernadsky Library as a guest of one of its staff members, meeting library staff and surveying library departments and operations. I was given a tour of modern facilities in the library. The library has extensive collections of scientific literature, copies of all Ukrainian publications, many special and archival collections, and several reading halls equipped with computers. To facilitate access to scientific information abroad, the library subscribes to many electronic databases, among them *Science Direct* and *Ebsco*. Within Ukraine it has pioneered online catalogs, electronic databases, electronic indexing of dissertation abstracts, and electronic access to articles in full text (Fig. 3).

Impressed by this spectacle of technology, efficiency, and customer service, I decided to return to conduct research for my forthcoming article on the Ukrainian library system. I had selected 10 relevant journal article citations and planned to acquire full text copies for my research. I arrived at 10 a.m. to the library hoping to accomplish the task before lunch with a colleague on the library's staff.

As the first step in what proved to be long process of acquiring copies of the needed articles, I had to queue up for 15 min in the library lobby to

Fig. 3.   Reading Hall Equipped with Computers. Photograph by Author.

register for a pass. The library is not open to the public. Passes are issued to provide access according to status. Students with suitable letters of introduction receive limited access, with additional privileges provided for faculty and for distinguished scientists. For my pass, I had to present a passport and proof of having earned my doctorate – in my case it was letter from the Fulbright office. This entitled me to a special foreigner pass, enabling me to browse and request materials but not to borrow them. I had to stand in line for 40 min before my application was approved.

I then tried to enter the library beyond the lobby, but I was stopped because I did not register my laptop. Use of registered laptops is permitted, but only when operated under battery power. A policy that laptops cannot be plugged in to the plentiful power outlets is in place that is rather unfriendly to researchers by American standards, and I have since been told that this policy exists to discourage the use of personal laptops connected to the network to download masses of text from commercial databases, and thereby running up large bills for the library. Scanners and cameras may not be used in the library. Registering the laptop yielded another pass authorizing its passage into the library. I noticed that the lobby and other common areas lacked seats or other points for social congregation.

I also was issued a "control ticket" of my own which I had to present at each entrance to a different room as I was moving within the library. The control ticket was stamped in each room by attendants stationed at the door of each of its 16 reading rooms. At the end of the day, I had to return it with a trail of stamps from the reading halls I had visited during my visit.

After receiving permission to enter the library, my first step was to go to the card catalog to retrieve call numbers for the publications I wanted. I struggled with the unfamiliar catalog system and politely asked for help from one of two idling librarians chatting nearby (Fig. 4). I was taken aback by the rude response "What? Do you want me to search the catalog for you? Here are the cards, go and find it yourself." Senior library staff later explained that the frontline personnel are significantly underpaid and suggested that this might explain their attitude. This recalls the classic Soviet-era aphorism, "They pretend to pay us, and we pretend to work." Generations of communist party rule left the USSR with one of the world's worst customer service cultures, and, in libraries, as in shops, hotels, offices, and restaurants most Ukrainians are accustomed to being treated as annoyances. However, I did find the call numbers for two journals. The next step was to obtain a request form to retrieve the appropriate issues. For each requested item (i.e., a single journal issue), a library patron must complete a form in duplicate. A patron can submit a maximum of four requests every two hours.

Fig. 4. Chatting Librarians in the Card Catalog Room. Photograph by Author.

While waiting for two hours to receive the first batch of journals and to file another request, I went to the current periodicals room seeking one of the current articles. I got my ticket stamped and retrieved one journal issue. Fortunately I had the right kind of pass since a prominent sign at the desk warned that only those with permanent library cards would be served there. However, even those patrons trusted with a recent journal issue cannot make copies of articles themselves, an echo of Soviet times in which photocopiers were carefully guarded and every copy made had to be authorized and accounted for to limit the spread of samizdat materials. The only legal way to copy an article is to leave the reading room and join the line in the basement to submit a copy request. In the middle of the day, I was lucky to wait only 20 min. Later in the day, queues were much longer. Although the logs of materials copied are no longer tallied they have persisted out of institutional habit (Fig. 5).

When I met my Ukrainian colleague, he revealed the existence of a computer catalog of call numbers covering materials from 1994 onward, so I no longer needed to struggle through the card catalog anymore. Searching the catalog required determination, as the librarian on duty in the computer room wanted to know exactly what I was planning to do on the computer and then insisted that I would not find what I needed. Fortunately, the system worked well and saved me much time. By then, my first four journal issues had arrived in the reading room. I had time to repeat the cycle once more before the library closed at 6 p.m.: submitting request forms, waiting

Fig. 5. At the Current Periodicals Desk the Librarian is Obscured Completely Behind a Large Sign Warning that Controls Tickets Must be Shown on Entry and that Users without Permanent Library Cards will not be Served. Photograph by Author.

to retrieve the journals, and queuing up to make copies. Unfortunately, the copy room closed an hour earlier than the library. Hiding behind a pillar in the lobby, I used my camera to photograph the text of the retrieved articles. After eight hours in the library, I had found seven journal articles and had copied just three of them legally. To accomplish this I had filled out 15 forms, and received four stamps on my control ticket (Fig. 6).

The contrast between the bold hopes expressed in the articles I retrieved and the process by which I procured them was jarring. The articles depicted a determined drive to open library collections to a broader population of researchers, to create user-focused culture, and to provide access to information. Technology to provide this change is available in Ukraine, and has been deployed more extensively in the Vernadsky than in any other library. However, the practices and assumptions of the Soviet era are embedded in many aspects of the library: its physical organization, service culture, limitation of access by user type, and proliferation of forms and permits. Librarians were more concerned with limiting access than facilitating it, actively discouraging the use of its ballyhooed electronic resources. To Western eyes, this library appeared hugely overstaffed, yet the staff

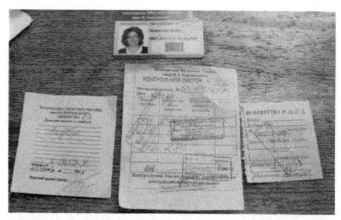

Fig. 6.   A Selection of Forms Accumulated After a Day of Library Use. Photograph
by Author.

members seemed to resent the presence of library patrons as an intrusion on
their routine. The Soviet-style control forms required to enter each room and
stamped to log the patron's every move, provided particularly striking
evidence of this micro-level continuity of practice despite a polar reversal of
official ideology. This was also evidenced by the centralization of copy
machines and the barriers to their use confronting users.

CONCLUSION

Attempts to restructure Ukrainian library education remain at the
experimental stage, with different approaches coexisting among the
country's institutions of library education. Impressive efforts are underway
to shift structures of LIS education toward Western European models,
including the introduction of master's degrees and a more modular
approach to course requirements. Explicitly ideological courses have been
removed, but Soviet culture, assumptions, and practices continue to exert
their influence in a subtle way. Although new approaches are being taught,
they have had a limited impact on practice as real change in the service
philosophy await the creation of a new generation of information
professionals. My examination of the actual user experience at the country's
most advanced library showed that shifts in rhetoric and an impressive

commitment to the adoption of international electronic resources have yet to fully shift practices from the ingrained habits of the Soviet era. Institutional cultures and practices can perpetuate themselves indefinitely. So far, the Vernadsky's institutional inertia has imposed its own patterns on the use of new technology, rather than being somehow transformed by the mere presence of computers, Internet connections, and databases. Yet my own opinion is that change is coming to Ukrainian libraries, albeit slowly. The new curriculum foregrounds electronic resources, and many Ukrainians are enthusiastic about the potential of open access digital libraries and journals for this relatively poor country. Within the country's largest libraries transformation may take place slowly, as a younger generation currently in mid-level positions gradually takes over. Smaller, more nimble libraries may be adapting more quickly, in terms of organizational culture if not in their technological infrastructure. Traveling the country in 2007 as part of my Fulbright fellowship, I was impressed by the commitment shown by many regional library directors to improve user services and make the physical layout of their libraries more welcoming. Improvising in an environment of scarce resources they recognized the importance of libraries as community centers and public institutions in a newly capitalist world. Struggling for survival has forced them to care about their users in a manner unimaginable during the Soviet era. For many smaller libraries the choice is between rapid evolution and extinction.

Ukrainian library educators face many of the same challenges and opportunities as their American counterparts, but they must guard against the assumption that the imposition of an American-style reliance on graduate Masters in Library and Information Science (MLIS) education is the only way forward. In the longer term, appropriate education for Ukraine's librarians will depend on the young nation's conception of what the purpose and mission of a library should be. Although Ukrainian library culture continues to reflect Soviet heritage, it already diverged dramatically from those prevalent in Putin's authoritarian Russia. I noticed at a recent major library conference in Crimea (14th International Conference "Crimea 2007: The Role of Digital Information and Digital Libraries in Advance to the Knowledge-Based Society") that Russian participants often began presentations by personally thanking Vladimir Vladimirovich Putin for his leadership and nurturing of libraries, a direct echo of Soviet rhetorical practice unknown in today's Ukraine. Ukrainian presenters at the same conference openly debated shortcomings and challenges with a well-founded skepticism toward the capabilities of their own government. As time passes, the shape of Ukraine's information institutions will both reflect and shape the efforts of its people to forge a consensus as to whether the Ukraine will finally be a liberal European democracy, a loyal satellite of a resurgent Russia, or something uniquely Ukrainian.

REFERENCES

Abramov, K. I. (1974). *Bibliotechnoye Stroitelstvo v Pervye Gody Sovetskoi Vlasti (1917–1920) (Building libraries during the first years of the Soviet power (1917–1920)*. Moskva: Kniga.

Abramov, K. I. (1980). *Istoria BD (Bibliotechnogo Dela) v SSSR (History of librarianship in the USSR)* (3rd ed., p. 351). Moskva: Kniga.

Apshay, N. (2004). Strategichni Zasady Rozvytku Bibliotek Vyschykh Navchalnykh Zakladiv (Strategic directions of higher education library development in the context of informatization). *Visnyk Knyzhkovoii Palaty* (6), 23–25.

Bilaniuk, L. (2005). *Contested tongues: Language politics and cultural correction in Ukraine.* Ithaca: Cornell University Press.

Biriukov, B. V. (2000). *Repressirovannaya Kniga: Istoki Yavlenia (Repressed book: Sources of origin)* (pp. 87–122). Moskva: Homo Legens.

Choldin, M. T. (1976). The Russian Bibliographical Society, 1889–1930. *Library Quarterly*, 46(January), 1–19.

Daniel, A. (2005). Istoki i Smysl Sovetskogo Samizdata (Sources and meaning of Soviet Samisdat). In: V. V. Egrunov (Ed.), *Antologiya Samizdata. Nepodcenzurnaya literatura v SSSR. 1950–1980. (Anthology of samizdat: Underground literature in the USSR, 1950s–1980s)*. Moskva: International Institute of Humanities and Political Research.

Demchyna, L. I. (2003). Strukturuvannia Dyszcplin Dokumentalno-Komunikazciynoho Zcyklu v Umovakh Stupenevoii Bibliotechno-Informazciynoi Oscvity (Structuring of the document management and communication courses in the conditions of tiered library and information education). *Visnyk Kharkivskoii Derzhavnoii Akademii Kultury (Kharkiv State Culture Academy Bulletin)*, 2003(11), 114–118.

Filipova, L. Y. (2001). Bibliotechni Resursy Internet dlia Naukovykh Doslidzhen (Library Internet resources for scientific research). In: B. Nauka (Ed.), *Osvita, Profesia u Demokratychniy Ukraini: Zbirnyk Naukovykh Prazc (Library science, education, profession in democratic Ukraine): Collection of scientific works* (Vol. 3, pp. 98–105). Kyiv: KDUKIM.

Golovko, A. G. (2003). Organizazcii ta Metodologichni Chynnyky Kompyuterizazcii Bibliotechno-Informazcyinykh Navchalnykh Dyszcyplin (Organization and methodology of computerization of the library-information education disciplines. *Visnyk Kharkivskoii Derzhavnoii Akademii Kultury (Kharkiv State Culture Academy Bulletin)*, 2003(11), 119–123.

Grigoryev, Y. G. (1975). Bibliotechno-Bibliographicheskoye Obrazovanie, Sistema Podgotovki Bibliotekarey i Bibliographov Vysshey i Sredney Kvalifikazcii. (Library and library-reference education, system for preparing librarians and reference specialists with higher and middle education qualifications). Moskva: Bibliotechnaya Palata.

Karetzky, S. (2002). *Not seeing red: American librarianship and the Soviet Union, 1917–1960.* Lanham, MD: University Press of America.

Kazanzceva, L. V. (1958). *Razvitie Bibliotechnogo Obrazovania v SSSR (Development of the library education in the U.S.S.R)*. In *40 Let Bibliotechnogo Stroitelstva v SSSR (40 years of library construction in the U.S.S.R)*. Moskva: Znanie.

Khlynova, N.F. (2001). Bibliotechna Polityka na Suchasnomy Etapi (Library policy on the current stage). In: Programy Rozvytku Regioniv i Bibliotechno-Informazcijna Polityka (Programs for development regions and library-information policy) (pp. 30–38). Kyiv: DAKKKIM.

Kimmage, D. (1992). *Russian libraries in transition: An anthology of glasnost literature*. Jefferson, NC: McFarland & Co.

Konyukova, I. Y. (2002a). Rozvytok Bibliotechnoii Profesii v Ukraiini: Sychasni Konzcepzcii ta Napryamy (Development of library profession in Ukraine: Current concepts and trends). Unpublished Thesis for "Kandidat Pedahohichnykh Nauk" (Candidate of Pedagogical Sciences), Kyiv National University of Culture and Arts, Kyiv, Ukraine.

Konyukova, I. Y. (2002b). Rozvytok Bibliotechnoii Profesii v Ukraiini: za Pidsumkamy Doslidzhennia 2000–2002 Rokiv. (Development of library profession in Ukraine: Results of a study 2000–2002). In: *Bibliotechna Nauka, Osvita, Professiya u Demokratychniy Ukraini: Zbirnyk Naykovykh Prazc. (Library science, education, profession in democratic Ukraine): Collection of scientific works* (4, pp. 50–57). Kyiv: KDUKIM.

Kostenko, L. Y., & Soroka, M. B. (2002). Biblioteka Informazciynogo Suspilstva (Library of an information society). *Bibliotechnyi Visnyk (Library Bulletin)*, *2002*(3), 33–38.

Krupskaya, N. K. (1934). Foreword. In: *Chto Pisal i Govoril Lenin o Bibliotekakh (What Lenin wrote and said about libraries)* (p. 4). Moskva: Gosizdat.

Kushnarenko, N. M., & Solianyk, A. A. (2001). Bibliotechno-Informazciyna Osvita: Perekhid u Novu Yakist (Library and information science education: Shifting to new quality). In: Bibliotechna Nauka, Osvita, Profesia u Demokratychnij Ukraiini: Zbirnyk Naukovykh Prazc (Library science, education, profession in democratic Ukraine): Collection of Scientific Works (Vol. 3, pp. 46–50). Kyiv: Ukrainian Ministry of Culture and Arts.

Likhtenshtein, E. S. (1978). *Slovo O Nauke (Word about science)* (p. 237). Moskva: Znanie.

Matvienko, O. V. (2000). Pidgotovka Specialistiv z Informazciynoi Diyalnosti v Galuzi Virtualnykh Komunikazciy (Preparation of specialists in the area of virtual communication). In: *Bibliotechna Nauka, Osvita, Professiya u Demokratychniy Ukraini: Zbirnyk Naykovykh Prazc. (Library science, education, profession in democratic Ukraine): Collection of scientific works* (Vol. 2, pp. 46–54). Kyiv: KDUKIM.

Mozyrko, L. E. (2000). Vyscha Bibliotechno-Informaciyna Osvita Ukraiiny (Higher library and information science education in Ukraine). In: *Bibliotechna Nauka, Osvita, Professiya u Demokratychniy Ukraini: Zbirnyk Naykovykh Prazc. (Library science, education, profession in democratic Ukraine): Collection of scientific works* (Vol. 2, pp. 61–66). Kyiv: KDUKIM.

Mozyrko, L. E. (2002). Reorganizazcya Bibliotechno-Informasciynoii Osvity v Kyiivskomu Nazcionalnomu Universyteti Kultury i Mystezctv: 2000–2002. (Reorganization of library and information science education in Kyiv National University of Culture and Arts: 2000–2002). In: *Bibliotechna Nauka, Osvita, Professiya u Demokratychniy Ukraini: Zbirnyk Naykovykh Prazc.(Library science, education, profession in democratic Ukraine): Collection of scientific works* (Vol. 4, pp. 130–137). Kyiv: KDUKIM.

Oleneva, Z. P. (1961). Stanovlenie i Razvitiye Vysshego Bibliotechnogo Obrazovania v SSSR. (Establishment and development of the higher library education in the U.S.S.R.)

Leningrad: Izdatelstvo Leningradskogo Bibliotechnogo Instituta imeni N.K. Krupskoy (Leningrad LIbrary Krupskaya Institute Press).

Oudshoorn, N. E., & Pinch, T. (Eds). (2003). *How users matter: The co-construction of users and technology.* Cambridge, MA: The MIT Press.

Raymond, B. (1979). *Krupskaia and Soviet Russian librarianship, 1917–1939.* Metuchen, NJ: Scarecrow Press.

Sheyko, V., & Kushnarenko, N. M. (2004). Kharkivska Vyshcha Shkola Bibliotechno-Informazcynoii ta Knygoznavchoii Osvity (Kharkiv Higher Education School of Library, Reference and Information in the context of past and present). *Visnyk Knyzhkovoii Palaty* (7), 29–33.

Shvakina, E. V. (2001). Avtomatizirovannaya Bibliotechnaya Sistema Donezckogo Nazcyonalnogo Universiteta (Automated library information systems of the Donetsk National University). In: *Virtualnye Biblioteki* (pp. 29–38). Kyiv: DAKKKIM.

Verzhbizkiy, H. (1924). *Trud i Kniga (Labor and book)* (2nd ed.). Moskva: Gosizdat.

Yates, J., & Maanen, J. V. (Eds). (2001). *Information technology and organizational transformation: History, rhetoric, and practice.* Thousand Oaks, CA: Sage.

Zhuk, V. M. (2004). Problemy Pidgotovky Specialistiv Specialnosti "Knyga, Bibliotekoznavstvo, Bibliogrphiya" (Problems in preparing specialists in "Book, Librarianship, Reference"). Paper presented at the Zvitna Naukova Konferenzcia Vykladachiv, Aspirantiv, Spivrobitnykiv i Studentiv RDGU, 20–22 Kvitnia 2004 (Report Science Conference Held for Faculty, Doctoral Candidates, and Students in Rivne State University, 20–22 April 2004), Rivne, Ukraine.

THE LIBRARY IN A MULTIETHNIC URBAN ENVIRONMENT: THE EXPERIENCE OF THE DEPARTMENT OF NATIONAL LITERATURES OF THE RUSSIAN NATIONAL LIBRARY (SAINT PETERSBURG)[☆]

Aleksei S. Asvaturov and Dmitry K. Ravinskiy

ABSTRACT

The Department of Nationality Literatures of the Russian National Library (RNB) in Saint Petersburg is a unique repository of publications in diverse languages of the peoples of the former USSR. In the collections are works in the Latvian language not to be found in Riga, works in the Tatar language not to be found in Kazan, and so on. Over the course of many decades academic researchers from all over the world have worked with these collections. Following the breakup of the USSR, the relevance of new functions for the department become apparent. First, as the

☆Translated from the Russian by William Graves III.

Advances in Library Administration and Organization, Volume 27, 25–47
ISSN: 0732-0671/doi:10.1108/S0732-0671(2009)0000027007

nationality communities in Saint Petersburg came to life, many people were drawn back to their own ethnic roots. The Department of Nationality Literatures serves, in its own way, as a national center for representatives of nationality communities. Second, the need to promote tolerance is important in Russia today. The Department brings into the public eye the cultural riches of diverse peoples and, in that way, promotes mutual understanding and tolerance. The results of a sociological study have been employed to determine the role of the Department in current changing sociocultural conditions.

INTRODUCTION

As in any other major Russian city, the basic ethno-cultural needs of the national and linguistic minorities of Saint Petersburg include the possibility of socializing and reading books and periodicals in their native languages. Given that the major libraries of the city provide, first and foremost, for the needs of the city dwellers in Russian and in a few European languages, what is, and what should be, the role in the national life of the city of the holdings of the Department of National Literatures (ONL) of the Russian National Library (RNB) – the largest collection of books, journals, and newspapers in the languages of the peoples of the former USSR?

LIBRARY SERVICES TO THE NATIONALITY COMMUNITIES OF SAINT PETERSBURG IN THE 19TH AND 20TH CENTURIES

Within an indisputably Russian-speaking populace, the linguistic environment of Saint Petersburg from the days of its very founding included foreigners as well as city dwellers from non-Russian communities within the Empire. A space of many nationalities has always been the hallmark of Saint Petersburg. Furthermore, the diverse nationality communities did not simply merge into an undifferentiated megalopolis. Their presences were reflected in a panorama of city events and given material expression in the signature style of Saint Petersburg architecture and artistic productions. At the same time, the diverse cultural forms of life of the nationality communities inescapably met and produced mutual influences as city dwellers of diverse nationalities, language backgrounds, and religious faiths entered into sustained communication with one another. Here we find it important to note that the entire history of this city produced no serious interethnic conflict and that Saint Petersburg was the site of the development of civilized forms of relations among different nationalities. This environment of multiple nationalities was characteristic of the print culture of the northern capital as well. Beginning in the 18th century, printing houses in Saint Petersburg printed books in the languages of the people of Russia and neighboring countries, and ethnic communities in the city published their own newspapers. Thus, in 1736 and 1737 the Academy of Sciences under Iosifom Sambeli directed a Georgian printing office. In 1785, a government office was established to print materials in Tatar, Arabic, and Chuvash. In 1788, an Armenian printing house was established by Grigoriy Khaldaryan. In 1780, one of the oldest books in the Tatar Collections of the RNB – Catherine II's edict "Institutions for the Governing of the Provinces of the All-Russian Empire" – was printed in Saint Petersburg in the Tatar language in the classical Tatar orthography.

However, Saint Petersburg is more than the publishing source for many books in the languages of the Russian Empire and neighboring countries from the 18th century onwards. We can also speak with certainty of the existence of collections of books from various nationalities in Saint Petersburg practically from the moment of its first appearance. Hundreds of lovingly bound volumes with elaborate ex libris notes handwritten in Georgian, Tatar, and other languages that were acquired from the citizens of Saint Petersburg are preserved to this day in the ONL of the RNB.

From the middle of the 19th century, specialized library services to the ethnic communities began to emerge in Saint Petersburg. Until this time (and, in some cases, even until the beginning of the 20th century), private libraries were a significant feature of diasporic cultural life. Among those private libraries possessing particular social significance were the collections of the Georgian Tsareviches Tejmuraz and Ioann Bagrationi (from the beginning of the 19th century)[1] and the private libraries of Khamidulla Khalitova and Mussa Bigieva (beginning of the 20th century).

The most important prerequisites to the emergence of library services to the multiethnic population were

(1) the actual presence of the ethnic group in the city;
(2) maintenance of ethnic identity by its members; and
(3) the presence of "high culture" (a writing system, literary language, formally educated community-members and, finally, book publishing in the native language).

Since these are significant characteristics of the contemporary situation as well, we need to examine these three prerequisites more closely.

The presence of ethnically and linguistically different reading publics within a dominant Russian population in Saint Petersburg is a significant feature of the historical development of the city. Representatives of more than 100 different nationalities played a role in the building of the city. Among these, in addition to foreigners, were Tatars, Mari, Chuvash, and Komi. "From the very founding of Peterburg, the main component of its linkage to Europe was the turmoil of Babel, manifesting itself in a terrible mixing of languages, customs and habits," so wrote Filipp Filippovich Vigel', Director of the Department of Foreign Religions and of German descent himself (Vigel', 1864, p. 29). In the first decades of the city "... the founding population of Peterburg was Russian, but foreigners provided an ethnic element" (Yukhneva, 1984, p. 9). By the beginning of the 19th century, foreigners made up almost 9% and non-Russians from Russia an additional 5% of the population of the capital (Yukhneva, 1984, p. 9). Until the very beginning of the 20th century, Germans constituted the largest ethnic group after Russians. As N.V. Yukhneva notes, "... the colorful ethnic diversity of the immediate surroundings of Peterburg, as well as the many nationalities of the Russian Empire, began to exert a pronounced influence on the composition of the population of Peterburg only in the second half of the 19th century" (Yukhneva, 1984, p. 15). The urban censuses of 1869, 1881, 1890, and 1900 provide support for this, showing that non-Russian residents of Saint Petersburg made up 16.8% of the total population in 1869 and 17.8% in 1900. During this period the numbers of such ethnic groups as Germans and Finns fell. The Germans, for example, made up 6.8% of the population of Saint Petersburg in 1869, but only 4% in 1900. During the same period, Peterburg witnessed a significant increase in the number of Poles, Lithuanians, Latvians, and Estonians. Research conducted by N.V. Yukhneva significantly adjusted the data from the city censuses. According to his research, by the 1850s, 3,500 Latvians and 5,400 Estonians lived in Saint Petersburg (the city census of 1869 gives the totals as 1,850 and 3,735, respectively). It is interesting that the first Lithuanian and Estonian reading rooms appeared precisely in the 1860s.

At that same time, Saint Petersburg played a noticeable role in the nationalist movements of these peoples. By the beginning of the World War I, as A. Kappeler notes, "The capital Peterburg remained the very mirror of this multi-national Empire, even as Moscow more clearly sharpened its features as a Russian city" (Kappeler, 2000, p. 238). In the particular conditions of large cities, surrounded by other cultures and other languages, ethnic processes have their own special characteristics. In every separate national community, these processes vary from the acceptance of external cultural influences to complete assimilation into the ethnically and linguistically dominant population. It should be clear, then, that there is no rationale for special library services for completely assimilated Tatars or Poles, for example. Various factors promote the maintenance of a group ethnic identity in the special conditions of a large megalopolis. These include preservation of enduring connections with the ethnic homeland, a regular flow of new immigrants, devotion to the traditional religion and way of life (this is to say kinship and family, dress, culinary habits, and many other things), and maintenance of the native language. In this case, however, representatives of "ethnoses" possessing their own political and cultural elites, a long tradition of literacy and communities of "young people" nevertheless found themselves in positions of inequality within the city. As they found possibilities for social mobility in the city, representatives of these "ethnoses," as a rule, fell under the assimilating influences of dominant ethnic groups: the Latvians and Estonians "germanized," the Lithuanians, Belorussians, and Ukrainians "polonized" or "russified" (Kappeler, 2000, p. 114).

   Certain organizational forms of national life made possible the preservation of the ethnic identity of members of nationality communities. Most important among these institutional forms were the distinctive religious faiths. Beginning in the second half of the 19th century, charitable societies and cultural-educational associations became the most widespread cultural organizations among nationality communities in the city. Among these were separate associations serving Belorussians, Georgians, Jews, Latvians, Lithuanians, Muslims, Germans, Poles, Slavs, Ukrainians, Finns, and Estonians. These societies and associations, as a rule, all had their own libraries. The book "National Societies of Saint Petersburg" notes the existence of libraries in 16 different societies from the middle of the 19th century to the revolution (Romanova & Mikhailenko, 2004). The goals of these societies and, in particular, their libraries, went beyond the maintenance of the spoken languages to include familiarization with the literary languages and support for the development of "high" national cultures.

   The majority of the cultural and scientific elites of Saint Petersburg loyally accepted the fact of multiculturalism in the city as in Russia as a whole. Experiencing, for example, cultural pressure in the homeland, in Saint Petersburg "Estonians and Latvians were met with unwavering goodwill" (Yukhneva, 1982, p. 32). "The Peterburg Russians make possible the existence of the Ukrainian national character and applaud it, as is characteristic of enlightened people of our time," P.A. Kulish, an activist in the Ukrainian nationalist movement, noted in a letter to S. Aksakov (cited in A.I. Miller) that " 'The Ukrainian Question' in the Politics of the State and the Russian Social Opinion".

The genuine growth of library services to the multiethnic population of the city was observed into the 1920s and early 1930s, even in conditions of rigid ideological pressure. Services were provided chiefly through the libraries of the national societies and the national Houses of Political Education (DPR). Libraries were located in the Finnish, Estonian, Polish, Jewish, Lithuanian, German, Hungarian, Latvian, Belorussian, Tatar, and Peoples of the East DPRs. The collections of the Estonian DPR, for example, included 8,530 books in 1932. Reading books, journals, and newspapers in the native languages allowed the multiethnic population of Leningrad to become familiar with the national cultures without the influence of intermediaries. "As with other organizational forms of cultural life for national minorities, the national libraries played an important role in the maintenance of their national self-identification and cultures in the Russian-language environment of the megalopolis" (Smirnova, 1998, p. 242). One of the consequences of a change in national policy of the All Union Communist Party in the mid-1930s was the complete suspension of all mass library services to ethnic communities in their native languages. Only at the end of the 1980s, after a 50-year hiatus, did such services begin to revive, and an entire network of independent, national libraries emerged with collections in the native languages of the city dwellers of Saint Petersburg. However, the majority of these libraries were short-lived, discontinuing operations primarily due to a lack of resources and available space.

THE DEPARTMENT OF NATIONAL LITERATURES OF THE RUSSIAN NATIONAL LIBRARY (ONL RNB) AS ONE ELEMENT IN THE STRUCTURE OF NATIONAL LIFE IN THE CITY

Representatives of approximately 130 nationalities live in Saint Petersburg. After the collapse of the USSR, the city experienced a new wave of migration out of Russia, as well as the former Soviet republics. According to the last census, the population of the city now exceeds 4.6 million people. Russians comprise 91.8% of the city dwellers (according to the census of

1989 – 89%), Ukrainians 2.3%, Belorusians 1.5%, Jews 1.3%, Tatars 0.8%, Finns 0.1%, and Poles 0.1% (Reference Book for Investors, 2001, p. 10). The nationality communities of Saint Petersburg now actively form their own cultural environments. The existence in Saint Petersburg of diverse cultural communities representing the peoples of Russia and the former USSR has become an obvious, empirical fact. These communities are distinctive not only in aspects of "high culture," but also in national dress, traditions of family and kinship relations, national culinary traditions, and much else that city dwellers encounter in daily life. With respect to intercultural communication, both positive and negative influences have resulted, from the adoption of new national cuisines, for example, to the psychological resistance of older city dwellers to the new immigrants. Ignorance of cultural norms of other peoples and a lack of tolerance and openness to others leads to negative socio-political consequences (right up to crimes on national soil). Saint Petersburg presents enormous resources for developing tolerance in city dwellers, as well as positive communication about diverse cultural forms, through the work of the internationally famous museums and theaters, as well as through the solid traditions of the study of languages and cultures of the peoples of Russia and the former USSR in the institutions of higher education of the city and, of course, in the work of the libraries. With respect to adjusting and providing support for processes of communication about national-cultural forms of life in the city (and even in Russia as a whole), The ONL, unique in the nature of its collections, plays a special role.

Today libraries remain the fundamental repositories of information resources about the histories and cultures of the diverse peoples of Russia. In information support for the study of the cultures of the peoples of Russia and support for their ethno-cultural development, the role of the RNB is paramount. The concept of the ONL as a place for discussing the cultures of the peoples of Russia and the former USSR defines its role and activities. Here we must distinguish between two fundamental, complementary directions. On the one hand, the Department assists in the preservation of the cultures of the nationality communities inhabiting the city (more will be said about this later). On the other hand, the Department provides the informational support required to promote public familiarity with and the study of the cultures of the peoples of Russia and the former USSR. The ONL serves as the institution of record for specialists conducting research on the peoples of Russia and the former USSR. However, this is of value to students and to readers with no background in higher education, for the study of cultures, languages, customs, and religious beliefs of different peoples contributes to mutual understanding and reduction of intercultural tensions and creates a tolerant worldview. This vector of activities of the ONL makes a contribution both to the prevention and battle against terrorism and extremism on national and religious soil.

However, what is the real possibility of acquainting the city dwellers with the cultural traditions of the peoples of Russia and neighboring countries under the dominating influence of American or Russian mass material culture? Does the possibility and, no less important, the need remain for personal self-realization through the linguistic, cultural, and historical traditions of the people? The fact that such a need does exist is demonstrated by the existence of functioning Georgian grammar schools, Armenian and Tatar Sunday schools, and temples of various religious faiths in the city. From the beginning of the 1990s, the mission of the ONL RNB has been to seek out and actively establish its place in the cultural, national life of the city. In those circumstances where the libraries of the national-cultural societies have very limited collections and where there is an absence of state public libraries with collections in the national languages, the ONL RNB secures the right of the citizens of Saint Petersburg to access information in their native languages. Preserving its importance as the authoritative base for scholarly work, the ONL also takes responsibility for the multicultural work of ensuring the preservation of the cultural traditions of thousands of citizens of Saint Petersburg who consider themselves Georgian, Tatar, Komi, or Estonian. As early as the end of the 1980s, in fact, the ONL was already providing patrons with resources in more than 100 different languages. With the revival of national life in the city, the ONL has become the center for the cultural revival of the Tatar community and a place where students of the Georgian grammar school gather to study their native literature. Here the relocation of the ONL from the suburbs of the city to the new location of the RNB inside the city in the 1990s played an immensely positive role. Conveniently located next to a metro station, the centralization of all reference and circulation services in one place (after many years of existence at four different geographical areas) and the availability of specialized reading rooms has created good conditions for library work.

Given the great importance of its information-providing function, the library is the place where every person may choose his own manner of immersion in the culture. As aptly noted in the professional literature, "The ultimate goal of library-bibliographic activity, which is essentially cultural activity, consists in its support for the spiritual self-realization of the person" (The Librarian's Reference, 2001, p. 142).

The success of the library-bibliographic activities and services to the multiethnic population of the city, in our view, is connected with the formation or modeling of a complete, integrated system, which can be envisioned as a positive, multicultural space. What makes this space "positive" is the possibility it presents for the maintenance of cultural identity given the frustrations of life in a megalopolis of many unfamiliar languages and ethnicities. Such a "positive" space transcends the physical walls of the reading room of the library. Although important, the library is only one element within this larger space and, without the cooperation of the other elements in the system, wholehearted library support to the multiethnic population cannot exist. Only as one element in the system can the library provide the possibility for citizens of different nationalities to take root in their native cultures, but also to provide open access to the great Russian cultural tradition and the cultural traditions of the other people of Russia. In other words, there is no interest here in creating a "cultural reservation." The point is to create a multicultural space. Principles for the modeling of this type of "positive" space exist both as firmly established principles of international practice and as the practical work of the ONL RNB.

The establishment of communications between the library and other elements of the system is the foundational principle. Above all, this is communication between the library and the national communities of the city. The cultural needs of the nationality communities and the role of the library in satisfying these needs can only be determined when these communications are clearly established. Communications become established in meetings between the Head of the Department and leading library professionals and representatives of the national communities and various organizations involved in the national life of the city, as well as representatives of city government and the media. And these kinds of meetings must be held as often as possible. It is important to remember that both national communities and members of institutes making use of literatures available in the ONL for the study of various aspects of the life of the country will constitute an important network of solid support for the ONL only when they feel that the ONL serves them well.

An immediate task for the ONL is the removal of obstacles to patron access to library services. First among these obstacles is ignorance of the existence in the city of a library with the richest collections in the native languages of the users, as well as ignorance of its location and services offered. From the end of the 1980s, nationality communities created their own cultural associations, approximately 50 of which were consolidated under the direction of the regional organization "House of National

Cultures" (DNK). There has been cooperation between the ONL and the "House of National Cultures" since the beginning of the 1990s. One of the tasks of the DNK has been to facilitate dialogue between the nationality communities and the city administration. In turn, the city provides accommodations for the national-cultural societies and assists in the resolution of any problems that arise in the communities. The functions of the DNK having been settled during the decade of the 1990s, the ONL has participated in scientific conferences organized by DNK, public functions dedicated to national literacy, and festivals organized by the various nationality-cultural associations. By and large, these various activities have been conducted outside of the library.

Communications between the ONL and the nationality communities has not been limited to coordination with the DNK. Indeed, there are more than 200 registered nationality-cultural organizations in the city; furthermore, the cultural life of the citizens of various nationalities of Saint Petersburg is certainly not restricted to the registered associations. Friends of the ONL, particularly those among our regular patrons, often propose such activities as, for example, a meeting of Ingush university students with an Ingush National Artist or an opportunity for Georgian students to learn about early, rare Georgian books. Participants in such activities are not, by and large, members of the nationality-cultural associations. These visitors to the library are not just coming to become familiar with their native culture, but to learn about the very rich collections and procedures for getting access to these. The very fact that the RNB, a state institution, is available for these types of activities does more to promote and preserve multicultural harmony than any type of official statute or declaration.

Diplomatic representatives in Saint Petersburg from the independent countries of the Baltic, Caucasus, Central Asia, and the Republics of the Russian Federation all provide support for the cultural life of the nationality communities of the city. Maintenance of cultural relations between the nationality communities and the historical homelands, concern for the cultural image of nationality communities in the Saint Petersburg environment, and cultural exchange all constitute the direction of cooperative work between the ONL and the representatives of the Republics. Book exhibitions in and outside of the library, as well as regular visits to the ONL by prominent cultural and scientific figures traveling to Saint Petersburg are very important results of this cooperation. At such functions members of the national-cultural societies and representatives of the media are in attendance and, thus, even citizens of Saint Petersburg who have not visited the library receive important objective information about the multicultural situation in

Saint Petersburg. The rich potential of the National Library, the guardian of the written memory of hundreds of peoples of Eurasia, needs to be promoted and advanced. The presence in the city of internationally recognized museums and widely celebrated theatrical and musical groups provides exceptional possibilities for demonstrating the cultural accomplishments of the people of Russia and neighboring countries.

For that very reason, the library needs to take the initiative in spreading the word about its own capabilities in this area. The combined associations of nationality societies in the city and official representatives of the Republics are the most important partners of the library in this work. Without the work of the national-cultural societies, it would be difficult to enter into sustained relations with diplomatic representatives. However, the attention of the official representatives of the Republics to the library and their participation in our activities serves to stimulate the cultural and educational activities of the nationality communities conducted together with the ONL. Thus, for example, the annual ONL book exhibition "Days of Islamic Culture" is regularly attended by colleagues and representatives of the Republic of Tatarstan in Saint Petersburg, as well as by members of the Tatar community. They have also participated in public readings in the history of Tatar literature held at the ONL. Therefore, it is not by chance that books from the RNB were exhibited together with treasures from the Hermitage in Kazan in 2001.

Relations with the leaders of various religious faiths in the city are very important. In 2001, at the request of the Armenian Apostolic Church, the ONL organized a public exhibition "Armenian Book Treasures" in the most prestigious exhibition hall (Count M.A. Korf) of the RNB. The Head of the New-Nakhichvan and Russian Diocese of the Armenian Apostolic Church, the Patriarchal Exarch in Russia, Bishop Ezras Nercicjan, attended the opening of the exhibition together with many representatives of the Armenian communities in Saint Petersburg and Moscow.

Apart from book exchanges and preparations for the bibliographic work of authority control for shared electronic catalogs, cooperation between the ONL and the National Libraries of the Russian Federation, the CIS and the Baltic nations has been expanded in recent years to include the organizing of joint book exhibitions assembled from the different library collections. A display of rare books in the Kazakh language from the RNB and from the National Library of the Republic of Kazakhstan has an emotional impact on the visitor, providing a graphic demonstration of the single, unified literary space of two countries and respect for the cultural heritage of our neighbors. Over the past two years the ONL has participated in similar joint exhibitions of books in the Komi, Kazakh, and Estonian languages, all held in the RNB. In August 2001, for the first time in the history of ONL, an exposition of prerevolutionary rare books from collections outside of Saint Petersburg. In Kazan, the RNB and the National Library of the Republic of Tatarstan held a joint exhibition "The Literary Heritage of the Tatar People." Such events attract the attention of the government to the business of preserving cultural heritage and enhances the prestige of libraries in society. Cooperation between the National Libraries of the Republics of the Russian Federation and the National Libraries of neighboring countries serves to maintain and develop a unified information space while helping to satisfy the cultural aspirations of the nationality communities of the city and promote familiarity with the cultural traditions of diverse peoples.

TOLERANCE AND BILINGUALISM

In the evolving practice of combining traditional forms of library services with nontraditional forms, closer relations between the ONL and the nationality communities of the city present increased demands on library staff. Tolerance toward people of different nationalities is an essential requirement for any librarian providing services to multiethnic patrons. Negative stereotypic perceptions of, say, natives from the Caucasus or Central Asia are absolutely unacceptable in library work. No level of professional competence can make a good librarian out of one who has feelings of this sort. Bilingualism and even multilingualism is as indispensable for library staff as it is to the organization of the reference section. Having bilingual library staff creates for the ONL patrons an atmosphere of trust and goodwill, removes psychological barriers between library staff and patron, and constitutes the essential characteristic of a multicultural library space. Of course, given a relatively small library staff, it is not possible to provide services in tens of different languages. Nevertheless, the present strong command by the library staff of Armenian, Azeri, Georgian, and Tatar permits visitors of all nationalities to experience an atmosphere of linguistic equality. There have also been unexpected psychological consequences of our promoting bilingualism in library services. A patron will now call ahead to learn the work schedule of any librarian who speaks his native language and will come to the ONL when he knows he can work with that librarian. In the past, library staff with no knowledge of other languages were psychologically unprepared to deal with such patron needs. Now we have had to come to terms with the fact that a small number of our patrons come to the ONL simply to unburden their souls.

With regard to the reference section of the ONL, there are no language problems of this kind because the catalogs of all the collections are organized alphabetically with descriptions in the languages and orthographies of the original texts. In the United States and in European countries in the 1990s, by contrast, the creation of similar catalogs in the languages of patrons of different nationalities presented significant difficulties, given the prevailing practices of transliteration or the use of English alone. Given the current language capabilities of the ONL library staff, language-related problems in searching book requests simply do not arise. Established in 1938, the unique, central catalog represents all of the different languages of the holdings in the ONL with additional author and title translations in Russian. The cards in the central catalog are sorted alphabetically by the Cyrillic translations of the titles.

JOINT MEASURES OF THE ONL AND THE NATIONAL-CULTURAL SOCIETIES AS A LIBRARY SERVICE

The cultural needs of the nationality communities of Saint Petersburg are determined by various factors, to include whether particular groups are temporary sojourners or natives of Saint Petersburg and the age and cultural and educational level of the most active part of the combined groups. Depending on the specific characteristics of the national-cultural associations, ONL library work together with specific groups taking the initiative to plan various kinds of activities. In conclusion, we will provide a few examples of nontraditional forms of services developed for users of the library.

The Tatars constitute one of the oldest nationality communities in the city and one of the most active and well-organized groups among our users. The majority of the members of the Tatar cultural society "Nur-Plus" either were born in Leningrad or have lived most of their lives in our city. Thus, the majority are not immigrants from Tatarstan and identify themselves as citizens of Saint Petersburg. For those who are middle-aged or older, the problem of national-cultural identification and the possibility of sustaining connections with each other is a very real need. It was precisely to address the needs of this audience that in 2000 we organized with the assistance of the Educational Center of the RNB a month and a half seminar on the study of the historical writing system of the Tatar people – the Arabic orthography. In the ONL, by the way, are preserved approximately 15,000 books and journals printed in the classic Arabic orthography in the languages of the Islamic people of the former Russian Empire. As a matter of fact, because of the historical change from Arabic to Cyrillic, patrons very rarely have requested these earlier publications in Arabic orthography. Yet our Tatar periodical holdings for the prerevolutionary period and the first years of the Soviet period contain very rich yet little-known materials about the lives of the Turkic peoples of Russia and the former USSR. Following our seminar on classical Arabic orthography, however, a number of the participants have become regular patrons of these collections.

In 2001–2002 for this very same audience, serials organized a regular monthly reading "The History of Tatar Literature," which attracted a much larger number of visitors. Other types of activities, including services for younger audiences such as meetings with actors, performers, writers, and journalists, have been organized in the reading room of the ONL or in the main offices of the director. Tea drinking, time set aside for informal, open conversation, and unrestrained code-switching between Russian and Tatar serve to create an atmosphere of warmth and goodwill for these kinds of meetings.

For the Veps, Komi, Mari, and other members of small minority groups not born in Saint Petersburg and spread throughout various regions of the megalopolis with no possibility of living daily life in their native languages, it is a real problem to find a place to meet with compatriots. Having heard about the ONL and coming to view an exhibition of books in their native languages, members of these immigrant groups then come to know the library and its full range of information provision and services.

The exhibition work of the ONL possesses exceptional potential to shape a positive cultural image of the nationality communities in the city. Organized under the initiatives of the national-cultural societies, exhibitions of Armenian, Georgian, Estonian, and Kazakh rare books from the collections of the ONL and its manuscript division attract the attention of the general public and generate a great many positive responses from the Saint Petersburg press.

The nationality communities themselves are heterogeneous. Although some see themselves as citizens of Saint Petersburg, others plan for the time they may return to the homeland. Furthermore, there are many students from different Republics of the Russian Federation studying in different educational institutions in the city who are living in the city temporarily.

Without having opportunities to meet their compatriots at the ONL, many of these students would never have learned about the existence of libraries in the city with collections in their native languages. Close to 200 people, most of them students, came to the ONL to meet the People's Artist of Ingushetia. For many temporary residents in the city, acquainting their children not only with the conversational but also the literary language and the cultural traditions of their people is of indisputable value. In 2002, the ONL conducted a series of meetings and activities with children entitled "Acquaintance with the National Book." Participants of these meetings were students from the Georgian schools, as well as Armenian and Tatar children. The Georgian schoolchildren are an excellent example. After graduating from the Georgian secondary school in Saint Petersburg, the young people have an opportunity to continue their education in their native language in the institutions of higher education in Tbilisi. The unprecedented wealth of the ONL's collections provides them with opportunities to become acquainted with genuine rare books and manuscripts. Our regular patron, the teacher at the Georgian school, conducts the lessons herself, working together with our curator of the Georgian collection to select materials for the lessons. The schoolchildren are presented with a rare opportunity to see such rare, first-edition books as "Warrior in the Tigerskin" from the famous collection of the Tsarevich Ioann. Thanks to the involvement of members of the national-cultural societies, researchers from the scientific and educational institutions and participants in the diverse library activities, the ONL has become an essential part of the life of the nationality communities of Saint Petersburg. As an institutional subdivision of the RNB, the ONL, in the strength of its specific collections and its library staff, also constitutes an essential element within the broader social structure – the national life of the city.

The radical changes in the life of the nation that have occurred over the past decades turned out to have the most direct influence on the activity of the ONL. The field of nationality relations in the Soviet period, viewed as successful and grounded in affirmations of "friendship among people" and "the rise of the new historical stage of society – the Soviet people" turned out to be dramatically more complex and conflict-ridden. Furthermore, in the USSR, the infrastructure of scientific and cultural institutions within which nationality problems were resolved was completely destroyed. Historically, within this infrastructure-organized relations between "the center" and the former Soviet republics possessed a completely different character. In the end, national life in the major Russian cities like Saint Petersburg underwent a completely new direction of development.

Consequently, the ONL from 2002 through 2005, in cooperation with the scientific research department of the RNB, conducted research on the patrons and users of the ONL in a focused attempt to reveal the real information and social needs compelling patrons to turn to the collections of the ONL.

To the extent that, in this case, traditional "hard" methods of sociological research of patrons and users proved to be clearly insufficient, we attempted to apply a series of supplementary research methods. We developed a questionnaire that the patrons of the ONL would fill out while they were working in the reading room. In addition, we conducted telephone interviews with patrons we were able to reach in Saint Petersburg. After this we conducted a series of interviews with representatives of the cultural-ethnic societies, regardless of whether they were patrons of the ONL or not. In addition, we conducted additional interviews with a number of specialists working in the areas represented by the ONL.

Analysis of registration forms by new patrons of the ONL provided valuable material. Finally, a library and information science analysis was conducted to establish a general picture of the roles and functions of the ONL in the overall information environment.

Analysis of registration cards revealed a series of characteristic features of the ONL patron base. The most important observation was that the majority of patrons of the ONL are visitors from abroad. Thus, of 95 visiting patrons, 16 were from the so-called "far abroad" countries (USA, Italy, Netherlands, Finland, Sweden, Germany, Japan, and Korea), 33 were from former republics of the USSR, and 46 were from Russia (including republics of the Northern Caucasus, Yakutia, and others). The visitors consisted of, naturally, scientific researchers, graduate students and, a bit unexpectedly, students. Furthermore, many were state employees from administrative and cultural agencies. Notably, a large number of visitors to the ONL were library staff, teachers from Institutes of Culture and bibliographers. Of those visitors living in Saint Petersburg, 20 were undergraduates and graduate students (12 graduate students; 9 under-graduates) from such higher educational institutions as the School of Eastern Studies at the Saint Petersburg State University, the Russian Pedagogical State University in the name of A.I. Hertzen and the State Polar Academy. A bit unexpected was the finding that among all of our visitors, there was not one undergraduate or graduate student from other higher educational institutions in Saint Petersburg who would have turned to the study of the culture and history of his own people for nonacademic reasons.

On the basis of our interviews, we attempted to categorize basic types of patrons of the ONL. Overall, we distinguished between two fundamental categories of patrons of the ONL: "Specialists" and "Representatives of Ethnic Communities."

Specialists

We found it useful to separate this category into two sub-categories: (a) academic specialists in the area of culture, language, and history of people represented by materials in the ONL and (b) students of higher educational institutions working with materials in the ONL related to their academic coursework.

Academic Specialists
The specific character of this sub-category (and this is confirmed by an analysis of the registration cards) is that the majority of these patron-academic specialists have come to Saint Petersburg from other areas, including other countries. We included in this group of patron-academic specialists not only those who came to the ONL to research issues directly related to their professional duties, but also those who came to the ONL to conduct professional research that complemented their professional duties. Judging from the registration cards, questionnaires, and interviews, such a situation is quite common (e.g., a chemist researching problems in Georgia and Abkhaziya, a Middle-East areal specialist researching the history of Estonia, and so on). It is clear that this situation is most common among people of retirement age. However, it is important here to emphasize that interest in the materials of the ONL is not restricted to problems of language, literature, history, and culture, but includes importantly interest in special regional and areal characteristics of research problems in the natural sciences. Thus, one of our respondents, a botanist by education and professional interest, has been researching materials in the Kirgiz language and materials related specifically to Kyrgyzstan in connection with his research into the cultivation of specific plants (in particular, the Greek walnut) grown in the area of Kyrgyzstan in the former USSR. In connection with this research, he is interested in many other aspects of the economy of Kyrgyzstan.

In the course of interviews, almost all academic specialists spoke of the unique character of the ONL collections (from time-to-time quite emotionally, in fact, "When I brought my Estonian friends to the ONL, they stared in disbelief – they have nothing of the kind in Estonia!"). This group, in contrast to all other groups, was important to us precisely because they could answer questions about how our collections compared to the collections of other libraries in the city. On the basis of information we have received, we confirm that a system of fully complementary collections is lacking – materials related to the thematics of the ONL can be found in the most unexpected institutions. Under these circumstances, the fact that the collections of the ONL of the RNB have been organized on an extremely systematic foundation of mandatory copy controls going all the way back to the prerevolutionary period has now become extremely significant. Academic specialists do note gaps in the collections of the ONL, it goes without saying; nevertheless, to the extent that they see the bigger picture, the most important fact for them is that our collections constitute a foundation or, as one of our respondents expressed it, "the backbone" of materials in the thematics of interest to them. Almost all of our academic specialists commented that the ONL collections were more important to them than the collections of the Academy of Sciences, libraries of the State University, and other libraries in the city.

Students
Students of the higher educational institutions who work with the collections of the ONL to fulfill course objectives are mainly students of School of Eastern Studies of Saint Petersburg University. In our massive collection of registration cards there are a few cards belonging to students of the Polar Academy, a new educational institution. However, all of these students live in dormitories and it is impossible to contact them by phone. Unfortunately, among the patrons of the ONL we were unsuccessful in finding even a single student from any of the specialized departments of the State University or State Pedagogical University. So far only instructors from the recently established Departments of Baltic Studies and Caucasus Studies have visited the ONL.

   One important discovery was that students are making use of materials in those national languages required for the study of the history of different countries. Thus, one student approached the ONL Iranian section with a request for materials in classical Armenian that she needed for coursework in the history of Iran. In the words of this student, her instructor had recommended that she come to the ONL since these types of materials are available only at the ONL of the RNB. Much to the point, it became clear that, although the library at the School of Eastern Studies did not have these kinds of materials, the library at the Institute for Eastern Studies did, but students were not permitted to use this library. From this we reach an important conclusion: the unique position of the ONL of the RNB in the overall information infrastructure of the city is not only a function of its rich collections, but of its democratism. In contrast to the academic and state bureaucratic system of libraries, the ONL is open to all students and "people off the street." In this particular respect, the ONL simply has no competitors.

Democratism acquires a special significance when we take up the second category – *representatives of the ethnic communities*. We must add here that in this instance we are not discussing academic specialists with ethnic backgrounds. Here the discussion concerns those nonspecialist patrons whose interests are of a personal, rather than professional character.

Here we found it expedient to divide these into two sub-categories: (a) active participants in the life of the community and (b) those who live "on the periphery" of the community. Although this might seem paradoxical, among all respondents identified by registration card, the majority turned out to be members of the second sub-category. It is not difficult to explain this, however. The community itself provides its members with a library of literary works and, most importantly, newspapers in the national languages, as well as popular works. Therefore, an active member of the community typically comes to the ONL to fulfill some special information need, which does not happen all that often. With respect to the nonactive members of the community, although the process of "ethnic mobilization" has motivated them, they find it simpler to come to the RNB than to the community library, which generally has more limited working hours. A typical example of this is the intellectual pensioner – the Tatar who does not know the Tatar language and has decided to begin the study of the language with children's books which she finds and studies at the ONL. Very often people who have been cut off from national life discover that "returning to one's roots" is accomplished more comfortably by making private visits to the library than by participating in community activities.

In connection with the fact that the role of the ONL in the multiethnic life of the city has become a subject of special attention by the library staff, the second stage of our research was based on a series of interviews with well-known representatives of nationality communities in Saint Petersburg to determine the actual and the potential place of the ONL in the life of these communities.

Practically all of the representatives of all of the communities noted with regret that literatures in the national languages were not enjoying great demand. Here is an excerpt from one interview with one leader of the Estonian community

And how often do people take advantage of the collection of books you have available for the community?

Well, not often, actually ... Practically no demand at all

Why?

In our community basically we are dealing with older people who left Estonia quite a long time ago. And they, as a rule, have lost active command of the language, the language has been lost, particularly among those who came to Russia before the war. Those who arrived after the war, they command the language, but, more often than not, still speak Russian at home. I know five families where they speak Estonian in the home, but this is out of a thousand people, Estonians, I know of living in Saint Petersburg. It is a widespread enough situation where an Estonian family, having lived for a long time in Saint Petersburg and having practically forgotten the language, want their own children to learn the Estonian language. In our community there is a Sunday school for children, there is a teacher, there are pupils, but, as usual, it is difficult to find suitable accommodations.

And here are the words of a representative from the Tatar community

There is a problem with the language. Many Tatars living in Saint Petersburg don't know the language, that is they are not able to read serious literature. Tatars generally as a people are very restrained, cautious, unwilling to talk about their problems. In the beginning at many of our activities people spoke Russian, but know they have already started speaking Tatar at our functions and they don't fall asleep when someone reads aloud some composition in the Tatar language. And so we sometimes hold our functions in the library and people from 80 years of age to small children all come. Interest in the culture is there, but much has been forgotten. The main problem was always that the children wrote poorly in Russian, so the Tatar families made an effort to speak Russian in the home, not Tatar.

Similar motifs were voiced by an Ingush woman in one interview

The Ingush all want to know history. To this very day the Ingush people do not have their own library, their own archives. Much was seized from us during deportation, and much of it was never returned to us. Students studying the Ingush language need dictionaries, self-study texts, so many come here. As for the adults, practically all know the Ingush language. But the youth, even in the Republic don't know the language. In school the language of instruction has always been Russian.

One Armenian spoke of similar problem

Use of the library depends on the composition of the population living now in this city. The Armenian community has ancient roots, ancient traditions here in Saint Petersburg. The old Saint Petersburg Armenians are mostly educated people, as knowledgeable about Armenian literature as they are about Russian. But the new immigrants, they, even in Armenian, read poorly. A significant portion of this contingent of new immigrants is semi-literate at best. Libraries are rarely used, and basically by students to fulfill academic requirements. Still, overall, most students are interested in the internet and television. For them the library is just a burden.

CONCLUSION

On the basis of our interviews we can conclude that for practically all of the nationality communities today, the main problem is a linguistic one. However, this problem exists, if we may phrase it this way, in an "inverted" form. The problem is not that the members of the ethnic communities do not know Russian or that they have a poor command of their native language. Even though there were representatives of such communities as the Armenian and the Ingush with many refugees and forced migrants among our respondents, what presents itself as more important than information is material and social support ("with no connections you will find no work"). For the refugee, it is practically impossible to preserve any professional status. Consequently, there is a loss of professional informational needs. Therefore, the formula adopted in European countries: the immigrant must have the opportunity to fulfill three needs: (a) to know about that which is happening in the native country; (b) to receive socially meaningful information, essential for organizing life in a new country; and (c) to have the opportunity to read for pleasure and for personal development literature in one's own native language – in the situation under discussion here, this last cannot become the conceptual foundation of information provision.

The main cultural problem in all nationality communities is that the youth do not know the native language, a situation made worse by the fact that youth are not oriented toward book culture in general. (It is true, as noted by our respondents, that even the adults are more likely to attend musical performances.)

The basic category of participants in the nationality associations are people who have lived many years in Russia and, due to circumstances, have become unaccustomed to reflecting on their ethnic roots. Today, however, when this has become possible (and in some sense even fashionable), they now willingly take up their national culture. It is typical, however, that those aspects of national culture in greatest demand are those that do not require knowledge of the language – concerts and musical activities. In some sense, we can also say of national languages exactly what is often said about English in Russia today: this is not so much the language of "social intercourse" as it is the language of "familiarity," a sign of belonging to a particular circle or, as in the case under discussion here, to a specific national community. People do not so much know a language as "want" to know a language.

(1) It is not surprising that the library and the ONL attract communities not just as a source of information, but as a "cultural space," a location for the realization of communal activities. Familiarity with one's own culture is often expressed in the visual form of monuments to book culture, of great importance to representatives of ethnic minorities, particularly in conditions characterized by cultural xenophobia.

(2) There is an obvious need to create an infrastructure of ethnic education in the city, not just ethnic enlightenment. More than anything, of course, we are discussing here the study of language, but also the acquisition of national customs and traditions that have significance to etiquette. Even though the theme of the return to the historical homeland arises most commonly today in reference to the Baltic countries, there is ample proof of the need for instruction and the recovery of traditions of "correct" conduct to permit the preservation of national and, indeed, personal identity in the conditions of a cosmopolitan megalopolis. The loss of language and national culture will cost many ethnic communities dearly.

(3) If there is agreement with the point of view developed in the course of this discussion that, in the libraries, we find among the representatives of ethnic communities "students and retirees" drawn into an educational process for one reason or another and also those who seek to "return to their roots," then it is apparent that one more category of library patron has remained outside of our field of vision. These are those who are called in foreign literatures "amateur researchers." This is the group that we have called "independent researchers" in the course of our sociological research into patrons and users of the RNB. These people are not members of any official scientific organizations or institutions connected to nationality communities, but on their own initiative conduct research into one or another problem often related to ethnic problems. The problem of the recovery of personal status, a painfully real problem for refugees and forced migrants, perhaps could be resolved by such a route.

NOTE

1. The private collection of Tsarevich Ioann which included manuscripts and printed books, Georgian manuscripts from the 12th and 13th centuries, and a personal list of the members of the Georgian imperial family was acquired by the Imperial Public Library in 1880.

REFERENCES

Kappeler, A. (2000). *Rossiya – Mnogonatsional'naya Imperiya (Russia: A multiethnic empire)* (p. 342). Moscow: Progress-Tradition.

Reference Book for Investors (2001). Available at http://www.ffrp.ru/issue/2001rus.pdf

Romanova, N. M., & Mikhailenko, V. V. (2004). *Natsiolnal'nye Obshchestva Sankt-Peterburga XVIII–XXIvv (Nationality Associations of St. Petersburg 18th –21st centuries)* (p. 210). St. Petersburg: SPN.

Smirnova, T. M. (1998). Natsional'nye Biblioteki v Leningrade (1918–1930 gg) (Nationality libraries in Leningrad 1918–1930). *Klio, 3*(6), 234–243.

The Librarian's Reference (2001). A. N. Vaneev (Ed.). Available at http://www.ffrp.ru/issue/2001rus.pdf

Vigel', F. F. (1864). Vospominaniya (Memoires), Part 2, Moscow, pp. 142–147.

Yukhneva, N.V. (1982). Peterburg – Mnogonatsional'naya Stolitsa (Peterburg: A multi-ethnic capital), Staryi Peterburg: Istoriko-Ehtnograficheskie Issledovaniya (Old Peterburg: Historical Ethnographic Investigations), L, 1982.

Yukhneva, N. V. (1984). Ehtnicheskiy Sostav i Ehtnosotsial'naya Struktura Naseleniya Peterburga Vtoraya Polovina XiX-Nachalo XX v. Statisticheskiy Analiz (Ethnic composition and ethnosocial structura of the population of Peterburg from the second half of the 19th century to the beginning of the 20th century. A statistical analysis) L, 1984.

BULGARIAN LIBRARIANSHIP: SURVIVING CHANGE THROUGH INTERNATIONAL COOPERATION

Tatiana Nikolova-Houston

ABSTRACT

The history of Bulgarian librarianship comprises a history of survival under change imposed by foreign rule. This chapter traces the historical development of Bulgarian libraries and LIS education through the lens of Bulgarian history. Part I presents an overview of Bulgarian history, focusing on four dramatic epochs. During Ottoman rule (1393–1878), Bulgarian libraries survived by hiding. The second epoch, European intervention, Russian, occurred under the Austro-Hungarian, and German rule (1878–1944). Bulgarian LIS survived by adopting European practices and the German academic model of library education. The third epoch, Soviet rule (1944–1989), saw a massive suppression of information, Bulgarian libraries survived by maintaining an undercurrent of dissent. The fourth epoch began in 1989 with the onset of democratic reforms. Bulgarian librarianship survived the financial crisis and anarchy of that epoch by adopting foreign practices and establishing partnerships with foreign library institutions. Part II describes agents of change acting within the Bulgarian LIS field during the radical change from Soviet to democratic rule. The change agents included the formation of a union, cooperation among Bulgarian libraries, and international cooperation with Western institutions.

Advances in Library Administration and Organization, Volume 27, 49–71
Copyright © 2009 by Emerald Group Publishing Limited
ISSN: 0732-0671/doi:10.1108/S0732-0671(2009)0000027008

Research for this chapter incorporated literature reviews, surveys of accredited Bulgarian LIS programs, interviews with Bulgarian and American LIS professionals, and bibliometric analysis of Bulgarian publications.

INTRODUCTION

The history of Bulgarian libraries and Library and Information Science (LIS) education mirrors the history of the Bulgarian nation. For over 10 centuries, Bulgaria nurtured the Slavic legacy of Sts. Cyril and Methodius. Bulgarian scribes wrote in Cyrillic (named for St. Cyril) to transmit the writings of the classical Greek and Byzantine civilizations to Bulgaria, centuries before the Renaissance. They translated, copied, and illuminated manuscripts under the patronage of tsars such as Simeon and Ivan Alexander, who established "Golden eras" of Bulgarian literacy and libraries in the 10th and 14th centuries.

Yet, Bulgarian history is a history of survival under foreign hegemony: Byzantine (1018-1185), Ottoman (1393–1878), Russian (1879–1886), Austro-Hungarian (1887–1918), German (1941–1944), and Soviet (1944–1989). As a result of the frequently totalitarian and repressive foreign regimes, Bulgarian library history remained virtually unknown in the West until 1990, when Bulgaria began its transformation from totalitarianism to democracy.

This chapter discusses the changes that occurred in Bulgarian libraries and LIS education during three dramatic episodes in Bulgarian history: the change from Ottoman rule to self-rule based on European models (1878), the onset of Soviet rule (1944), and democratization (1989). It then discusses the agents of change that were at work during democratization and their results.

PART I: A HISTORY OF CHANGE

Ottoman Imperialism (1393–1878)

The Ottoman conquest of Bulgaria resulted in occupation, wars, and neglect that destroyed thousands of manuscripts. Perhaps 5% of all manuscripts survived, being taken into hiding or into foreign lands such as Russia, Moldavia, and Mount Athos in Greece (Matejic, 2005, personal communication). Scriptoria and libraries survived during the Ottoman period, situated in remote mountain monasteries where the Orthodox Church organized the process of manuscript production and custodianship (Nikolova-Houston, 2008). Over the years, self-educated secular scribes joined ecclesiastical scribes in composing and copying manuscripts. This broadening of authorship from clerical to secular resulted in manuscripts being written in a simple spoken language, the evolving vernacular of the times (Nikolova-Houston, 2008).

In 1762, the Bulgarian monk Paisii of Hilandar wrote the simple but powerful *History of the Slavo-Bulgarians*, based on his research at foreign libraries and archives. All Bulgarian historians, including Mihail Arnaudov, Vladimir Topencharov, Hristo Hristov, Nadezhda Dragova, Bonyo Angelov, Bozhidar Raikov (Boycheva, 2002, p. 5) believe that Paisii's book inspired the 18th–19th century Bulgarian cultural and political revival, including the establishment of public reading circles and libraries (*chitalishte*, plural *chitalishta*).

Western Library Models (1878–1944)

The Liberation from Ottoman rule (1878) allowed new ideas from Europe to enter Bulgaria. In 1869, before the liberation, the first Bulgarian academic library, the Bulgarian Academy of Science, appeared in Braila, Romania. Following liberation, the National Library Sts. Cyril and Methodius was founded in Sofia, being followed 10 years later by the University of Sofia St. Kliment Ohridski library (SU). The first Bulgarian library institutions employed the foreign models of education and library practices of their founders, librarians who had received their education in the West or in Russia and in Germany and Austria (Black, 1943, p. 507; Dobrev, 2005, p. 13).

Foreign ideas and practices continued to influence Bulgarian librarianship education during the 20th century. Dimitur Agura introduced the French model of library education and librarianship in 1905 (Yanakieva, 2008a, p. 9). The French influence, however, was overshadowed by the German-Austrian, perhaps because Bulgaria allied with Germany and Austro-Hungary, during the World War I. Stoyan Argirov visited German and Austrian libraries and began in 1905 to advocate the German-Austrian model of library and archival practices and particularly the perception of library science as an academic discipline. He introduced into the SU curriculum the first "elective" course in librarianship in 1919. Library

Theory followed, to become a permanent course in 1922–1923. Both courses presented organization and use of library materials, library architecture, library administration, cataloging, and library history. Argirov strongly believed that professional librarians should possess subject expertise: academic degrees and specialization in particular areas of study (Yanakieva, 2008a, p. 12).

I speculate that the German-Austrian model reflected the political affiliation of Bulgaria to the Austro-Hungarian Empire until the end of the World War I, and to Germany until the end of the World War II. This affiliation would have facilitated Bulgarian academic visits to libraries and archives in Germany, where Bulgarian scholars adapted the German model of library education to Bulgarian higher education. The defeat of Axis forces in Bulgaria in 1944 allowed the Soviet-sponsored Georgi Dimitrov to impose totalitarian rule over Bulgaria, ushering in a new era influenced greatly by Soviet librarianship.

Soviet Ideological Control (1944–1989)

Soviet control of Bulgaria in 1944 introduced a totalitarian Marxist-Leninist communist ideology that imposed central planning and a brutal suppression of individual expression and personal freedom. Bulgarian libraries and archives became "ideological institutions" (Gergova et al., 1997, p. 8). They restricted information, for example, with *spetsfonds* (special closed stacks, accessible only to Communist Party members). The Bulgarian government established the *Bibliotekarski Institut* (Library Institute) in 1949 to eradicate the German-Austrian influence on librarianship (Yanakieva, 2008b, personal communication). At the Library Institute, curricula in librarianship included ideologically charged historical aspects of libraries, books, and bibliography, contradictory to the kind of librarianship practiced in most other countries. Courses such as Marxist-Leninist theory, esthetics, ethics, dialectic materialism, and scientific communism persisted until 1990. Russian became the required foreign language, although this was not unusual – Russia and Bulgaria shared common historical and literary heritages. The didactic style of teaching in library courses did not encouraged students to participate and favored memorization rather than creative or critical thinking. Students did not interact with faculty (Atanasov & Todorova, 1990, p. 31; Stoikova, 1990, p. 26).

The Soviet model demoted librarianship to a vocation and librarians to paraprofessional status, reducing the social standings and power of librarians. The government also restricted contact with any colleagues except those in the Soviet Bloc: Prague, Warsaw, Krakow, Budapest, and East Berlin. Professors could attend conferences and students could perform internships, but only in Soviet Bloc countries. Travel outside the Bloc required special approval (Yanakieva, 2008b, personal communication). Occasionally, professors had clandestine contact with Westerners, but such contacts did not influence policy in Bulgaria. Subscriptions to Western library periodicals and IFLA (International Federation of Library Association) publications were scarce. Yanakieva recalls that the Communist Party monitored and censored personal correspondence between Bulgarians and Western colleagues.

However, The German model, principles, ideas, and curriculum remained. Like Argirov, Todor Borov studied library science and bibliography at Berlin University (1924–1927) and introduced additional German library theory and practices into Bulgarian library education (Yanakieva, 2008a, p. 13). He established the specialization of "Library science and bibliography" at the SU Department of Archival Studies in 1953 to prepare librarians for work in academic and special libraries. The curriculum included courses in history and organization of librarianship, organization of library practices in Bulgaria, theory and practice of librarianship, planning and reporting of library work, library practicum, librarianship, general bibliography, special bibliography, general and applied library science, theory and practice of archival studies, museum science, introduction in the history of science, and foreign language. Borov also insisted that librarians should have a degree in a particular academic major in addition to a specialization in library science, a concept quite revolutionary and innovative for his time for the entire East European Bloc (Yanakieva, 2008b, personal communication). Borov incorporated courses in bibliography and book-related disciplines that balanced theory and practice in librarianship, whereas teaching library history and bibliography for the Department of History and Philology.

In its opposition to the German model, the Bulgarian government imposed further obstacles to librarianship education. The government created internal tensions by institutional fragmentation when it split the administration of higher educational for librarians, giving the university *visshe* (higher, academic), including Bachelor's and Master's degrees, to the Council for Higher Education, and the Library Institute *poluvische* (semihigher, vocational, paraprofessional), or Associate's degree, to the Committee of Culture. Librarians became "cultural-educational cadres" with a new ideologically laden, nonprofessional status and low salaries

(Yanakieva, 2008a, p. 25). For more than 30 years, the Soviet-sponsored Library Institute fought the German model, but the German model prevailed (Yanakieva, 2008b, personal communication).

Democratization, Financial Crisis, and Survival (1989)

The collapse of the Communist regime in Bulgaria in November 1989 led to power struggles and constantly changing administrations. The chaos of the transition broke the authoritarian shell of the Soviet system but left a vacuum of values and public resistance to further change. The economy nearly collapsed, requiring remarkable innovations in the library community.

The political changes and financial crisis caused catastrophic unemployment, inflation, and a cessation of government subsidy of libraries and archives. Libraries closed, or they fired staff, reduced salaries, and canceled subscriptions to periodicals and other acquisitions. For example, the National Library decreased its subscriptions from 183,997 (1989) to 53,782 (2001). Book acquisitions decreased by 2/3 compared to those before 1989 (Dimchev, 2001, p. 144). For the period 1989–2000, the number of libraries dropped from 10,442 to 6,942 (Dimchev, 2008). According to the Bulgarian National Statistical Institute, the number of libraries in 2005 had dropped further to 4,552. The number of "readers" decreased by 30% to 1,300,000 (Dimchev, 2001, p. 145).

As a result of the political reforms, however, Bulgarian libraries received more autonomy, increased public access to information and resources, and began to interact with Western institutions. Bulgarian libraries opened their doors and stacks to foreign visitors and colleagues. American library and information professionals visited Bulgarian academic and research libraries during this time and witnessed the crisis. Edwards (1998) remarked on the shortage of funds at the University of Rousse in 1996–1997, calling the situation an "information crisis." The library could not afford new monographs and teaching resources or the implementation of computer technology in classrooms or in the library. Scholarly journal subscriptions dropped from 1,000 to 700. Librarians retrieved textbooks from closed stacks and restricted their use to the reading room, due to high demand and short supply. Professors self-produced multiple copies of course materials for their students. In the Winter of 1996–1997, the University of Rousse academic library was forced to close, because it was unable to pay its fuel bills.

Four years later, Smith (2001) described the continuing impact of the financial crisis on the Central Technical Library in Sofia, the main provider of scientific research publications in Bulgaria and a part of the National Center for Information and Documentation. The librarians, highly competent and fluent in foreign languages, felt powerless to solve the funding issues and confessed to Smith that the crisis had "transformed them into philosophers," struggling with bare bookshelves but many houseplants. Subscriptions of periodicals decreased from 10,000 (1990) to 105 (2001), and monographs from 6,000 (1990) to 435.

The history of survival under change imposed by foreign rule took several forms. Bulgarian libraries survived under Ottoman rule by hiding. They survived under Austro-Hungarian rule by adopting European practices. They survived under Soviet rule by maintaining an undercurrent of dissent. They survived democratization by again adopting foreign practices and establishing partnerships with foreign library institutions. Part II describes survival during the change to democratization of Bulgarian libraries.

PART II: AGENTS OF CHANGE IN BULGARIAN LIBRARIANSHIP

This section discusses the various agents of change in Bulgarian librarianship that were at work during the 1990s change from totalitarian to democratic rule. The change agents included the Union of Library and Information Science Officers (ULISO), the academic library of the American University in Blagoevgrad (AUBG), the American Bulgarian Library Exchange (ABLE) project between American and Bulgarian public libraries, the leadership of LIS program at SU, international educational standards (the Paris and Bologna accords), international cooperation between LIS programs, the GLOBENET Conferences, and LIS research and publishing.

The Union of Library and Information Science Officers

In 1990, Bulgarian librarians realized the dream of the pioneers of Bulgarian library science education Argirov and Borov with the establishment of a professional union, like the American Library Association, called the ULISO. ULISO denounced censorship and advocated open stacks instead of *spetsfonds*. ULISO also encouraged Bulgarian libraries to design their services to meet the needs of their patrons rather than political ideologies. According to the mission statement of ULISO (ULISO Website, 2008), adopted during the Union's 8th Congress in 2005, ULISO works to:

- develop and assert positions in defining and implementing national library and information policy;
- support harmonization of library bills and regulations with European Union directives;
- work toward implementation of international technological standards in library and information services;
- coordinate and support partnership initiatives between libraries in carrying out their activities;
- launch new projects and events with local, national, and international significance about general library issues as well as in specific priority areas;
- continue its activities as a leader of continuing education for librarians and information specialists by strengthening the Center for Continuing Education for Librarians; and
- collaborate with similar NGOs and support the integration of the country's book publishing and disseminating sector.

Left to their own meager resources, the library officers of ULISO turned to foreign support and informed the international library community about the crisis in Bulgarian libraries. Assisted by the American Embassy in Sofia and the Soros "Open Society Foundation," ULISO received funds for purchasing computer equipment for Bulgarian libraries. In the early 1990s, the Open Society donated $550,000 for basic library automation and $1,000,000 for automation of research libraries. ULISO and the Open Society collaborated to organize national and international professional conferences and promoted the concept of library consortiums to survive the shortage of funding. Together with the LIS department at SU, ULISO worked to establish in 2001 the Center for Continuing Education for Librarians (Doncheva, 2004, p. 161). ULISO arranged for and coordinated donations of books and gift subscriptions to foreign journals from foreign partner libraries. Provided with funds by the Open Society Foundation, ULISO generated in 1997 the strategic National Program for the Preservation of Library Collections.

AUBG Library as a Model and Agent for Technological Change and Leadership

Some Bulgarian academic libraries used international cooperation to become agents of technological and social change. For example, the AUBG, a branch of the University of Maine, introduced a new set of values characteristic of American society, being the first to abolish ideological control and censorship (Alexandrova, 2005, pp. 59–60). The AUBG library also pioneered the implementation in Bulgaria in the 1990s of other modern library practices such as self-service copying machines, e-mail and Internet access, open stacks, and bibliographical instruction for patrons. AUBG created Bulgaria's first online electronic catalog, library Internet portal, and an integrated library system.

The financial crisis and budget cuts inspired AUBG to form the Bulgarian Information Consortium (BIC) in 2002 in alliance with the New Bulgarian University, Sofia; the Technical University, Sofia; and the Economic Academy, Svishtov (Terzieva & Todorova, 2006, online). BIC provided Bulgarian libraries with access to electronic databases such as EBSCO Host, Emerald Full Text, the GALE Virtual Reference Library, and Oxford Reference Online (Bulgarian Information Consortium, 2008, online). To encourage use of the BIC resources, the AUBG library organized the Technology Day for Bulgarian librarians and other technology training workshops (Alexandrova, 2005, p. 59).

Public Libraries as Agents of Social Change: The ABLE Project

Cooperation between Bulgarian and American public librarians also created social change, specifically, patron-oriented paradigm for Bulgarian libraries. This paradigm was one of the changes initiated by the joint project known as the ABLE project, linking the Colorado Association of Libraries to ULISO in 1996 (Bolt, 2002, p. 1). Nancy Bolt, of Nancy Bolt & Associates, initiated this cooperative venture to help Bulgarian librarians observe, meet with, and train with American counterparts. Bolt organized annual Bulgarian jewelry sales to support the project and to send books to Bulgarian libraries. Her organization applied for and received a $198,000 grant from the Bureau of Education and Cultural Affairs, U.S. Department of State (Bolt & Ianeva, 2004, p. 103). In 2002, eight Bulgarian members of ULISO interned at six model U.S. Community Information Centers (CICs). Then, American librarians visited six Bulgarian libraries to provide training. During conferences organized by ULISO, the participating Bulgarian and American librarians shared their experiences with other Bulgarian librarians. In 2004, American librarians trained staff of ABLE Bulgarian libraries to become CIC (Bolt, 2004, p. 7). Eleven CICs opened in Bulgarian cities. The project later expanded to include 18 CICs (Popova, 2008).

The ABLE project helped to transform Bulgarian public libraries into places of social interaction, much like the reading clubs, *chitalishta*, of the 19th century. Those community centers were the predecessors of Bulgarian public libraries. A number of libraries opened foreign language reading rooms, and launched free conversational English courses and Friends of the Library clubs (Bolt, 2002; Velkova, 2006, p. 4). During the time of transitional financial crisis and massive unemployment, public libraries provided free lessons in English, and preparation for taking the TOEFL, and the SAT exams. ABLE libraries offered children's activities, services to disadvantaged people, and free Internet access. Transformed into modern CICs, those libraries offered online information about local community activities. The ABLE Internet portal now hosts community information approximately 18 topics: Local and state government; European integration; Media; Social security; Education; Work, Jobs and continuing education; Law & legislation; Health care; Business & Finance; Culture & Arts; Quick Reference; All about the USA; Society; Libraries; How to search the Internet; For school children; Tourism; and Entertainment, hobby, and sports. The portal links to 700 other sites (Popova, 2008).

In another important innovation, the ABLE partnership made Bulgarian public libraries more visible to local governments. American partners met with Bulgarian municipal officials and convinced them of the importance of public libraries (Bolt, 2008, personal communication). The Americans also trained Bulgarian librarians to lobby for their patrons' and libraries' interests. As a result, Bulgarian libraries have greater visibility and support from local governments through increased budgets for salaries, technological equipment, and book acquisition (Popova, 2008, report). The National Library Week and National Library Day, organized by ABLE partners and ULISO, lobbied for public libraries at the national level, attracting the attention of international foundations such as the Bill and Melinda Gates Foundation (Bolt, 2008, personal communication).

In exchange, the ABLE project changed profoundly the views of American librarians through learning about another country, visiting Bulgaria, and establishing friendships (Bolt & Ianeva, 2004, p. 104). For Bolt, ABLE changed her life "incredibly" when she felt in love with Bulgaria, its people, and its libraries to the extent that she now dedicates her efforts to international relations, realizing the impact of "making a difference in libraries" (Bolt, 2008, personal communication).

Other programs such as PUBLICA and PULMAN also opened new horizons of understanding about the social role of libraries as CIC. In this social role, the libraries helped people to cope with the problems of daily living and facilitated community participation by bringing people together to discuss common issues and to learn from foreign experience in resolving them (Durrance, Pettigrew, & Fisher, 2002).

Bulgarian libraries rediscovered their mission as agents of social change, following their predecessors, the *chitalishta* (Gergova et al., 1997, p. 7). They developed an appreciation for this mission in large part by merging old traditions with new foreign experience as they worked with their ABLE partners. As a result, Bulgarian public libraries became service providers to their local communities and patrons.

LIS PROGRAMS AT BULGARIAN UNIVERSITIES AS AGENTS OF CHANGE

Immediately after the overthrow of the Soviets in 1989, as a result of the privatization of higher education and institutional autonomy from the government, LIS programs began to offer expanded courses in library and information science and library management. The international cooperation with Western library institutions affected this change in library school curricula as academic training of Bulgarian librarians began to conform to Western accreditation standards. New courses addressed the information technology revolution and the resultant exponential growth of electronic information resources.

The establishment of an independent LIS program in the Philosophy Department of SU in 1993 came in response to a new LIS program at Veliko Turnovo University the year before. This competition between the two universities encouraged other library programs to update curricula and balance library practice with theory. The LIS program at Sts. Cyril and Methodius University began to offer two specializations: Book Publishing, and LIS (Yanakieva, 2005, p. 46).

The SU curriculum emphasized the role of Bulgarian libraries as social institutions and the role of information specialists as handling complex information sources and media to meet the variable needs of patrons. The Master's degree program, for example, became interdisciplinary, borrowing from other fields and offering dual credit courses in information copyright law, the marketing of cultural institutions, information-seeking behavior, and information brokering. The Department of Journalism and the History Department created new specializations such as Book Publishing and Archival Studies. Since 1993, the SU LIS course curriculum has changed three times to create new disciplines associated with new digital and online information resources.

Change also affected the Library Institute in Sofia. In 1997, its name changed to the College of Library Science, and since 2004, the college has offered a three-year Bachelor's degree in librarianship, increasing the social status and image of its graduates. The college teaches library science, bibliography, book distribution, information brokering, information technologies, and historical information resources to 250 full-time and 300 part-time students annually.

After the collapse of communism, privatization of higher education introduced changes and competition in other Bulgarian universities. Private universities competed with public universities for students. Nine of the 32 Bulgarian private and public universities now offer training in information science and technology (Yanakieva, 2005, p. 46). Shumen University offers IT and LIS programs. The New Bulgarian University in Sofia offers the M.S. in Information Science. Varna Free University offers the M.S. in Information and Computer Science. Rousse University has degree in Information and Computer Sciences, and Southwestern University in Blagoevgrad offers degree in Computer Systems and Technologies. The Technical University in Gabrovo offers specializations in Automation, Information and Control Systems, and Computer Equipment and Technologies.

The shortage of adequately trained faculty affected the quality of education in provincial LIS programs. Without coordination among LIS programs, the quality of instruction and the amount of time that each instructor could give to each course decreased significantly, because "traveling instructors" lectured at several locations to survive financially (Yanakieva, 2005, p. 45). Resultant tight schedules for the instructors caused them to compress and intensify their lectures, making the work of the students more difficult.

International Standards as an Agent of Change for LIS Education

European agreements about higher education resulted in standards that Bulgarian educational institutions needed to meet to integrate successfully into the European Union academic system. Since its formation in 1993, the LIS program at SU has been a leader and catalyst for change in establishing European accreditation standards in Bulgarian LIS education. SU transformed its LIS curriculum, standards, and degrees to promote across Europe the mobility and employability of its graduates. Other Bulgarian LIS schools followed.

The integration of Bulgaria into the European Union on January 1, 2007 required compliance with European standards, including the Joint Declaration on Harmonization of the Architecture of the European Higher Education System, signed in Paris on May 25, 1998 (Sorbonne Joint Declaration, 1998, official web site) and the Bologna Declaration on the European Space for Higher Education (The Bologna Declaration of 19 June, 1999, official web site), ratified by European ministers of education on June 19, 1999. The Paris declaration emphasized the social role of knowledge produced in European universities as a factor for the development of the European Union. These two accords encouraged a shared system of standards and accreditations to make European institutions mutually compatible and able to participate in exchange programs.

The new standards for organizing and providing access to information influenced Bulgarian LIS education (Dimchev & Angelova, 2003, p. 1). For example, the changes in LIS curriculum at SU addressed the impact of new information technologies, creation of a knowledge-based economy, and development of the field of knowledge management. In agreement with Western accreditation standards, the LIS program at SU began to offer three degrees in LIS education: Bachelor's, Master's, and Ph.D., with mandatory core courses for all Bulgarian LIS programs and elective courses related to a student's specialization.

The Bachelor's degree provides the fundamental knowledge and skills for librarians, archivists, museum workers, information brokers, and media designers. Each year, the regular program accepts 40 students and the correspondence program accepts 30 students. The programs consist of 32 core and 15 elective courses over 8 semesters (240 credit hours) (Nedkov, 2009; Yanakieva, 2008a).

The Master's degree provides an interdisciplinary LIS curriculum of specialized training for professional librarians, conservators and preservation administrators, web site developers, managers of information centers, and facilitators of international cooperation. Approximately 20 to 30 students enter the Master's program, consisting of 90 credit hours over three semesters (Nedkov, 2009; Yanakieva, 2008a, p. 34).

The Ph.D. degree trains researchers, university professors and future directors of libraries and museums. Students complete 180 credit hours in 3–4 (correspondence) years of study (Yanakieva, 2008a, p. 34).

Modern Bulgarian LIS education has undergone dynamic transformation. This transformation has come as a response to the pressing requirements of European educational accords and standards. The current curricula have become interdisciplinary, patron-centered, and technological oriented, balancing LIS theory and practice and keeping up with current foreign experience.

International Cooperation as an Agent of Change in LIS Education

In 1999, Bulgarian higher education adopted the new European Credit Transfer System (ECTS) in accord with the Bologna Declaration (ECTS, 2006, official web site). The ECTS, introduced in 1989 within the Erasmus-Socrates Exchange framework, facilitated the creation of international academic partnerships and student exchanges according to the systems' intent to increase the employability and mobility of European university graduates. SU officially adopted the ECTS in 2003 (Dimchev & Angelova, 2003).

The Socrates-Erasmus Exchange Program and the ECTS standards created opportunities for student participation in international exchange. During summer training seminars, Bulgarian students traveled to the cities that ratified the cooperative contract of the program: Hanover, Devender, Warsaw, Vilnius, and Bordeaux. In exchange, over 25 German, Dutch, Polish, and Lithuanian students have studied in Bulgarian LIS programs (Dimchev & Angelova, 2003; Yanakieva, 2008a, p. 39). The resultant friendships formed with foreign colleagues facilitated intercultural learning and acquiring foreign language skills. Students praised this program for expanding their knowledge of foreign library theory and practice and their "communication skills and ability to respond to challenges" (Angelova, Przastek-Samokowa, & Kisilowska, 2006). Participation in the program also provided students with a chance to conduct research. In addition, Bulgarian LIS programs exchanged lecturers with Western European and North American LIS programs. Twenty-five foreign professors have taught in Bulgaria, and Bulgarian LIS faculty has taught at foreign universities (Yanakieva, 2008a, p. 38).

GLOBENET Conferences as Agents of Change for Professional Development

The Paris and Bologna accords facilitated participation in international conferences. In 2000, Emporia State University (Kansas) and SU (Bulgaria) collaborated in organizing an international conference that has become another catalyst for change in Bulgarian LIS education and Bulgarian libraries. The conference allowed Bulgarian librarians and LIS professionals to meet with foreign colleagues, exchange ideas, and establish networks (Yanakieva, 2008b, personal communication). The conference was successful and has been repeated every two years, providing visibility for Bulgarian library professionals and helping them to integrate into the European Union and internationally. By participating in these conferences, librarians united around their common concern for the future of libraries (Achleitner & Dimchev, 2001, p. 3). Christened GLOBENET, each conference has focused on a particular theme, listed in Table 1. The globalization theme has appeared at three consecutive conferences, each time with a different approach to explore related phenomena and issues in the LIS profession. In 2004, a preconference conference entitled "New librarians-challenges and opportunities" assembled 13 students from the U.S., Czech Republic, Germany, and Bulgaria. The students discussed the need for international cooperation and networking in times of change. The 2006 conference invited students from Bulgaria, the U.S., Croatia, Greece, Italy, Latvia, and Ukraine to participate in poster sessions. Table 1 lists the topics and collaborations of the GLOBENET conferences.

Table 1 demonstrates that attendance increased at each conference, indicating a growing popularity among Bulgarian and foreign library professionals. For every two conferences, the number of participants doubled: 31, 38, 64, 68, and 119. The number of Bulgarian speakers also increased: 8, 9, 21, 17, and 25. Collaborative, multinational presentations constitute another feature of this conference. Such collaborations have included librarians from Bulgaria and the US, Greece and Great Britain, US with France, Croatia, and Italy, and Portugal and Spain. Three consecutive conferences (2002, 2004, and 2006) highlighted the ABLE project between Bulgarian and American public librarians. The theme of globalization during the recent three conferences drew a wider international audience, following a pattern of progressively broadening appeal.

The conference encouraged Bulgarian library professionals to develop their foreign language skills and to share their experiences and issues with foreign colleagues. For Bulgarian speakers, the conference provided an affordable venue to present and share their research, ideas, and professional issues. On the informal side, the conference encouraged empathy, friendship, and tolerance between citizens of different nations. At the 2004 conference, library professionals emphasized the increasing social role of the library profession in the development of society (Gergova, 2004, p. 92). The range of presentations reveals the richness of the profession, for example, as

Table 1. Topics, Attendance, and Collaboration Projects of the GLOBENET Conferences.

Year	Conference Theme	Number of Participants	Collaborative Presentations and Projects	Bulgarian Participation Topics
2000	Libraries in the age of the Internet	Bulgarian 8 Foreign 23 U.S. 10 Total 31	4 Papers England–Greece collaboration	Bulgarian libraries-global network, Internet and collection development, Open Society and Bulgarian libraries, academic libraries and cooperation, IT and challenges for cataloging, Internet and reference, and survey of LIS curriculum
2002	Libraries, civil society, and social development	Bulgarian 9 Foreign 29 U.S. 9 Total 38	7 Papers Bulgaria–U.S. collaboration	Integration of libraries in national infrastructure, the new economy of knowledge, library as provider of social integration, tolerance and human dignity, ABLE project, reforms in Bulgarian librarianship, hybrid libraries, academic libraries, and knowledge transaction
2004	Libraries, globalization, and cooperation	Bulgarian 21 Foreign 43 U.S. 14 Total 64	17 Papers Bulgaria–Belgium Bulgaria–U.S. collaborations	LIS education, electronic information literacy, e-learning, special libraries cooperation, ABLE project, eIFL.net and cooperation, National libraries cooperation, cooperation between history department and academic library, copyright, digital preservation and access of cultural heritage, digital library strategy, and electronic publishing
2006	Globalization, digitization, access, and preservation of cultural heritage	Bulgarian 17 Foreign 51 U.S. 13 Total 68	12 Papers Bulgaria–U.S. collaboration	Cultural heritage and the electronic environment, Bulgarian NL digital library, virtual museums, preservation, ABLE project, bibliographic control and digitization, the future of Bulgarian book heritage, MARC21 in BAS, access to electronic information for people with disabilities, LIS and digitization, national and international information policies, and European projects for digitization
2008	Globalization and the management of information resources	Bulgarian 25 Foreign 94 U. S. 18 Total 119	14 Papers Bulgaria–U.S. Portugal–Spain U.S.–France U.S.–Croatia U.S.–Italy collaborations	Database management, metadata, cataloging traditions and challenges, Slavic medieval heritage on the Web, LIS legislation and policies, National library and IT, knowledge in cognitive systems, virtual collections and information architecture, information literacy and globalization, LIS and digitization of cultural heritage, national statistical digital library, Wikipedia, digital libraries, national bibliography, national agricultural scientific database, and access to electronic resources

Sources: Achleitner and Dimchev (2001, 2004, 2005, 2007, 2008 online source).

knowledge workers, instructors, mentors, social workers, health information and community information providers, and the traditional role as preservers of cultural heritage. The forum provided an opportunity for Bulgarian librarians to discuss practical ways that foreign colleagues managed change, sometimes through experiences quite similar to the Bulgarian experiences. Bulgarian librarians discovered that issues such as budget cuts and low social status apply to librarians worldwide.

LIS Research and Publishing as an Agent of Change

Before 1990, the Library Institute did not require research and publishing from faculty (Yanakieva, 2005, p. 47; Johnson, 1993, p. 12). *Biblioteka* (library), the publication for library professionals, emphasized library history and library practices. The chapters remained descriptive in nature and focused on domestic issues (Dipchikova, 1990–2006). The democratic reforms in Bulgaria created opportunities in the LIS community for research and publishing. The financial crisis required libraries to analyze current issues and discuss them openly with colleagues at professional conferences. Bulgarian LIS authors increased their research and publications in scholarly publications. Reforms in the publishing industry and book trade facilitated this process as well.

Publications of the LIS faculty, SU

To understand the trends in publishing, I analyzed the publications of 14 members of the LIS faculty at SU, as listed in the publication *Annual of the LIS program at SU* (Yanakieva et al., 2008; Tsokeva & Yanakieva, 2008, pp. 105–224). These members included three generations of LIS faculty, representing both pre- and post-Soviet eras. These faculty played leadership roles in ULISO, international projects, and conferences. After 1990, the SU LIS faculty increased the rate of their publishing, as well as the number, type, and diversity of subject matter of those publications. Articles began to emphasize international cooperation, exchange, and foreign experience. The topics of those scholarly and popular chapters discussed included library history, theory, and practice. The results of my analysis appear in Table 2.

Bulgarian LIS faculty also published in foreign languages at an increasing rate and number of languages. Before 1990, Russian and other Slavic languages were the predominant languages of foreign publications. After the democratic reforms, participation in joint projects and international

Table 2. SU Faculty Publications, Pre- and Post-1990.

Type of Publications Periodization	Before 1990	Percentage	After 1990	Percentage	Total
Monographs	25	21	95	79	120
Scholarly articles and studies	59	22	213	78	272
Popular articles	169	36	305	64	474

conferences required authors to communicate their research and experiences in West European languages. Bulgarian LIS faculty joined most European LIS associations and the IFLA and published in foreign journals. For example Ani Gergova, as the President of ULISO (2000–2002) and the International Association in Bibliology (2002–2006), published in six languages (Russian, Polish, German, French, Italian, and Czech). Krasimira Daskalova, lectured at Central European University and Technical University in Hanover, Germany, served as an editorial committee member of international journals and a member of the International Federation for Research in Women's History and the International Federation of University Women, and published 25 articles in English. Alexander Dimchev, as a representative of SU for the Alliance of Universities for Democracy and for People to People International and co-organizer of the GLOBENET conference with Herbert Achleitner published four conference proceedings and 22 articles in English.

Publications of LIS Professionals (Biblioteka)

In addition to LIS faculty, other Bulgarian library authors increased their productivity after the reforms of 1990. Between 1990 and 2006, these authors published approximately 1,047 articles in *Biblioteka*. A bibliometric analysis of *Biblioteka* for the 1990–2006 period revealed that the subject areas of published articles followed closely the established LIS curriculum. The most popular subject areas appeared as in Table 3.

This ranking demonstrated that *Biblioteka* preserved its emphasis on the traditional subjects of librarianship and book production. Within those particular subject areas, however, traditional articles decrease over the years. Table 4 demonstrates the steady decrease in these traditional subject areas and the relative stability but fluctuation of topics such as international exchange.

As international partnerships between Bulgarian and Western authors increased, Bulgarian authors published more about international partnerships.

Table 3. Ranking of the Most Popular Subject Areas According to
Biblioteka.

Subject Area of Publication	Number of Articles	Percentage
Literary and library personalities	147	14.0
History of books	140	13.4
International exchange	107	10.2
Libraries and their role	105	10.0
Information technology	96	9.1
Book reviews and publishing industry	85	8.1
Bibliography	72	6.8

Table 4. A Chronological Survey of *Biblioteka* Articles about History of
Books, Literary and Library Personalities, and International Exchange
(1990–2006).

Subject Area Year	90	91	94	95	96	98	99	00	01	03	04	05	06	Total
History of books	20	19	23	11	6	11	16	6	13	13	4	6	1	140
Literary and library personalities	20	20	20	17	12	4	10	5	6	12	10	6	5	147
International exchange	5	18	14	22	3	5	12	8	1	7	3	2	7	107

This may explain the high number (107) of articles in the international exchange subject area, 10.2% of the total. Typical articles described the PULMAN Network of Excellence conference, the international summer student seminar in Poland, and the international conference "Libraries and the Woman." These articles, featuring international librarianship and cooperation, demonstrated an increased use of English language source materials. At the end of the period (2006), the topic of "international exchange" was equally popular. The least featured topic was preservation and conservation of books and archives.

CONCLUSION: 19 YEARS LATER

Nineteen years have passed since the democratic reforms in Bulgarian society. The Bulgarian library system and LIS education survived through financial crisis, transforming themselves from traditional preservers of national heritage into people-oriented community information centers. Still, only 16% of the public utilized traditional library resources, most of which have become outdated. Bulgarian librarians, even the expert librarians and archivists at the National Library, still receive low salaries.

During the economic crisis, the Bulgarian library community became active and aware of its social role, mobilizing around its professional union ULISO and forming international partnerships. Currently, ULISO is promoting a new law, which will provide an incentive for more support from the local entities responsible for libraries. American ABLE partners showed Bulgarian public libraries how to lobby for salaries, resources, and technical equipment to establish CICs. Bulgarian ABLE libraries then promoted the CIC model to other Bulgarian libraries. The AUBG library promoted the Western people-oriented model of academic libraries and created a national consortium with other libraries to finance the high cost of electronic database subscriptions. Built on the success of these partnerships, Bulgarian libraries learned to apply successfully for grant funding. The Open Society and recently the Gates Foundation have helped to bridge the digital divide in Bulgaria by providing computers and Internet access to local communities (Kranich, 2008, report).

Bulgarian LIS education is addressing the dreams of its pioneers, Argirov and Borov, by providing a more humanistic education to professional librarians. Today, professional Bulgarian librarians have a subject expertise degree in addition to their LIS degree. The LIS programs of SU hold accreditation in compliance with European and international standards and provide leadership for other Bulgarian LIS programs. As a result, Bulgarian LIS education has become "convertible" internationally, and its students and professors participate successfully in exchange programs such as Socrates-Erasmus, PULMAN, and PUBLICA. They create partnerships with LIS programs at foreign universities and hear foreign lecturers, learn in foreign LIS schools, and participate in international conferences.

The Bulgarian library community, like the Bulgarian nation that existed for over 1,300 turbulent years and nurtured Slavic literacy, survived the changes of the reforms of 1989–1990 and the resulting crisis. Lessons learned from 700 years of foreign domination taught Bulgarian librarians to adapt to foreign ideas and to accept international support. I am optimistic that a third "Golden Age" of Bulgarian libraries and library education will return as Bulgaria becomes better known and better integrated into the international community.

REFERENCES

Achleitner, H. & Dimchev, A. (Ed.). (2001). *Libraries in the age of the Internet*. Papers from the international conference held in Sofia, Bulgaria, 8–10 November 2000. Sofia: Union of Librarians and Information Services Officers, Bulgaria.

Achleitner, H., & Dimchev, A. (Ed.). (2004). *Libraries, civil society and social development*. Papers from the International Conference held in Sofia, Bulgaria, 14–16 November, 2002. Sofia: St. Kliment Ohridski University of Sofia.

Achleitner, H., & Dimchev, A. (Ed.). (2005). *Libraries, globalization and cooperation*. Papers from the International Conference, Sofia, Bulgaria, 3–5 November 2004. Sofia: St. Kliment Ohridski University of Sofia.

Achleitner, H., & Dimchev, A. (Ed.). (2007). *Globalization, digitization, access and preservation of cultural heritage*. Papers from the International Conference, Sofia, Bulgaria, 8–10 November 2006. Sofia: St. Kliment Ohridski University of Sofia.

Achleitner, H., & Dimchev, A. (Ed.). (2008). *Globalization and the management of information resources*. Conference program, Sofia, Bulgaria, 12–14 November 2008. Available at http://globenet.emporia.edu/sofia2008/Sofia2008Program.pdf. Retrieved November 20, 2008.

Alexandrova, B. (2005). AUBG library's practices and shared experiences: A key factor in the emancipation of Bulgarian libraries. *Libraries, globalization and cooperation* (pp. 55–60). Papers from the International Conference held in Sofia, Bulgaria, 3–5 November 2004. Sofia: St. Kliment Ohridski University of Sofia.

Angelova, K., Przastek-Samokowa, M., & Kisilowska, M. (2006). A Slavonic librarianship phenomenon? The Polish–Bulgarian cooperation case study. *World Library and Information Congress, 72nd IFLA General conference and council*, 20–24 August 2006, Seoul, Korea. Available at http://www.ifla.org/IV/ifla72/papers/145-Anguelova_Przastek-Samokowa_%20Kisilowska-en.pdf. Retrieved 30 October 2008.

Atanasov, L., & Todorova, E. (1990). Some issues of the professional preparation. *Biblioteka, 1*, 30–32.

Black, C. E. (1943). The Influence of Western political though in Bulgaria 1850–1885. *The American Historical Review, 48*(3), 507–520.

Bolt, N. (2002). A Bulgarian and Colorado Library Project. *International Leads*, 1–2.

Bolt, N. (2004). The ABLE Project: American/Bulgarian Library Exchange. *International Leads*, 7.

Bolt, N. (2008). Survey of Bulgarian LIS education and librarianship. Personal communication by email, September 29, 2008.

Bolt, N., & Ianeva, S. (2004). Bulgarian/Colorado Library Partnership Project: A Model for Partnership. *Libraries, civil society and social development* (pp. 98–106). Papers from the International Conference held in Sofia, Bulgaria, 14–16 November 2002. Sofia: St. Kliment Ohridski University of Sofia.

Boycheva, V. (2002). *Sv. Paisii Hilendarski I Novobulgarskoto Obrazovanie*. Sofia: Askoni-izdat.

Bulgarian Information Consortium. (2008).Available at http://www.bic.bg/EN/. Retrieved 20 October 2008.

Dimchev, A. (2001). Bulgarian libraries under the conditions of a global network. In: H. Achleitner & A. Dimchev (Eds), *In libraries in the age of the Internet*. Sofia: Union of Librarians and Information Services Officers.

Dimchev, A. (2008). Policies in preparing LIS specialists in the Republic of Bulgaria. *ULISO conference proceedings "The library profession during the 21st century-changes and challenges"*, June 19–20, Veliko Turnovo. Available at http://www.lib.bg/konferencii/nk2008/prezentacii/adimchev.pdf. Retrieved 28 October 2008.

Dimchev, A., & Angelova, K. (2003). *New possibilities and chances for cooperation*. Available at http://www.lib.bg/dokladi2003/dimchev-angelova.htm. Retrieved 30 October 2008.

Dipchikova, A. (Ed.) (1990–2006). *Biblioteka*. Sofia: National Library Sts. Kiril and Methodii.

Dobrev, I. (2005). Introduction. In: A. Angelova & L. Petkova (Eds), *Kolektsia Slavika: Redki I tsenni zaglavia po slavistika to bibliotekata na Sofiiskia universitet Sv. Kliment Ohridski (1519–1922)* (pp. 7–15). Sofia: Universitetsko Izdatelstvo Sv. Kliment Ohridski.

Doncheva, A. (2004). Reforms in librarianship in Bulgaria after 1990. *Libraries, civil society and social development* (pp. 160–165). Papers from the International Conference held in Sofia, Bulgaria, 14–16 November 2002. Sofia: St. Kliment Ohridski University of Sofia.

Durrance, J., Pettigrew, K., & Fisher, K. (2002). *Online community information: Creating a nexus at your library*. Chicago: American Library Association.

ECTS-European Credit Transfer and Accumulation System. (2006). Education and Training, European Commission. Available at http://ec.europa.eu/education/programmes/socrates/ects/index_en.html. Retrieved 11 November 2008.

Edwards, A. (1998). Bulgarian university libraries in a time of transition. *Information Outlook*, pp. 7–9.

Gergova, A., Dipchikova, A., Dimchev, A., Kazandzhiev, A., Ljudskanova, V., Kapitanova, M., & Marcheva, R. (1997). *National program for the preservation of library collections*. Sofia: Union of Librarians and Information Services Officers.

Gergova, A. (2004). The library as provider of social integration, tolerance, and human dignity: Questions. In: H. Achletner & A. Dimchev (Eds), *Libraries, civil society and social development*.

Johnson, I. M. (1993). *Education for librarianship and information work in Eastern Europe*. Report on visits sponsored by the European commission on TEMPUS program, 1992 and 1993. School of Librarianship and Information Studies, Aberdeen, Great Britain. Available at http://eric.ed.gov/ERICDocs/data/ericdocs2sql/content_storage_01/0000019b/80/13/35/5d.pdf. Retrieved 10 October 2008.

Kranich, N. (2008). *Report for the United States Department of State, U.S. Speaker Program*. Visit by Nancy Kranich, Past President, American Library Association, 10–15 May 2008. Washington, DC.

Matejic, P. (2005). Preservation and survival of Bulgarian manuscript heritage. Personal communication at the Hilandar Research Center, Ohio State University, July 2005.

Nedkov, S. (2009). Bibliotechno-informacionni nauki. *Filosofski fakultet SU "Sv. Kliment Ohridski*. Available at http://forum.uni-sofia.bg/filo/display.php?page = bibliotekoznanie. Retrieved 20 December 2008.

Nikolova-Houston, T. (2008). *Margins and marginality: Marginalia and Colophons in South Slavic manuscripts during the Ottoman Period (1393–1878)*. Austin: The University of Texas at Austin.

Popova, A. (2008). *Evaluation of the Community Information Centers*. Report by Anna Popova.

Smith, A. (2001). Making the transition: Bulgarian libraries struggling in a past communist world. *Information Outlook*, 5(12), 24–29.

Sorbonne Joint Declaration. (1998). *Joint Declaration on harmonization of the architecture of the European higher education system.* Paris: The Sorbonne, 25 May 1998.Available at http://www.bologna-berlin2003.de/pdf/Sorbonne_declaration.pdf. Retrieved 25 October 2008.

Stoikova, D. (1990). About the professional preparation of librarians. *Biblioteka, 10,* 25–28.

Terzieva, N., & Todorova, R. (2006). Electronic publications and library cooperation: Bulgarian experience. *Proceedings ELPUB 2006 conference on electronic publishing,* Bansko, Bulgaria, June 2006.Available at http://elpub.scix.net/data/works/att/208_elpub2006.content.pdf. Retrieved 28 October 2008.

The Bologna Declaration of 19 June 1999. Joint Declaration of the European Ministers of Education, 19 June 1999. Bologna, Italy. Available at http://www.bologna-berlin2003.de/pdf/bologna_declaration.pdf.

Tsokeva, V., & Yanakieva, T. (2008). Library and information science specialty. Bibliography guide of faculty publications. In: T. Yanakieva, et al. (Eds), *In Godishnik na Sofiiskia universitet Sv. Kliment Ohridski* (pp. 105–224). Sofia: Universitetsko Izdatelstvo Sv. Kliment Ohridski.

ULISO – Union of Librarians and information services officers, Bulgaria. (2008). Available at http://www.lib.bg/. Retrieved 6 November 2008.

Velkova, D. (2006). A Bulgarian's view of American libraries. *International Leads, 20*(1)4, 7.

Yanakieva, T. (2005). Educational concepts in the LIS field in Bulgaria. *Libraries, globalization and cooperation* (pp. 43–50). Papers from the International Conference, Sofia, Bulgaria, 3–5 November 2004. Sofia: St. Kliment Ohridski University of Sofia.

Yanakieva, T., et al. (Eds). (2008). *Godishnik na Sofiiskia universitet Sv. Kliment Ohridski, Filosofski fakultet, Kniga Bibliotechno-Informatsionni Nauki* (Vol. 1). Sofia: Universitetsko izdatelstvo Sv. Kliment Ohridski.

Yanakieva, T. (2008a). Creation and development of library and information science at St. Kliment Ohridski, Sofia University. Specific features and integration into the academic community. *Godishnik na Sofiiskia universitet Sv. Kliment Ohridski* (pp. 5–44). Sofia: Universitetsko Izdatelstvo Sv. Kliment Ohridski.

Yanakieva, T. (2008b). Survey of Bulgarian LIS education and librarianship. Personal communication by email, October 11, 2008.

DIGITAL LIBRARIES NEED DIGITAL LIBRARIANS

Zsuzsanna Toszegi

ABSTRACT

This chapter summarizes the library history of Hungary, with the main focus on the decades preceding the regime change in 1989. The country has been a member *of the* European Union since 2004. *One of the consequences of joining the EU was that Hungary had to implement the three-tier system of higher education defined by the Bologna Declaration. This new system of library and information professional education and training that began in the 2006–2007 academic year is discussed in detail. The first students to begin their studies in the new, two-tier system of higher education will be awarded the BA degree in the first half of 2009. The best of them will be able to continue their studies at the MA level at one of the four universities that were approved for new MA programs in 2008.*

Where seek tyranny? Think again: Everyone is a link in the chain; Of tyranny's stench you are not free: You yourself are tyranny.[1]

Illyés; Gyula

Advances in Library Administration and Organization, Volume 27, 73–98
Copyright © 2009 by Emerald Group Publishing Limited
All rights of reproduction in any form reserved
ISSN: 0732-0671/doi:10.1108/S0732-0671(2009)0000027009

INTRODUCTION

Throughout Europe, Library and Information Science (LIS) schools must face the same uncertainty and the same problems: they are in a transitional period between modern industrial society and postmodern information society; and it is yet unknown what the future will bring for the library and information profession and for the LIS academic sphere. Naturally this is the case in Hungary, too, where the regime change in 1989 took place at the same time when the traditional work processes in the library were changing radically everywhere due to the development and implementation of info-communication technologies.

Hungary is situated in the middle of the European continent; inhabited by the Hungarian people for the past 1,100 years. This nation survived many depredations during its stormy history; but still kept its unique language; which is very different from those of all surrounding nations. The key to our survival has always been our strong cultural and national identity and traditions. The Hungarian people are proud of their country's continuous history of more than 1,000 years. Saint Stephen; the founder of the Christian Hungarian kingdom was crowned in 1000 AD in the bishopric town of Esztergom.

Like other European nations, the Hungarians first learned about books as a consequence of the spread of Christian religion and culture. In this, Hungarian librarians can take pride in the fact that they can look back to a law regulating libraries that is a thousand years old. Saint Stephen, our first king, ordered that every 10 villages had to build a church, and the bishop was responsible for furnishing it with the necessary books. It is partly in tribute to that ancient tradition, that a decade ago a CD-ROM was published about the great tradition of Hungarian librarianship, titled "Hungarian Libraries in the Mirror of a Millennium" (Tószegi, 1999).

A BRIEF HISTORY OF HUNGARIAN LIBRARIES

Looking back over this millennial history of Hungarian libraries, the first library that is usually mentioned is the Library of the Benedictine Archabbey of Pannonhalma. This Library is more than a thousand years old, and its building is among the most beautiful of structures in all of Hungary.

The rich and famous Corvina library of our King Matthias was one of the biggest and most valuable book collections in Europe during the

Renaissance period. Unfortunately, most of the collections were dispersed during the frequent storms of our national history. At present, only one-fourth of the 53 original codices remain in Hungary.

During the 16th and 17th centuries, the Age of Reformation, the basic collections of the most prominent protestant schools were founded. These schools are still in operation. The next two centuries saw the foundation of the great aristocratic book collections. Fortunately, two of these collections have remained intact: the exceedingly rich and beautiful Helikon Library in Keszthely, founded by Count György Festetics, and the Teleki Téka, bearing the name of the founding Teleki family, in Marosvásárhely, now a part of Romania.

The beginning of the 19th century was flush with ideas of nationalism, the nation-state and national self-consciousness and many European countries established their National Libraries then. In Hungary, in 1802, Count Ferenc Széchényi donated his priceless private collection to the nation for the purpose of founding up our National Library. It still bears his name, and has been housed in the imposing building of the former Royal Palace since 1985.

His son, Count István Széchényi, offered all revenues from his estates for a period of one year for the purpose of founding the Hungarian Academy of Sciences. Following the generous examples of the Széchényi family, Count József Teleki donated his own priceless private collection to establish the library of the Academy of the Hungarian Academy of Sciences.

Among the university libraries that are still working, the Library of Eötvös Lóránd University has the longest past. It was founded in 1561 by Miklós Oláh, the Archbishop of Esztergom. The predecessor of the current university was founded in 1635 by Péter Pázmány, a Jesuit cardinal in Nagyszombat. The university and its library moved to Buda in 1777 and then later to Pest. The library of Budapest University of Technology, the flagship of Hungarian engineering education, was donated by Baron József Eötvös in 1898.

When the Revolution of 1848 and the War of Independence in 1849 ended in the defeat of Hungary, years of Habsburg despotism followed. This ended in 1867 with the Austro-Hungarian Compromise that gave partial autonomy to Hungary. The state established many important libraries at that time – the Library of the Hungarian Parliament, the Hungarian Central Statistical Office Library, the National Educational Library, the Library of the Museum of Fine Arts, and the Library of the Technical Museum.

The last years of the 19th century brought an economic boom to Hungary. As the national economy prospered, national pride skyrocketed.

In 1896, glorious festivities were held to commemorate the 1000th anniversary of the arrival of Hungarian tribes to the Carpathian Basin. The years preceding this anniversary celebration were years of feverish construction in preparation. Great new roads were built and magnificent buildings were erected. This historical period favored the establishment of many public institutions and libraries, as well. The first national survey of libraries conducted in 1885 listed 1,357 public libraries and 913 significant private collections (György, 1886).

One of the most significant public figures of the period before the World War I was Ervin Szabó. Szabó started to promote the national adoption of the English-American model of the public library system as early as 1910. His goal was to create a system of open public libraries with a network of branch libraries. He was able to realize only part of his plan during his lifetime, but his intellectual influence can be felt even now, 100 years later. Today the public library network of the capital is named after him and, recently, the structure of its central library has been redesigned to serve its functions better.

Before the World War II, the number of academic and special libraries and the larger public and school libraries all together numbered 1,008. By the end of the 1930s, 1,227 farmer's libraries and 1,629 people's libraries had been founded (people's libraries are small libraries open to the public, but their collections are small and usually ideologically biased). Industrial workers could use approximately 250–300 workers' libraries run by trade unions, private companies or private associations. Registries from that era did not list smaller school and association libraries, so the total number of existing libraries can be estimated at around 4000 (Kovács, 1961). However, when interpreting statistics from this period, it is important bear in mind that the Trianon Treaty of 1920 assigned 72% of our country's territories to neighboring states. Thus, immediately after the World War I, 5,961 people's libraries were registered in Hungary, but after the Trianon Treaty, 46% of them remained on territories lost to Hungary. Of the 485 libraries deemed nationally significant, 55% were now in the territories of other countries (Szabó-András, 1966).

The World War II visited devastation on our country, but the damage caused by the political regime that took power after the War was worse than anything in Hungarian history.

In 1946–1947 plans were still in effect to create up-to-date, English-American type public libraries, but after 1949, when the darkest years of the communist regime begun, regional, municipal, and village libraries were created on the transplanted Soviet model. Library-founding fever (Kovács, 1961)[2] was such that each and every village had its own libraries by the middle of the 1950s, all of them supervised by the local councils. The function of most of these new people's libraries was political propaganda. The scope of their collections was narrow and collections development targeted less-educated people for the purpose of ideological education.

During this same period of rapid creation of people's libraries, a number of books and even entire sections of collections deemed ideologically harmful were destroyed. Then, after a time, the policy was changed to have such items withdrawn from circulation, though not destroyed. Ecclesiastical libraries, having a long past and particularly valuable collections, were especially targeted. Fortunate were the ones whose collection remained intact with "only" a total loss of public status (HORVÁTH, 1978).[3] During these same years large numbers of documents deemed politically harmful were destroyed. One spectacular manifestation of the arrogance of political power was the publication of indexes in 1949–1950. Based on the "guidance" of the communist regime, all works deemed harmful were listed in the published indexes and had to be removed from all library collections (*ibid.* p. 235).[4]

Approximately 10 years after the Revolution of 1956, significant national political changes were signaled by the fact that ideas of creating up-to-date public libraries began to supplant the prominence of the ideology of people's libraries. Important professional discussions were taking place by the middle of the 1960s, on the surface, at least, about open-shelving systems and classifications. These debates began to focus attention on readers' demands and the interconnectedness of the activities of local, workplace, and university libraries. On the whole, the function of the library and the whole system of libraries was beginning to be redefined.

BULGAKOV VS. MITCHELL – THE LIBRARIAN AS ARBITER OF PUBLIC TASTE

But what were readers' demands in the 1950s or in the 1970s, for that matter? And what was the role of the librarian, according to the political authorities? This problem is so complex and so obscure that here only a few basic facts can be outlined to provide an overall picture of official expectations of librarians before the post-communist regime change.

Throughout the socialist era, two basic, official expectations of librarians were clearly and loudly proclaimed:

• to elevate the level of culture to promote socioeconomic equality and
• to elevate the level of general and professional education.

However, during the 1950s there had been yet another primary expectation: to re-educate readers to create a "socialist type of human being." The "socialist type of human being" was supposed to think and to work in the socialist manner. This meant total acceptance of Marxist–Leninist ideology, the shedding of all "philistine values," and insistence on the primacy of the interests of the collective over the interests of the individual.

Librarians, then, were instructed to give patrons readings that would stimulate the formation of socialist ways of thinking and a socialist work ethic. However, no one could have answered the question: Why would a worker work harder and faster if he Gorky the night before instead of a "clerical-reactionary" writer? But the situation was very simple: such questions were not allowed to be posed at all.

The work in the many new libraries created in the 1950s were under total political control. Most of the library employees have little more than secondary-school education and no professional training at all. They forced the compulsory books required for proper ideological development on everyone, regardless of what readers actually wanted to borrow.

In socialist Hungary, effective power was in the hands of the working classes. The peasantry played a decidedly secondary role in political life, and the middle-class was totally excluded from it. Children from intellectual families suffered discrimination and were forced to yield to children from working class or peasant families. In fact, the authorities openly stigmatized 18-year-old young people, and opened or closed the gates of universities and colleges, the essential vehicles of upward mobilization, based on the applicants' family backgrounds.

However, the main target group of ideological re-education was always the working class, since the peasantry was much less important in the eyes of the authorities. This led to the amazing paradox that while the working class leaders of the country continually touted the superiority of the, "victorious working class," they apparently had very bad opinion of the tastes and ideological sophistication of the workers themselves, for they ordered their continual compulsory re-education.

The ideological struggle, enforced through political terror, was most intense in the 1950s, subsiding gradually from the 1960s onwards until it reached a relatively acceptable state in the 1970s and 1980s. This was the era that won Hungary the pan-soviet title of "the happiest barracks in the camp."

The forcefully and hastily created people's libraries then started to close down. The changing social situation in the 1970s made open discussion about problems possible. It is interesting that the analysis of readers' tastes have now become an important professional question. Published surveys, one after another, have made it clear that librarians in the 1970s, most of them with professional credentials by that time, knew what writers they should have liked and should be reading. Still, the surveys also showed that they claimed to prefer reading best-sellers, instead of the classics it was often claimed they favored. Margaret Mitchell's popular best-seller *Gone with the Wind* became an emblematic example of this trend when it turned out to be more popular among librarians than, for example, the classic novel *The Master and Margarita* by Mikhail Bulgakov.

So how could librarians have raised the cultural level of the people, when even they did not rise above the level of popular literature? And movement toward actual socioeconomic equality, though not in regression, showed no improvement, either, though truly there were not many things librarians could have done about any of this, in any case.

LIBRARIES IN THE 1970s and the 1980s

After years of almost inconceivable tyranny through the 1950s, it seems scarcely believable now that hardly 20 years after the Revolution of 1956, Hungarian professionals could work on adapting the ISBD essential for the introduction of international data exchange formats. The ISBD for books were published in 1978 in Hungary, only 7 years after its first publication. That was an outstanding achievement for any country. Following this, the ISO standards of librarianship and reference work were published one after the other. By the end of the 1980s, the status of library and documentation standards, with its long history in Hungary, was deemed high-quality internationally.

The modernization of libraries had begun. Just as in the application of bibliographic descriptions, it was a new era in automation as well. The National Széchényi Library began to use computers to create entries for the Hungarian National Bibliography, as well as for a central catalog of foreign periodicals subscribed to by special libraries in Hungary. Personal computers and CD-ROM drives appeared first in the more important libraries just one or two years before the regime change in 1989.

Village and municipal libraries were in a special position. They did not have to endure central control and supervision any more, but the price of this liberty was the disappearance of professional help. Libraries have been totally at the mercy of their home organizations, and their budgets have always been smaller than they need. The home organizations of libraries did not establish any professional requirements or standards and the libraries themselves had no formal strategic plans. Different cultural institutions in a given town or village regarded each other as rivals, rather than possible partners. Managers were selected on the basis of friendship and family ties, not professional competencies. "Instead of high professional level, the characteristic feature of the work of these libraries has been poverty and amateurism with the mask of goodwill on them" (Vidra Szabó, 2002).

REGIME CHANGE

The era of the regime change is dated usually between 1989 (the year when Imre Nagy, the Prime Minister executed in 1956, was ceremonially reburied, and the Hungarian Republic officially declared) and 1991 (when the Soviet Army left the country). During and after these years, libraries were in a difficult position. Hundreds of company libraries, most of them holding significant collections of professional literature, were liquidated due to the accelerated pace of privatization. The number of librarians decreased drastically.

Most of the new political leaders at every level had no leadership experience at all. Family and friendship ties had a much greater impact than ever before on the process of appointing leaders and making decisions about staff. This was true not only of the first government after regime change, but of all the politicians after them, replacing each other every four years.

The democratic process began in the country in the middle of very difficult economic conditions. Libraries remained isolated and unsupported, many librarians losing their jobs. Nevertheless, positive changes started to take place after a few years, and the position of libraries became stable after the turn of the century, even though the amount of financial resources available has continually decreased.

THE TURN OF THE CENTURY

The Library Act of 1997 brought significant changes to Hungarian librarianship, and not only in comparison to the preceding two decades. This was the very first law in our history that regulated open public library provision. The most important principles of the law are the following:

- Citizens' rights to information, education, culture and entertainment, as guaranteed by our Constitution, can be exercised through the system of open public libraries.
- The library system is indispensable for the operation of a democratic constitutional state and information society because it can affect the free flow of information for everybody.
- Running library services is a strategically significant goal of the state.
- The aim of the open public library system is to serve the citizens' interests.

This law regulates the national system of document provision, the central services that are compulsory responsibilities of the government, the basic function of the national library and the Library Institute, the tasks and rights of organizations maintaining open public libraries, the necessary requirements of open public library provision, the professional requirements of libraries, the rights and conditions of library use, and so on.

The law has induced unambiguously positive changes in Hungarian librarianship, among them the most important ones may be the following:

- quick technological and informatics development has begun;
- important digitizing programs have been started;
- new library buildings have been built and many older ones have been redesigned;
- a central union catalog for all the collections of the biggest libraries of the country has been developed; and
- practicing librarians can now participate in organized professional training to achieve mastery of the new requirements of the profession.

In addition, libraries have initiated several national campaigns, such as the Internet Fiesta, the Autumn Library Days, and The Big Read campaign. These campaigns have met with considerable success, becoming increasingly well-known and popular in return (Hegyközi, Murányi, & Tószegi, 200).[5]

Meanwhile, Internet penetration in the country has significantly increased. In 1999, the Goethe Institute initiated a survey: "Information and Publicity." According to this survey, in 1999, 18% of Hungarian families had a computer, but only 1.5–1.6% of the 3.8 million households of the country had Internet access. By the first part of 2007, however, 23% of the population had access to the Internet from home, this number growing to 28% in the second half of the same year. In 2007, the percentage of households owning a computer rose from 43% to 48%. And in the first half of 2008, Internet penetration reached 46%.[6]

Thanks to these favorable changes, Hungarian libraries grew and became comparatively strong, until 2004 when the country joined the European Union.

THE EDUCATION AND TRAINING OF HUNGARIAN LIBRARIANS

Although since the 15th century Hungary has known many excellent librarians, the systematic education and training of librarians started only in 1898. However, since 1874 librarians working in the University Library of Budapest had to pass a professional exam. The first law regulating the training of professional librarians working in research libraries was passed in 1922. Library Science has been taught at the University of Kolozsvár since 1901, and at the Pázmány Péter University in Budapest (the legal predecessor of Eötvös Loránd University) since 1914. The independent Library Studies major was started in the academic year 1948–1949 in Budapest. In the 1960s, more universities followed its example. The new doctoral program offering the PhD degree was started in 1997 in Budapest.

The 1980s and 1990s brought substantial changes to the education and training of librarians. First, Informatics gained more ground in the library. Second, information institutions other than libraries began to employ information professionals. Institutes of higher education reacted to these changes by revising their former curricula and offering more courses in Information Science.

In 1997, a Cultural Act was passed that regulates, among other fields of culture, the operation of public libraries. This law mandated the continuing professional education of librarians. In 2000, the Ministry of Culture instituted a system of professional education for credentialed librarians and decreed that this system would be financed and administered by the state. Now among all of the courses offered in this system of continuing education, one of the most popular subjects is the application of IT technologies in the library.

As I write this article, almost 10,000 people are working in librarian positions in 5,400 libraries in Hungary. On average, 450 librarians leave the profession every year, whereas approximately 350 students graduate yearly from the 11 accredited LIS schools.[7]

Joining the European Union and the Bologna Process

Lately, profound changes have taken place in the higher education system of Hungary. One of the consequences of joining the EU was that the country had to implement the three-tiered system of higher education as defined by the Bologna Declaration. Consequently, today all students begin their studies in this new system. In the new system, after three years of full-time study, students receive the BA degree. After two more full years of study, they receive the MA degree. The PhD degree may be obtained after an additional three years of study.

The new Higher Education Act regulating the Bologna Process in Hungary passed in 2005. By this Act, after September 1, 2006 all new courses had to meet the requirements of the new system of higher education. The cornerstone of the Bologna system are the national qualification guidelines that define the educational requirements and learning outcomes of every major and specialization, the knowledge, skills and competencies students have to acquire, and the tasks they should be able to fulfill after completion.

THE NEW SYSTEM OF EDUCATION AND TRAINING FOR LIBRARY AND INFORMATION PROFESSIONALS IN HUNGARY

The Ministry of Education and Culture, the supervising body of higher education, has been publishing the qualification guidelines for all majors accredited under the new educational system since 2005. The LIS educational requirements and learning outcomes defined in those guidelines are based on proposals provided to the Ministry by the schools providing LIS education. The requirements for the BA degree were published first. The requirements for the MA degree in Library and Information Science were published in the Spring of 2008.

BA-level Qualification Framework for Library and Information Studies

LIS is now defined as one of the Interdisciplinary Social Sciences. During the 6 semesters of the program, students have to complete 180 credits. At the bachelor's level the degree is called "Informatics Librarian" and each degree granted must indicate field of specialization.

Professional Skills at the BA level
The aim of the program is to train library and information professionals who have up-to-date knowledge and are able to fulfill professional positions in various types of libraries and other information institutions. They are also able to do tasks in connection with collection maintenance, cataloging and classification, and storage and retrieval of different types of documents. In addition, they are able to organize library processes. Those graduating in this major are capable of providing information services using computer-based professional information retrieval systems, and they have the necessary knowledge to enter the MA program.

Graduates at the BA level are familiar with

- Hungarian and EU system of library and information economy, and the system of legal regulations;
- basic principles of evaluation, cataloging and classification of documents, of collection management, of running and developing information retrieval systems, and of the organization and design of services;
- the effective use of IT tools and technologies;
- the basic principles of maintaining and developing digital information systems and the principles of creating digital documents;
- methods of using various learning resources; and
- fundamental knowledge necessary to do such tasks in the library as organization, marketing, communication, design, project leadership, and quality development and human resource development.

They are capable of

- fulfilling tasks in the field of their specialization;
- organizing and processing information;
- acquiring and developing those written, oral, and presentational skills necessary for their work;
- communicating in at least one foreign language;
- applying conflict-resolution methods efficiently; and
- understanding, processing and presenting texts, data, tables and visual texts containing visual signs, and typographical elements and icons.

They must have the following qualities and skills:

- service orientation;
- quality awareness and success orientation;
- organizing, enterprising, and cooperating skills;
- basic competencies in pedagogy and andragogy;

- critical assessment of their own work; and
- skills necessary to make a decision as well as to work as a member of a group.

The Core Curriculum
Basic subjects:

- philosophy and sociology;
- basics of communication theory;
- history of writing, books, and press and libraries;
- basic computer skills;
- communication skills and communication development in their mother tongue;
- sociology and pedagogy and psychology of reading; and
- research methodology.

Professional core subjects:

- information resources and bibliographic control;
- information retrieval and query languages and classification systems;
- content description;
- library organization;
- reference services;
- basics of library management;
- information theory and information systems;
- building and using databases, library automation, and networks; and
- basics of pedagogy and psychology.

Specific professional skills are defined for each different specialized education. The website of the Ministry of Culture and Education enumerates the following specializations:

- Based on library type: Electronic and Digital Libraries, EU Information Libraries, Academic Libraries, Children's Libraries, Public and Professional Libraries, Special Collections, and Book History.
- Others: Information and Knowledge Management, Content Provider, Web Designer, and Web Programmer.

Of these 13 specializations authorized by the Ministry of Education and Culture, in the 2007–2008 academic year, 11 of them were offered in one or more of the LIS schools in Hungary.

An internship is obligatory for every specialization. This can take place in a library or in another information provider institution. The BA degree will be awarded only if the student has passed a C-type (both written and oral) intermediate level, officially accredited language exam in a modern language or has equivalent language certification from a secondary institution.

Requirements and Qualifications at the MA level

The MA curriculum is one of the branches of the Multidisciplinary Social Sciences. Students have to complete 120 credits over the course of four semesters to finish the degree. Those graduating with the MA will have a degree called "Informatics Librarian," which also must indicate the field of specialization.

The Ministry of Education and Culture authorized the following specializations: Human Informatics (Content Provider), Information and Knowledge Management, Internet Technology, School Libraries, Library Quality Management, Public Libraries, Special Collections, Media Science, Linguistic Informatics, Health Sciences Libraries, Old Prints Collections, Professional Information Management (Research and Development), Content Development Management, Business Information Management, and Web Technology.

Professional Skills on the MA level

The aim of the MA program is to educate professionals who can develop their skills and deepen their knowledge of informatics and library management acquired in the BA program and are able to fulfill their job in various basic institutions of the information society, such as libraries and other public collections in the fields of science, business and cultural life, state administration and civil service, and other information-providing institutions. They will be able to use the whole range of IT tools and technologies and perform the following tasks at an advanced level:

- content creation and description;
- development and management of content services;
- providing information for users;
- management of content-providing institutions;
- conducting scientific research; and
- mediating culture.

The MA curriculum

- up-to-date theories of Library and Information Science;
- technology of handling information;
- up-to-date theories of economics of information, financial and legal frameworks, and standardization;
- traditional and modern technologies of representing knowledge in the library: bibliographic control, information retrieval query languages, text procession, etc.;
- laws regulating the operation of libraries, the use of informatics systems and applications, and content provision;
- basic characteristics of the information economy and the information market;
- fundamental techniques and methods of scientific research; and
- basics of scientific thinking.

Graduates at the MA level

- have profound, sophisticated comprehension of philosophy of science, hermeneutics, sociology, economy, etc.;
- understand the current operational processes of the Hungarian and international library systems and IT technologies and the current laws and ethical problems of content provision; and
- have deep professional knowledge about users' habits, needs, and survey methods.

Graduates of the MA program are capable of executing the following tasks:

- creating and managing marketable library and content services, quality assurance, and innovation;
- using modern IT technologies;
- creating and running traditional and digital libraries and services;
- planning, creating, running, and maintaining databases;
- analyzing trends on information market and economy;
- learning the methodology of user training and education;
- applying efficient management techniques when communicating with users, members of the market, and patrons;
- executing performance evaluations in the library;
- performing research to solve the problems of content management;
- collection, cataloging, classification, and regular publishing of documents both in Hungarian and other languages;

- satisfying information needs in the fields of economy, politics, administration, culture, and science;
- building professional connections abroad; and
- doing scientific work, developing and updating their literacy and their professional knowledge, and learning to apply the latest scientific results and methods.

MA graduates have the following skills and competencies:

- Personal skills: helpfulness, responsibility, empathy, independence, creativity, discretion, and sensibility.
- Interpersonal skills: openness, communicability, efficient negotiating skill, cooperation, leadership competencies, good communicative, and pedagogical skills.
- Problem-solving skills: exactitude, decision-making ability, coherence, steadiness, perseverance, and alternative thinking.

Graduates of the MA program will have the following professional skills and attitudes:

- Systematic theoretical and practical knowledge making them capable of understanding and analyzing the trends and development of LIS and of solving newly emerging problems efficiently.
- Motivation to continually enhance the knowledge acquired during the MA program to be able to understand the newest developments in LIS as well as other branches of science.
- Strategic approach, service orientation, capability of decision making, quality awareness, success orientation, innovation, critical sense, and dynamism.

MA Core Curricula
There are some subjects that enhance and deepen general knowledge acquired at the BA level, such as History and Basics of Society, Communication, Economy, Philosophy, and Law.
Compulsory elements of the core curriculum are:

- management of library services;
- modern tools of library services and bibliographic control; and
- content management in libraries.

There are also elective courses in the curriculum that can be chosen according to the student's chosen specialization. The general qualifications framework lists the specific subjects and fields of knowledge relevant to every specializations.

Specialization in human informatics (content provider)

- Applied Mathematics and Statistics
- Calculus
- Architecture of information systems, informatics algorithms, data and system models, and knowledge-based technology
- Semantic Web and data mining
- E-learning, E-management, and the information economy
- ECDL computer skills
- Organizing databases in the library, electronic documents and their formats, sociology, and pedagogy and psychology of reading
- Processing natural language texts;
- Legal frameworks of content provision
- Learning and research methodology
- Human Resource management, self-knowledge, career choice, decency, and etiquette and protocol in the library
- Applying artificial intelligence in Health Sciences
- Shape recognition, topology, and genetic algorithms

Specialization in information and knowledge management

- management basics and theory;
- apparatus of information and knowledge management and system of concepts and connections;
- info-communication systems and networks and technologies of information and knowledge organization;
- applications in knowledge society and knowledge technology solutions;
- organizing projects on information and knowledge management;
- E-learning;
- media didactics;
- online community building; and
- professional terminology in English.

Specialization in internet technology

- strategy of information society; ethical and legal concerns;
- strategic planning;
- theoretical and practical issues of information and project management;
- planning and development of network structures;
- technologies; standards and protocols behind the Internet;

- design and development of web-based services;
- IT security; data security; encryption;
- E-government and E-commerce;
- data and text mining; and
- professional terminology in English.

Specialization in school libraries

- basics in pedagogy and psychology;
- history and theory of pedagogy;
- theory and development and organization of curricula;
- E-learning and management and information organization;
- pedagogical information systems;
- guidelines for operating school libraries, knowledge management in the school and school library management;
- service management and quality direction program;
- media pedagogy and subject pedagogy;
- history and characteristics of children's and young adults' literature;
- research and pedagogy of reading;
- guidelines of media and school equipment; and
- media analysis and research.

Specialization in quality management in the library

- national and international innovation trends and systems and models of quality management;
- strategic planning, resource management, professional and supervising activity, and communication and quality strategies;
- documentation of quality, standards, and legal regulations;
- methodology of quality management, quality supervision, and Total Quality Management;
- organizational management, performance measurement, and problem and conflict resolution;
- user demand survey, user training and education, and service management; and
- marketing and project management.

Specialization in public libraries

- social and public services, national and international innovation strategies, and the system and network models of public services;
- public service system in small villages and settlements, management of regional cooperation, and management of libraries with double functions;

- public service, cultural databases and services, and informatics and web development;
- providing audiovisual content and document provision;
- Internet access in libraries, telehouses, and E-points;
- E-administration, laws, professional supervision, and methodology; and
- knowledge management.

Specialization in special collections

- music collection, local history collection, other thematic collections, and collections of unique documents;
- bibliographic control and retrospective cataloging in special collections;
- audiovisual and electronic documents and different types of small prints;
- research methods and technologies in information and knowledge organization;
- problems and solutions of document conservation;
- organizing exhibitions and public events; and
- resource management in digitizing projects and digitizing and project management in special collections.

Specialization in mediamatics

- EU directives on E-content;
- media communication and multimedia systems;
- program design;
- copyright law;
- information processing and managing information processes;
- digital conservation and wideband services;
- development of web-based services and media content management; and
- virtual reference services; knowledge management.

Specialization in linguistic informatics

- basic concepts and branches of linguistics: phonology, laboratory phonology, syntax, formal languages, semantics, formal semantics, and pragmatics;
- basics of experimental linguistics;
- computer-based text processing;
- introduction to artificial intelligence; and
- expert systems and logical programming.

Specialization in health sciences libraries

- basics of physiology and pathology and applied psychology;
- special terminology and reference service on Health Sciences;

- evaluation of information resources and research organization;
- library ethics and value assessment;
- didactics of mentoring;
- bibliometrics;
- professional use of the Internet; and
- desktop publishing.

Specialization in old prints collections

- history of intellectual schools and trends;
- history of reading and writing and books;
- history of censorship;
- history of printing techniques and book illustration;
- related disciplines: paleography, basics of archives, and topography;
- European and Hungarian library history;
- bibliographic control of old prints and reference books of their bibliographic description; and
- strategies of book publishers and basics of antiquarianism and book restoration;
- Latin language.

Specialization in professional information management (research and development)

- current Hungarian macro- and microeconomy and science policy;
- role of library innovation in scientific and cultural information management;
- national and international reference services and devices and institutions;
- reference services in Medical and Health Sciences;
- reference services in Social and Sciences and Humanities;
- reference services in Law and Economy;
- reference services in Natural Sciences and Engineering;
- reference services in Arts; and
- reference services in Environmental and Agricultural Sciences.

Specialization in content development management

- network society;
- management of nonprofit organizations;
- Internet and PR;
- multimedia and web technology;
- basics of programming and HTML;
- basic principles of networks and network services;

- structured texts and metadata;
- organizing databases and full-text databases; and
- handling digital texts.

Specialization in business information management

- market economy and librarianship in the information society;
- basics of business and law and marketing;
- professional information retrieval and dissemination;
- theory and practice of business information;
- up-to-date methods of information management;
- information economy in organizations;
- information counseling;
- charged information services in the library;
- workshops on financial resource collection and tender writing;
- basics of information protection;
- starting a business enterprise; and
- business administration systems.

Specialization in web technology

- guidelines in Web development;
- namespaces; ontologies and semantic Web;
- basics of frameworks;
- application development;
- database design and data security;
- SQL, XML, CSS, Flash, and CMS and design solutions;
- programming languages (PHP, PERL, and others), Javascript, and AJAX; and
- E-governmentand E-commerce.

An internship is compulsory on the MA level, as well. Requirements of the internship are specific to every LIS school. To graduate, students must have at least one C-type intermediate level, officially accredited language exam in a modern language, and an additional C-type basic-level language exam in a different language.

The Program of Specialization in Digital Libraries

One faculty in the legal predecessor of the University of Kaposvár has been training librarians since 1994. Graduates were awarded a college degree ("fõiskolai oklevél") under the old system. In 2006, the new, Bologna system of higher education was implemented there as well, beginning with new BA programs. In the first three semesters students finish the basic subjects and the core curriculum, after which they can specialize either in Public Libraries or in Digital Libraries.

Basic Subjects of the BA Program at the University of Kaposvár

- Philosophy, ethics, sociology, and theory of communication and information;
- introduction to LIS, history of writing, and books and libraries;
- basics in informatics and computer skills;
- communication in the library, IT technology in the library, and sociology of reading; and
- speaking techniques and research methodology.

The common core curriculum before specialization

- history and theory of pedagogy and theory of education;
- introduction to psychology and social psychology;
- bibliographic description: resource types and description of traditional and electronic documents;
- content description: classification and information retrieval query languages;
- library organization: collection organization, services, and system of libraries;
- library management: strategic planning, and project management, quality assurance, PR, and user training;
- reference services: theory of reference services and information resources;
- library informatics: information and information retrieval systems, building and using databases, library automation, and integrated library systems;
- ethical and legal regulation of information society and copyright law; and
- professional terminology in English.

In addition, students have to choose one of the following subjects: Cultural History, Politology, History of Hungary, History of Science and Engineering, and Basics of Scientific Thinking.

Subjects of the specialization in digital libraries

- Organizing a digital library: new ways of information dissemination, E-resources, collection organization, archives, organizing and building databases, digital library services, surveying and analyzing user demands, and user training and education;

- basics in multimedia and digitizing and DRM technologies;
- Internet technology: advanced Internet skills, metadatabases, metadata standards, and markup languages (SGML, XML, etc.); and
- basics in programming and SQL and static and dynamic Web design.

Naturally, the subjects listed earlier are all in accord with the national qualifications framework as defined by the Ministry of Education and Culture. As a member of the EU, it is highly important to compare the program of the education of library and information professionals in the University of Kaposvár with those of other LIS schools in the European Higher Education region, to ensure that the educational program of specialization in Digital Libraries is of adequate content and quality.

A project document published in 2006 with the title "European Curriculum Reflections on Library and Information Science Education" described a detailed survey concerning the integration started by the Bologna Process, and outlined an educational program of high standards (Kajberg & Lørring, 2005). Analyzing the principal frameworks, the structure of the program and its subjects, we can proudly say that students graduating with a BA specialization in Digital Libraries from the University of Kaposvár have the necessary current knowledge and professional competencies, and they have excellent job prospects, not only in libraries, but in the whole range of information institutions.

Building on the strengths of this new BA program, the Departments of Social Sciences and Library Sciences have now received accreditation for the new MA program that will begin in the Fall of 2009 with a specialization in Internet Technology. This new MA program will offer new possibilities for BA graduates to continue their professional studies. The new MA program will also provide new options for professional librarians interested in expanding their professional continuing education work into new content provision areas.

A SUBJECTIVE AFTERWORD

The first students to begin their studies in the new, two-tiered system of higher education will receive their BA degrees in 2009. The best of them will now be able to continue their studies at the MA level since four universities were granted permission in 2008 to start MA programs.

However, one question remains unanswered. What can be expected from a young generation born during or after the regime change, who started their university studies in a new historical era when Hungary was already the member of the EU? Their professional future is obviously directly connected to the future of libraries, about which many different theories exist at the moment. One thing is indisputable. The future of libraries and the future of LIS education in Hungary is strongly linked because Hungarian librarianship will be formed by those professionals who will be awarded their degrees in the coming years and decades.

What will the professional careers of these new students be like? What about the generation following them? Degrees in informatics librarianship with at least one foreign language competency will probably be marketable. Those who complete one of the specializations that trains not only for traditional library work but also for tasks typical in content-providing industries, generally, will probably be in high demand.

The number of people using the Internet has increased dramatically in recent years. Forty-six percent of the population was using the Internet regularly in 2008. This quickly growing group of Internet users must be provided with content and, specifically, Hungarian content. Those who study web development, the provision of digital library services, and other tasks related to the content industry will be able to meet these new demands.

And what will the library of the future be like? There are two typical answers to this question. One begins to envision a future with no printed documents, but no patrons either, since people have no reason to go to a specific location for information. The other answer tries to imagine libraries with enhanced functions, becoming real community spaces where people love to come together and learn together.

However, 20 years after the regime change it is very difficult to grasp an unclouded vision of the future in Hungary. It is possible to chase dreams about everybody becoming a library user, choosing the library as a place for information, education and entertainment as well. But now the country is in the midst of one of its most serious economic crises in decades. It is difficult not to note that one-third of the population lives under the poverty line, that almost 15% of our students leave the school system functionally illiterate, and that librarians have to cope with situations that they never have been trained for, such as the growing problem of homeless people using the library for shelter during the day.

The financing of Hungarian libraries is insufficient compared to the requirements and the international trend of inflation. However, it must be acknowledged that it is not easy to run 10,000 libraries, pay monthly salaries to all librarians, and pay for the education of 350 informatics librarians a year[8] from the small amount of tax revenues available.

One of the biggest challenges facing university teachers is to come to an understanding about what to prepare their students for. Should they teach high-level, purely professional knowledge, thus serving that elitism that takes it for granted that 80% of the globe's resources are used by 20% of its population, and so "the rest" must be content with the 20% left to them? It is notable, in fact, that the number of users registered in the library system mirrors this ratio almost exactly.

The author of this chapter is convinced that the most important function of universities – besides passing on the most up-to-date, high-quality professional material and broadening the intellectual horizon of their students – is to promote the development of responsible intellectual behavior.

It is also important to promote lifelong learning. Young people must understand that they have chosen a career path that requires continual maintenance of their professional skills and ceaseless self-education. Teachers must try to create responsible intellectual behavior based on strong ethical norms that do not evade social responsibilities.

The three strong pillars of the new type of university education are *knowledge, ethics,* and *responsibility.* We can only trust that the politicians of our future attend universities where the same principles prevail. That would mean the end of those restrictive politics that accompanied Hungarian librarianship all through its history in the Gutenberg Galaxy. Let's hope that in the Neumann Galaxy, the principle declared in the library act will not be just a dream any more: "the library system is indispensable for the operation of a democratic constitutional state and the information society because it can effectuate the free flow of information for everybody" (Act CXV of 1997).

NOTES

1. The complete poem (A Sentence on Tyranny) is available in Hungarian and in English at http://visegrad.typotex.hu/index.php?page = work&auth_id = 123&work_id = 504&tran_id = 921

2. "Based on the data provided by the last statistical survey in Hungary, 18,577 public libraries are operating; and possessed altogether 39.4 million documents of different types. The 2,187,791 registered users borrowed 25.8 million volumes; and read an additional 3 million volumes in-house; so altogether 28.8 million volumes have been used by them. Libraries employed 2,680 full-time and 891 part-time librarians; besides 11,833 honorary librarians and thousands of volunteers helped their work. (Based on the data provided December 31, 1957.)" According to the

1956/5 Act regulating Hungarian librarianship, public libraries are the libraries run by national offices and companies by trade unions and other similar organizations and by co-operatives.

3. Two significant ecclesiastic collections, those of Zirc and Gyöngyös, were pronounced "libraries of museal value," so they could remain intact and in their buildings. Three large monastic libraries; among them the Library of the Benedictine Archabbey of Pannonhalma mentioned in the introduction were accepted from nationalization.

4. "The National Library Center started to collect the documents of nationalized collections in 1949, and finished largely in 1952, though the work was continued by its legal successors, the Center of People's Libraries and the National Széchényi Library as well."

5. Downloadable from *http://www.goethe.de/z/30/infomoe/ungarn/deung00.htm*
6. http://einclusion.hu/2008-09-8/46-szazalek-internet-penetracio-2008-elso-felev/
7. http://tmt.omikk.bme.hu/show_news.html?id = 4501&issue_id = 475
8. The referendum of March 2008 rejected the government's plan for installing compulsory tuition fee, so participation in higher education can still be free of charges.

REFERENCES

Act CXV of 1997 on Protection of Cultural Heritage and Museums and on Public Library Provision. Available at: http://www.1000ev.hu/index.php?a = 3&param = 9559

Gyory, A. (Ed.) (1886). *Magyarország köz- és magánkönyvtárai 1885-ben* (Vol. 1). Budapest: Athenaeum.

Kajberg, L., & Lorring, L. (eds) (2005). European curriculum reflections on library and information science education. Copenhagen: The Royal School of Library and Information Sciences. Available at http://biblis.db.dk/Archimages/423.12.05.pdf. Accessed on September 6, 2007.

Kovács, M. (1961). A magyar könyv- és könyvtárkultúra a szocializmus kezdeti szakaszában. In: *Magyar Könyvszemle.*

Szabo-Andras, E. (1966). *Könyvtári adatok (1884–1962)* (76, 81pp.). Budapest: NPI.

Toszegi, Z. (Ed.) (1999). *A magyar könyvtárak egy ezredév tükrében. Multimedia CD-ROM.* Budapest: Neumann Kht.

Vidra Szabo, F. (2002). A minőség szerepe; jelentősége a magyar könyvtárügyben. In: *Könyv; Könyvtár; Könyvtáros* Október. Available at http://epa.oszk.hu/01300/01367/00034/vidra.html. Accessed on January 6, 2009.

LIBRARIES AND LIBRARIANSHIP IN CZECH REPUBLIC

Stanley Kalkus

ABSTRACT

This chapter presents a brief historical overview of Czech libraries and librarianship with special attention paid to the ways in which this history laid the foundations for present postcommunist developments. This is followed by a more detailed discussion of important changes in the wake of the "Velvet Revolution" from my perspective as library user and as active participant in the process of postcommunist change in the library world of the Czech Republic.

HISTORICAL BACKGROUND

The cultural development of libraries and librarianship in what were the Lands of the Czech crown, once part of the Austro-Hungarian Empire, shared the same trajectory with the rest of the Central Europe. The Czech Republic itself is only 10 years old, formed by the division of Czechoslovakia into two independent states: Czech Republic and Slovak Republic. Czechoslovakia was proclaimed an independent state after World War I and during its 70 years of existence endured many turbulent times and political changes. Occupied by Germany during World War II, the so-called

Advances in Library Administration and Organization, Volume 27, 99–107

Copyright © 2009 by Emerald Group Publishing Limited

All rights of reproduction in any form reserved

ISSN: 0732-0671/doi:10.1108/S0732-0671(2009)0000027010

Protectorate of Bohemia and Moravia was created. Slovakia seceded from Czechoslovakia at that time to become a separate state collaborating with Nazi Germany for six years. During the war there was a popular uprising in Slovakia against the pro-German regime. This was suppressed by the German Army, but the uprising nevertheless revealed the true feelings of the majority. At the end of World War II, there was a brief period of quasi-democratic rule which lasted three years and ended in communist coup d'etat in February 1948. The communists then assumed power for the next 40 years. All of these historical events exerted considerable influence on libraries in the Czech Republic.

Since the 10th century, collections of mainly religious books existed in the monasteries and in the castles of the nobility. As town collections of documents and local chronicles developed, municipal libraries began to appear. In 1348, Charles University was established and, although very modest, the first university library then came into being.

In the 18th century public reading rooms began to appear, and in the 19th century the first public libraries came into existence. These public libraries were actually the result of the private efforts of citizens, who instituted these public libraries on the basis of collective cultural interests. After Czechoslovakia was proclaimed and independent state in 1918, the first national "library law" was passed in 1919, leading to the widespread, systematic establishment of public libraries in cities, towns, and larger communities throughout the country. This national library law of 1919 resulted in the creation of one of the most modern public libraries systems in existence at that time.

In the post–World War I period, documentation centers, technical libraries, were developed. The new state of Czechoslovakia, one of the political entities of the former Austro-Hungarian Empire, then contained more than 70% of the empire's industrial resources. This included such world-renowned manufacturers as Skoda, CKD, CZ and many others.

In the 1920s formal library education began. At first, only general courses for library workers were offered, but in 1927 professional librarianship began to be taught at the university level in the Faculty of Philosophy of Charles University.

However, the development of Czech libraries and librarianship was brought to a halt by the German occupation. Public libraries still existed and some specialized libraries continued to offer services, but the university, the Institute of Technology, and their libraries were all closed. To a certain extent, their collections were disturbed. Censorship was instituted and "unsuitable" books were discarded and destroyed.

At the end of World War II, life was beginning to return to normal, at least in libraries, if not on the political scene. However, a new totalitarian regime was on the horizon. A February 1948 communist coup initiated a new era of censorship and totalitarian state control. All school libraries suffered the consequences almost immediately. At the universities and at the National Library, books were not removed, but special collections were created to make many items accessible only to those approved by the communist party. Many private libraries were confiscated and in some instances these valuable collections were sold abroad.

After the 1950s, the situation changed for research and technical libraries. The regime recognized the need for scientific information, not only for scientific and technical development. In fact, the end of the communist era found all scientific and technical libraries relatively well equipped and stocked. In fact, the only difference between these libraries and the best scientific and technical libraries in the West was the library personnel. Ideologically acceptable people had been selected for positions of leadership in the library world and they were not always the best in the library profession.

The Post-Velvet Revolution Period

Public libraries in Czechoslovakia between the Wars had always subscribed to very high standards. One of the reasons for this is that they were used to promote the Czech language after the Habsburg Empire ceased to exist and Czechoslovakia was established as a nation-state.

However, after the "Velvet Revolution" a poor work ethic and morale from the previous regime were quite obvious, but this was not limited to libraries. As many have no doubt also discovered, when I asked a simple reference question at one of the leading public libraries, I had the definite feeling that I was "bothering" the reference staff. This disinterest in providing service was not limited to dealing with users, either. After the "Velvet Revolution," such disinterest was felt in all areas of library work. General resistance among staff to all change was normal, particularly when change meant more work. However, this was beginning to change in the 1990s.

In the 1990s, enthusiasm for the coming changes and general hope for rapid progress led to increase support for new institutional and administrative rules requiring a commitment to renewed personal effort. However, accepting personal responsibility was the biggest problem encountered in almost all institutions and this had the effect of minimizing creative responsiveness to accelerating change. In many cases, the newly emerging private companies were best able to respond effectively to changing needs. For example, when the new Prague International School was built, the architects and builders required new, special library furniture that did not exist in the Czech Republic at that time. But the new private companies designed and built the new types of furniture needed by working with photographs the School provided. Since almost no school libraries existed in the Czech Republic at this time and children's sections of public libraries also were receiving more public attention, this specific company profited greatly from its willingness to experiment and learn.

After the "Velvet Revolution" of 1989 a new democratic era began. Censorship was a very common topic of public discussion, although practically nonexistent in the new postcommunist period. The censorship actually practiced in the postcommunist period dealt concerned publishers' discussions and decisions about what materials should or should not be published. Since librarians did take a strong stance against all forms of censorship, changes in library collections and in collections development became quite noticeable almost immediately. Previously banned books were returned to the shelves, and books from the West were added to the collections. At first all of these books came to the libraries as donations. Later they were included in budget calculations and added to collections as funds became available.

Two specific early changes that had the greatest impact on libraries and librarianship in the Czech Republic were decentralization and laws prohibiting censorship. As it turned out, prohibiting censorship created no social problems at all, for everyone welcomed that initially. Later minor problems were encountered, such as children's access to questionable materials, but these were minor social problems. Decentralization, although welcomed by most librarians, presented another problem entirely. Traditionally, those in charge of libraries were not used to making important decisions about the collections. Under the communist system, all important decisions were made centrally and under party administrative control. Because of this, librarians were, in the old British phrase, "keepers of the books." Under the new regime of decentralization, differences in abilities and competencies of individual librarians suddenly became quite noticeable in libraries everywhere. However, these human resource problems were resolved fairly easily and quickly, leaving the most significant problem today: the best allocation of finances.

At first, learning to develop and manage budgets was difficult for most librarians. However, the real challenge for most librarians in the new period was learning how to develop grant proposals. As a result of decentralization, new students of Library and Information Science were required to learn more about management and administration. This became all the more important because the new labor laws affected the operation of libraries more than the new revised library laws.

In fact, since the 1920s there had always been some library law in effect and this was well known to librarians who were well prepared to administer and manage libraries from this perspective. The specific mission of today's libraries is based on the right of free access to information, based on the new national law No. 106/1999Sb concerning citizens' rights to free access of information.

THE CZECH REPUBLIC, 1993 –

Perhaps the most interesting changes have involved the development of modern automated processes in libraries and the handling of online information systems. The revolution in new technologies and new software systems has had a considerable influence on Czech librarianship. The first and most popular system from abroad was TINLIB, followed by development of the Czech systems LANIUS and SMARTLIB. Then a grant from the Mellon Foundation helped to create the project CASLIN (Czech and Slovak Library Information Network). The first participating libraries were the National Library of the Czech Republic, the Moravian Regional Library, the Slovak National Library and the Library of the University of Bratislava. The CASLIN project provided for full automation of all of these libraries and, thus, established the foundation for development of national union Catalog for Czechoslovakia. Initiated at a time when Czechoslovakia was still a united country, the CASLIN project, nevertheless, has continued to serve both the Czech Republic and the Slovak Republic.

Automation and use of online information systems varies with the type of libraries involved. In the university libraries, the special libraries and, of course, the national libraries automation is practically complete. The public libraries are making good progress in obtaining automated systems and implementing online services. An important impetus was the Open Society Fund's offer to bring any public library to the Internet. Many libraries took advantage of offer and today many public libraries offer Internet services to their users. However, public access to the Internet is not free in most libraries. Furthermore, some libraries serve such small communities that they probably will never, or at least not in the foreseeable future, be able to offer and maintain such services. Many libraries serving small communities still do not have the technologies and lack of funds to obtain and maintain such systems.

Another good deed of the Open Society Fund was a grant to provide EBSCO full-text services to all academic and research libraries. The agreement was that the Open Society Fund would pay the subscriptions fees for the first year, after which the Ministry of Culture would begin paying the fees. Needless to say, this offer was accepted primarily by institutions of higher education, the national libraries, regional libraries and some large public libraries.

In general, it can be said that all libraries are open to modernization and the progress in this respect depends to a large degree on the library staff and to an even larger degree on available funds. Furthermore, changes in both staffing and budget are quite volatile at this time, changing for most libraries on an almost daily basis.

One of the most modernized libraries in the Czech Republic is the Parliament Library. As early as 1990, the Parliament Library received substantial financial and technical assistance from the Congressional Research Service of the Library of Congress. By 1995, the Parliament Library had initiated their own project "The Electronic Library," which is probably the most ambitious project of its kind among all of the parliamentary libraries of Eastern and Central Europe.

The basic goal of this project was to have all parliamentary proceedings, including shorthand records dating back to 1861, digitized at the present technological level and made accessible to the general public. The historical part of this project is almost complete.

I mention this particular library because although it is relatively small, it is technologically very advanced, but it also illustrates an important point about the automation of libraries in the Czech Republic. Many in the West, especially, anticipated that automation and the implementation of new computer technologies in libraries would encounter human obstacles. However, cases such as the automation of the Parliament Library demonstrated quite early on that library staff, in general, has been very fast and very eager learners, welcoming automation from the days of its earliest appearance in the library world.

In general, we know the least about the new special libraries in the private sector. Obviously the major companies, some of them named earlier, do continue to build collections of relevant technical and scientific information. The smaller companies and business organization tend to follow the general trend these days: hiring credentialed information specialists. The very fact that 80% of the students graduating from the Institute of Information Studies and Librarianship of Charles University now work for these large and small private enterprises, thus not filling the needs of the public, school and even university libraries, speaks for itself. In most cases, though, this is nothing more than simple economics. Private organizations pay a lot better. Furthermore, special private libraries are not a strange or new phenomenon in the Czech Republic.

Finally, we must include in this group of special libraries the government special libraries. All of the ministries have libraries, for example, and practically all of them hire our students to work there.

LIBRARY EDUCATION

As everywhere else in the library world, the curriculum at the Institute of Information Studies did change considerably during the 1990s, as did available space and equipment. At present, programs are offered are at the baccalaureate, masters and doctoral levels with specializations in library management, as well as information management for all types of institutions and enterprises responsible for access, creation, selection and use of information sources. Furthermore, classical disciplines such as descriptive bibliography, indexing of documents, acquisition, organization and main-tenance of collections are not left out.

In addition to the Institute of Information Studies, there is an Institute of Bohemistics and Librarianship at the Silesian University in Moravia. This academic institution offers three-year bachelor's programs in Librarianship, and Library Science and Information Services with the option to continue studies at the master's level at the Institute of Information Studies and Librarianship at Charles University in Prague.

There are a few other programs at other institutions, such as the Masaryk University in Brno and the Graduate School of Economics in Prague. However, the most interesting and innovative program is that of the Special School of Information Services in Prague. Its three-year program is comparable to the British polytechnics or the German "Fachhochschule." This school did not confer any degrees in the past, but it will soon begin offering the Bachelor's degree in the field of librarianship and information management. Continuing education programs are in increasing demand and all the aforementioned institutions include provision for such programs.

One thing is very clear. All of the past formulas for "scientific truth," definitions of "world scientific opinion" and "socialist and communist thought" have been dropped from their previous center in all academic curricula. Many of students, too, participate in study-abroad programs with universities with which we maintain exchange agreements. Some students participate in such programs as ERASMUS.

In my humble opinion more needs to be done in the field of training school librarians; however, that should be of equal concern to the education departments of institutions of higher education.

PROFESSIONAL ORGANIZATIONS

There are few professional organizations in the Czech Republic. SKIP (Svaz Knihovniku a Informacnich Pracovniku – the Association of Librarians and Information Professionals of Czech Republic) is the best known and has the largest membership: approximately 1,500 members organized in 10 regional committees. The description "professional" may be a little loose by western standards, but that is not the real problem.

This organization was established during the Prague Spring in 1968, only to be abolished in 1970. The present SKIP organization operates very much along the lines of the old system. It depends heavily, if not totally, on financial support from the government, primarily from the Ministry of Culture, but also from Ministry of Education, and for international activities (e.g., International Federation of Library Associations IFLA) from Ministry of Foreign Affairs. This makes SKIP dependent on the government and, therefore, very vulnerable. Furthermore, for just these reasons SKIP tends to be very unattractive to the younger generation of professionals.

Government grants and subsidies do keep the organization going, but more effort should be made to make it more independent and truly representative of the profession. This is not to say that it should not cooperate with the appropriate government organizations, but that it should have a stronger voice in professional affairs and work to gain more respect for the profession itself.

This, then, would lead to greater financial awards. The present salaries for professionals are very low by any standard and this goes hand-in-hand with general lack of respect for the profession. Establishing the independent voice to resolve these problems should be the primary mission of the organization.

There are other tiny organizations in the field: the 89 members of the Association of Libraries in the Czech Republic, the official English title "Association of Library Directors of the Czech Republic" providing a more accurate description of the membership. Then there is the

(Sdruzeni Universitnich Knihoven – Association of University Libraries SDRUK) – The Czech Republic Library Association – and the Nadace Knihoven (Library Foundation). These all have their specific functions and goals, but in the end there is far too much fragmentation. There has been some talk of merging professional organizations and that would most certainly be a step in the right direction. Simply said: there is a need for stronger and more independent professional organizations in the Czech Republic.

CONCLUSION

Generally speaking, the libraries, librarianship and information centers, as the new technical libraries are called, are all making good progress in spite of common problems, the most pressing of which are budgetary concerns. Inflation in the new economy has outpaced all increases in library budgets and salaries. The special libraries have the least problems, mainly because they do not have the same financial problems and, therefore, can afford to purchase better equipment and to hire the best people in the profession.

The new organization of government offices has now transferred the responsibility for public libraries from the central offices (ministries) to the local government (towns, cities, and county offices). This requires much more active "marketing" on the part of professional librarians, especially those who work in the public libraries.

FROM THE OLD-FASHIONED LIBRARY TO THE PUBLIC LIBRARY: CHANGES IN THE CULTURAL FUNCTIONS OF POLISH ACADEMIC LIBRARIES

Miroslaw Gorny

ABSTRACT

The chapter discusses the transformation of the functions Polish academic libraries fulfill. Once inaccessible for ordinary people, the libraries now have become real public libraries. However, their main problem is the lack of adequate staff. This prevents the libraries from acting as effective providers of "memory outsourcing."

INTRODUCTION

As late as the 1980s, Polish academic libraries were functioning almost in the same way as they had in the period between the two World Wars. This was due to a number of factors – the technological "lag" in prewar Poland (until 1939, Poland had one of the poorest telephone networks in Europe), the

Advances in Library Administration and Organization, Volume 27, 109–122
Copyright © 2009 by Emerald Group Publishing Limited
All rights of reproduction in any form reserved
ISSN: 0732-0671/doi:10.1108/S0732-0671(2009)0000027011

massive destruction caused by World War II, and the fact that communist governments underestimated the costs of developing communication and computer technologies.

Postwar Poland, however, saw a rapid increase in the total number of libraries. This resulted from the fact that the authorities in power at that time viewed education as one of their top priorities. Nevertheless, the technological level of library infrastructure remained practically unchanged for some time thereafter. It was only the political changes of the 1980s and 1990s that indirectly caused significant technological change in the Polish library science field. These political changes involved commitments to the construction of new libraries, new storage techniques, communications upgrades, and the introduction of computer technologies.

These changes also occurred concurrently with changes in the functions of libraries. However, although technological changes were rather clear, obvious, and easily noticed by both librarians and decision makers, the ways in which those changes were transforming the functions of libraries went almost unnoticed, and unfortunately, their impact was underestimated. One can say that the resulting situation was unusual because librarians usually accept new technologies, but they still find it difficult to adapt to changes in the tasks assigned to those working in the library. Of course, there is a small group of librarians who do understand the necessity of considering new models of librarian functions. However, they commonly encounter serious resistance. It will probably require a generation change to accomplish the work of redefining library work in Poland.

THE OLD-FASHIONED LIBRARY

The prestige of the library in the immediate postwar period rested on the quantity and quality of its resources. Above all, this was connected with the necessity of rebuilding the collections destroyed during the war. This was certainly in accordance with the beliefs of those who were in positions of authority in the immediate postwar period. Poland had always been a nation of scholars and science and education were promoted quite highly, in part, to broadcast the message to the postwar world that the Polish People's Republic was an enlightened country. This had its advantages and disadvantages. On the one hand, some very valuable new book collections were created. On the other hand, library shelves also became loaded with many low-value publications.

In addition to expanding the collections of books within existing libraries, new libraries were founded. New institutions of higher education institutions were established and it was necessary to develop more libraries to serve them. Unfortunately, this was not accompanied by the development of new library service programs. As early as the 1960s, Polish academic libraries faced the problem of shrinking storage areas. One consequence of quickly growing collections in shrinking, inadequate spaces meant that developing an open-stack system was simply out of the question. The most critical shortcoming, however, was the fact that the average citizen did not have the opportunity to take full advantage of the rich collections of Polish academic libraries. Both for political reasons (e.g., secure sources related to the Eastern Borderlands of the II Republic of Poland) and for technical and management reasons (e.g., the size of maps or theater posters and other common documents of social life) stacks were not open to the general public. Furthermore, because these academic libraries were located in large cities, people from the provinces had to make time-consuming journeys to use these collections. Such visits were possible only infrequently, and since users could not borrow books (this was only offered to students and university faculty and staff), checking out materials for use in the reading room typically required multiple visits to the library. To make things worse, the number of readers who actually could use the library at the same time was limited by the number of seats in the reading rooms. Photocopiers also were not available for readers. Libraries had low-speed photocopiers for staff use only, and even in the 1970s these machines were not available to the public.

Consequently, libraries were almost exclusively for the elite, most often students, faculty, and other professional researchers. But even this relatively small group of library users could access no more than 15–20% of the necessary foreign holdings. Users of Polish materials were in a much better situation, yet using the library was still very time-consuming at best. For academic work in the Liberal Arts, time spent in the library amounted to 70% of the total time devoted to preparing a master's thesis, a doctoral dissertation, an article, or a monograph. In the case of historical research, many researchers spent years developing personal collections that they would then use for the rest of their lives for teaching and research. They would make extensive notes during multiple visits to different libraries over a long period of time. However, libraries did have special reading rooms for professors to provide them a comfortable environment for studying and reading literature for many hours at a time.

Of course, there were fewer inconveniences for those working in the Sciences. Books and periodicals used by scientists were typically purchased at their own request, and released immediately after being catalogued. In addition, articles were also directly accessed by using publications like *Current Contents*. For the Liberal Arts, however, the library model did not change for decades. Researchers in the Liberal Arts in most cases had only limited access to the world's literature.

The fundamental weaknesses of academic libraries in 1970s and 1980s were:

- The large number of the sources was purchased without clear acquisitions criteria;
  - Poor equipment;
  - Space limitations;
  - Poorly educated staff who had little commitment to the profession;
  - Small foreign holdings due to lack of foreign currencies;
  - No interlibrary cooperation because there was no collection coordination at any level;
- Very infrequent interlibrary lending and borrowing.

From the beginning of the 1970s, Polish academic libraries concentrated on managing the collections and they performed this task very well. Unfortunately, collections were available only to a small group of specialists and students and, even then, with serious restrictions. Both conditions of access to the library and completeness of collections left much to be desired.

THE LIBRARY OF THE TRANSITIONAL PERIOD

The beginning of the 1990s was marked by the purchase of integrated library systems (VTLS, Horizon, and Aleph). These purchases were financed, in part, with grants from the Mellon Foundation. The introduction of the first online catalogs that could be accessed via the Internet marked the beginning of significant changes in Polish library science.

Computer systems improved the library circulation process. Many books, once thought to have been lost, were being returned to libraries. The phenomenon of keeping books illegally was largely eliminated and the management of library collections greatly improved. A systematic process of weeding unnecessary or unwanted items from the collections also commenced. At the same time, access to the Internet made it easier for librarians and readers to become familiar with the world's literature, a fact that definitely improved acquisition policies. Online catalogs slightly shortened the time necessary for using libraries. Readers could check from home to see which books were actually on the shelves, rather than wasting their time coming to the library for items already checked out. In turn, the library did not have to continue to use staff to assist patrons with such routine requests.

The most important change, however, was the fact that online catalogs made it possible to check the collections of any particular library at any time and from any place in the country. This contributed to a significant "revival" in the use of library collections and interlibrary lending became much easier. Furthermore, many interesting publications became available to individuals who previously had had little or no access to library collections (e.g., amateurs and hobbyists of various kinds).

The Public Library

However, the real communication revolution in Polish academic libraries did not commence until the beginning of the 21st century. It is was then that digital libraries came into being, organized according to the recommendations of the Library Science faculty at Poznan University. At present, there are two central digital libraries (the National Digital Library Polona, http://www.polona.pl, and the Polish Internet Library (PBI), http://www.pbi.edu.pl). The PBI was established as an independent institution; its collections are mainly classics of Polish literature.

There are also 17 regional digital libraries in Poland:

- The Digital Library of Wielkopolska (http://www.wbc.poznan.pl)
- The Kujawsko-Pomorska Digital Library (http://kpbc.umk.pl)
- The Digital Library of Zielona Góra (http://zbc.uz.zgora.pl)
- The Dolnośląska Digital Library (http://dlib.bg.pwr.wroc.pl)
- The Digital Library of Jelenia Góra (http://jbc.jelenia-gora.pl)
- Podlaska Digital Library (http://pbc.biaman.pl)
- The Pedagogical Digital Library (http://www.ap.krakow.pl/dlibra/)
- Silesian Digital Library (http://www.sbc.org.pl)
- The Digital Library of Wejherowo (http://biblioteka.wejherowo.pl)
- The Digital Library of Małopolska (http://mbc.malopolska.pl/)
- Swietokrzyska Digital Library (http://sbc.wbp.kielce.pl/dlibra)
- Podkarpacka Digital Library (http://www.pbc.rzeszow.pl/dlibra)
- Nowa Huta Digital Library (http://cyfrowa.biblioteka.krakow.pl/dlibra)
- Elblag Digital Library (http://dlibra.bibliotekaelblaska.pl/dlibra)
- Lodz Regional Digital Library (http://bc.wimbp.lodz.pl/dlibra)

- Baltycka Digital Library (http://bibliotekacyfrowa.eu/dlibra)
- ABC Digital Library (http://abc.krakow.pl/)

And 8 digital libraries at universities:

- The Digital Library of Wrocław University (http://www.bibliotekacyfrowa. pl)
- The Digital Library of the Technical University of Łódź (http://ebipol.p. lodz.pl/)
- The Warsaw University of Technology Digital Library (http://bcpw.bg. pw.edu.pl/)
- The Cracow University of Technology Digital Library (http://www. biblos.pk.edu.pl/bc)
- The Digital Library of Warsaw University (http://ebuw.uw.edu.pl)
- UMCS University Digital Library (http://dlibra.umcs.lublin.pl/dlibra)
- The Digital Library University of Łódź (http://bcul.lib.uni.lodz.pl/dlibra)
- Lublin University of Technology Digital Library (http://bc.pollub.pl/ dlibra)

The PBI and the National Digital Library are financed by the state and are under the authority of the Ministry of Culture of the Republic of Poland. In contrast, the regional libraries are merely organizational–technical platforms that allow academic and other libraries to publish their collections in a digital form. For this reason, many academic libraries now have assumed the functions of a public library, and readers have finally obtained tools for using library collections on demand.

At present, logs and correspondence show that over 60% of the users of the Digital Library of Wielkopolska (DLW) are nonacademic readers. They are usually the inhabitants of smaller towns in Poland located anywhere from 50 to 200 km from Poznan. Twenty-three percent of the users are readers from abroad. Records show that the number of readers accessing the DLW at the same time ranges from approximately 100 to 700 reader.

Approximately 90% of paid visits to the DLW by foreign readers is related to research into kinship and family connections. These readers routinely search the approximately 40 books for address records of Poznan, certain towns in Wielkopolska province, and even the whole of Poland during the interwar period. These readers often request additional information that is not available in the online address books. They often look online for additional information from newspapers, but since they most often do not know Polish, they have to ask library staff for help. Later these people often come to Poland to pursue their family research.

Domestic readers, on the other hand, tend to search publications on the history of their home region. Sometimes these same readers will donate to the library copies of their own private publications and results of their own personal research.

SOCIAL ATTITUDES TOWARD BOOKS AND LIBRARIES IN POST-SOVIET TIMES

Changes that followed the fall of communism in 1989 and the introduction of a capitalist economy were comparable in scope to those which took place after 1945. Democracy was introduced, censorship was abolished, and a free press developed. For the first time in 60 years, Poles could freely elect their parliament. In this new situation, it might have seemed that libraries would play a greater social role than under the previous system and that the post-Soviet authorities would strive to realize a broader, more robust cultural development of all social institutions.

In fact, those in power did declare that libraries would be assigned a key public cultural role, but, in reality things turned out differently. The financing of public libraries was entrusted to local authorities, so many libraries were closed in for local budgetary reasons, whereas those that remained open were forced to operate with very small budgets. Between 1995 and 2006, the number of public libraries fell from 9,500 to 8,500, the number of library service points dropped from 4,400 to 1,700, and the number of books held by libraries fell from 136.7 million to 135.5 million. But at the same time, the number of readers remained the same over the same period with 7 million borrowers annually. Notably, the total number of items borrowed from libraries fell from 157.4 million in 1995 to 134.4 million in 2006.[1]

The commercialization of life and the increase in unemployment had a pronounced effect on Polish cultural life. Poles bought fewer books and went to the library less often. Entire social groups – both workers and intellectuals – simply stopped reading. The traditional place of books was taken over by the rapidly developing tabloid press. State television, which under communism generally broadcast high-quality cultural and educational programs, now faced competition in the form of private television stations broadcasting only entertainment. On the other hand, satellite television now provided access to foreign-language channels, including significant amounts of popular science programming.

The book market also was commercialized. A large number of for-profit publishing houses came into existence and there was a very serious decline in the standard of translations, often done on commission by amateurs for private publishers.

It was the case that these significant changes made possible the development of a popular, entertainment-based culture that began effectively to supplant so-called high culture. In 2006, when asked whether they read books (i.e., had contact with at least one publication in the course of the year), one-half of Polish respondents answered in the affirmative. There were more readers among women (53%), inhabitants of towns (55%), and persons with at least a high-school education (61%). Among those who had completed secondary or tertiary education, 77% were readers, and among young persons aged under 30, 81% of those in the 15–19 age range and 56% of those in the 20–29 range declared themselves to be readers.

At the same time, the majority of men (54%), rural dwellers (60%), persons over 30 (58%), and persons with no more than basic vocational education (68%) did not show any interest in books at all. Overall, nonreaders made up the largest single group among all respondents (50%), whereas sporadic readers, declaring that they had read no more than six publications in the last year, made up almost one-third of the total (32%), and readers with a greater interest in reading (at least seven books annually) found themselves in the definite minority (just over 17% of the population).

The most widely read books were thrillers and crime stories (20% of readers) and schoolbooks and textbooks (also 20%). Fifteen percent read romances and novels, whereas there was only slightly less interest in encyclopedias and handbooks (14%), as well as specialist publications (12%).

Similar levels of success were enjoyed by nonfiction and youth literature. The first category, which includes memoirs, biographies, autobiographies, and journalistic accounts, "Books of the Moment" about current or recent events and gossip relating to the lives of celebrities, often by the celebrities themselves, attracted 11% of Polish readers. Youth literature, the second category, was read by 10%.

Less widely read were fantasy literature (8%), religious books (also 8%), essays, categorized as journalism (3%), and esoteric works including "ufology" and predictions and horoscopes (1%). In terms of a percentage of the total population, the most popular categories (thrillers and crime stories, and school books and textbooks) recorded a popularity rating of 10% (Straus, Wolff, & Wierny, 2007, p. 4).

On the other hand, those who seek contact with higher culture acquired new outlets. This refers especially to the ease of access to foreign sources via the Internet and the ability to buy foreign books and magazines thanks to the convertibility and current higher value of the zloty. It should be remembered, however, that this particular group has significantly diminished in numbers due to mass emigration (approximately 3% of Poland's population have emigrated in recent years).[2]

THE SIGNIFICANCE OF THE INTERNET

The development of the Internet in Poland has had great significance. The number of households with home access to the Internet exceeded 5 million in 2007 (41% of the total), and the number of households with broadband connections is rising rapidly: in 2007 there were 3.7 million such households (30% of the total). Since 2006 this number has increased by almost a million (8%), and it is rising faster than the total number of households with Internet access (up by 5%), which means that practically all new Internet connections are now broadband links.[3]

In 2006, 69% of Internet users answered in the affirmative when asked whether they read books, whereas of the 39% of those who were not Internet users only 37% claimed to have any contact with books. In 2006, the Internet was used by 36% of Polish residents over 15 years of age, most often at home (28%), sometimes at work (10%), but more rarely at school or college (6%). There was clearly a larger proportion of Internet users among university graduates (65%), but the number of Internet users was also above average among people with only a high-school education (45%).

The smallest numbers of Internet users were recorded among persons with only a primary education (25%) and those who had completed only vocational schools (15%). Internet use was dominant in the age groups 15–19 (70%) and 20–29 (57%), whereas in the 50–59 age group only 20% used the Internet, and among the over-60 age group the percentage was just 3%. In 2006, the Internet was used by 45% of those living in towns but only 21% of those living in rural areas. In 2006, almost 30% of Internet users said that they read the news and media releases on the Internet, both web-published journals and online versions of traditional newspapers and magazines. One in five Internet users in 2006 accessed online books of all types in various electronic formats, including literary works, handbooks, scientific books, and books for specialists, amateurs, and hobbyists. Half of these Internet users declared that they had used this form of access to books more than a few times. Ten percent of all Internet users stated that they found and read books in various types of digital libraries and the remainder indicated other sources, such as portals or other specific websites.

The Internet is also becoming a more frequent source of information about traditional books. In 2006, 27% of Internet users stated that they used the Internet when seeking information about new publications, as well as opinion, reviews, extracts, recommendations, or simply prices of books, including 11% who declared that they did more often.

The final interesting question concerns the extent of Internet downloading of various types of files, including books. The actual proportion of Internet users taking advantage of file downloading in Poland is only 38%. Music, film, and video files are downloaded most often, but only 12% of Internet users downloaded any text files (documents, press articles, etc.). The fewest number of Internet users downloaded files with books (5%) (Straus et al., 2007, p. 6).

BOOKS, LIBRARIES, AND THE EDUCATIONAL SYSTEM

It would appear that interest in books and libraries might be expected to rise in Poland due to the increase in the number of people learning and studying. Students made up 55.3% of 19–24-year olds in 2006/2007, compared to only 45.4% in 1995. There was also an increase in the 16–18 age group: from 88.7% in 1995 to 95.5% in 2006/2007.[4] The number of students in post-secondary educational institutions rose from 794,600 in 1995 to 1,941,400 in 2006/2007. Teaching staff in institutions of higher education rose from 67,000 in 1995/1996 to 100,200 in 2006/2007.[5]

Academic libraries have been particularly affected by increases in student borrowing. Nevertheless, these have been almost exclusively increases in the number of textbooks circulated. Unfortunately, interest in journal resources in electronic form has remained low. This is in spite of the fact that libraries are able for the first time in their history to offer readers such rich collections of foreign-language publications and have made them so easily accessible (they can be used at home at any time).

On the other hand, the academic community has shown little interest in the rich resources now offered by academic libraries. The rapid development of private colleges has led to an enormous demand for teaching staff. Their number has indeed increased, but not enough to meet the needs of hundreds of new private schools. For this reason, many teaching staff work concurrently at several institutions, taking advantage of the situation to augment their earnings. As a result, Poland is suffering a continuous decline in standards of academic research and new publications actually reaching only local readers.

The academic significance and quality of new academic publications in most cases is negligible. The list of the world's 500 best universities includes only two Polish institutions. These enter the list only at 400th place.[6] Over the past ten years, Polish academics have produced 121,061 publications, ranking Poland 19th in number of publications, but in terms of number of citations (658,927) and average number of citations per article (5.44), Poland finds itself outside of the top 20. Two countries in 20th place, in contrast, are Finland with 948,501 citations and Austria with an average of 10.33 citations per article.[7]

The role of libraries in Poland – both public and academic – unfortunately has declined markedly since 1989. However, it is also true that the material situation of libraries has significantly improved. All Polish academic libraries purchase thousands of foreign journal titles in digital form from EBSCO or ProQuest and they are buying e-books much more frequently. Libraries are attempting to take action under the Open Access Initiative to build repositories.

However, Polish academics do not show any great interest in these undertakings. Quite the contrary, it is clear that what is happening in Polish libraries is happening at the initiative of a small number of librarians. These professionals are motivated by concern for the decline in the importance of libraries in society and a fear of losing their positions. Some librarians, in turn, see such projects as opportunities for career advancement, attendance at foreign conferences, employment experience, and so on. One clear example here is the high level of interest in the LIBQUAL+ project, whose practical importance is negligible, given current conditions in Poland.

AND WHAT NEXT?

Polish scientific libraries face a difficult task. They have to accept the role they assumed earlier in Poland's history. The time of experiments has ended. Readers have started to take digital libraries very seriously and have growing expectations about them. They use these libraries frequently and expect to do so at any time.

A digital library, as any other library, must guarantee that its collections will be available at all times and for everyone. Since the academic library now has become the public library, it must ensure access to many publications that have never been made publicly available before because of security issues. It also must broaden the description of these publications because the public readers are not the small group of specialists who had not required that type of help using the library collections. Indeed, the specialists often knew more than the librarians. The general public, however, must receive additional information about publications. Otherwise, they may not be able to use them.

If the DLW makes available to the general public approximately 750 legal acts related to the town of Poznan issued in the years 1254–1790, readers must receive the kind of enhanced information which will help them understand the functioning of the old Polish legal system. It is often necessary to overcome the resistance of many librarians to publish their collections on the Internet, and to convince them that digital libraries should be a part of a statutory, routine activity of libraries. But before this can occur, approximately 20% of the library budget would have to be devoted to digital resources and programs.

It is also necessary to convince librarians that they should not be afraid of publishing visual and media collections (photographs, postcards, etc.) on the Internet. Today, a very common concern is that someone might reproduce the postcards and sell them.

We are only at the beginning of the new path. The largest regional digital library in Poland, DLW, has barely 60,000 publications. The biggest academic library of Poznan, the Adam Mickiewicz University Library, spends only two percent of its budget for digitization. It will have to increase spending ten times to be able to fulfill an important social function. Digitization will be an important element in so-called "memory outsourcing."

Provided that a global information infrastructure is in place, digitization will facilitate permanent, reliable, and easy access to factual, documented information. Information users will start to behave like traveling tourists who expect to find hotels and restaurants at every step on a journey – having to carry food and a tent becomes unnecessary. Requiring students to produce facts and figures from memory will also slowly become unnecessary. Facts will be available anywhere and any time.

There is no doubt that the information infrastructure necessary to ensure easy and uninterrupted delivery of information to all who need it anywhere will be developed very soon, for this is in the interest of big telecom companies and the manufacturers of computer equipment. But are libraries prepared for this? Unfortunately, they are not. The main problem is the lack of adequate personnel. The librarians of today are well prepared for the "indoor" types of tasks. Tomorrow, however, they will be required to fulfill "outdoor" types of functions. They must quickly digitize huge collections in their possession, which requires further development of technological databases, yet this is a financial burden. Still, the necessary means are relatively small and probably can be obtained without much difficulty.

However, the biggest problem is adequate organization of collections. The current organization is designed for conducting searches with elements of a bibliographic description, which is only effective when searching specific publications or publications that are grouped under a specific topic. However, the future user will need more and richer information, although this will undoubtedly be subject to authentication and some type of authority control. Guaranteeing the authenticity and reliability of new information resources will have to be ensured by the library as a scientific institution. But the larger question of how to find the way through the current jumble of publications is still very much open. Thus, it will be necessary to conduct thorough assessments and provide clarifications and comments on new information sources. This requires a great deal of knowledge and much work.

Libraries will have to use their collections as a basis for anticipating and preparing to meet specific educational needs adjusted to the level of the users. Let us imagine, for example, a primary-school student looking for library materials on folk customs in the Wielkopolska region. Today, such student can find many publications that, however, may be difficult or impossible for him to read. This is because many of these types of library materials are either written in Old Polish, or they are technical documents prepared by ethnographers for specialists. If, however, a librarian anticipates this problem and prepares selected texts for such students (in fact, they can include links to the original publications), providing annotations and appropriate supporting materials, the student will not find it difficult to read and analyze the material.

Polish scientific libraries are at the beginning of this new path. The total number of digitized items libraries have made available to the public so far is just 190,000. But there is a generation of young librarians who fully intend to modernize Polish libraries. The success we have enjoyed so far is due to the fact that regional libraries have established a consortium and have started to cooperate on these new library tasks.

NOTES

1. Concise Statistical Yearbook of Poland 2007 GUS Table 3 (166). See http://www.stat.gov.pl/gus/45_2144_ENG_HTML.htm. Główny Urząd Statystyczny, Warszawa 2007, p. 271.

2. Wpływ emigracji zarobkowej na gospodarkę Polski, see http://64.233.183.104/search?q = cache:Ku0MY5IzmAQJ:www.msz.gov.pl/files/docs/DKiP/Material_nr3 Analiza_Ministerstwa_Gospodarki.pdf+emigracja+zarobkowa+w+Polsce&hl = pl&ct = clnk&cd = 3&gl = pl. Ministerstwo Gospodarki, Warszawa 2007, p. 13.

3. Use of IT and telecommunications technologies in households and by private individuals in 2007. See http://www.stat.gov.pl/gus/45_3733_PLK_HTML.htm. Główny Urząd Statystyczny, Warszawa 2007, p. 2.

4. Concise Statistical Yearbook of Poland 2007 GUS Table 3 (136), pupils and students by age groups. See http://www.stat.gov.pl/gus/45_2144_ENG_HTML.htm. Główny Urząd Statystyczny, Warszawa 2007, p. 236.

5. Concise Statistical Yearbook of Poland 2007 GUS Table 1 (134). See http://www.stat.gov.pl/gus/45_2144_ENG_HTML.htm. Główny Urząd Statystyczny, Warszawa 2007, p. 232.

6. Academic Ranking of World Universities 2007. Top 500 World Universities (305–402). See http://ed.sjtu.edu.cn/rank/2007/ARWU2006_305-402.htm (downloaded on April 2008). Institute of Higher Education, Shanghai Jiao Tong University, 2007.

7. Essential Science Indicators from the November 1, 2007. Update covering a ten-year plus eight-month period, January 1997–August 31, 2007. See http://in-cites.com/countries/2007allfields.html. The Thomson Corporation, 2008.

REFERENCES

Academic Ranking of World Universities. (2007). Top 500 World Universities (305–402). Institute of Higher Education, Shanghai Jiao Tong University. Available at http://ed.sjtu.edu.cn/rank/2007/ARWU2006_305-402.htm. Accessed on April 2008.

Concise Statistical Yearbook of Poland. (2007). Główny Urząd Statystyczny, Warszawa. Available at http://www.stat.gov.pl/gus/45_2144_ENG_HTML.htm

Essential Science Indicators from the November 1, 2007. (2008). Update covering a ten-year plus eight-month period, January 1997–August 31, 2007. The Thomson Corporation. Available at http://in-cites.com/countries/2007allfields.html

Straus, G. Wolff, K., & Wierny, S. (2007). Czytelnictwo, zakup książek i wykorzystanie Internetu w Polsce w 2006 – Research report (manuscript). Biblioteka Narodowa, Warszawa. Available at http://www.bn.org.pl/doc/konferencje/komunikat20070309.doc

Use of IT and telecommunications technologies in households and by private individuals in 2007. (2007). Główny Urząd Statystyczny, Warszawa. Available at http://www.stat.gov.pl/gus/45_3733_PLK_HTML.htm

Wpływ emigracji zarobkowej na gospodarkę Polski. (2007). Ministerstwo Gospodarki, Warszawa. Available at http://64.233.183.104/search?q = cache:Ku0MY5IzmAQJ: www.msz.gov.pl/files/docs/DKiP/Material_nr3Analiza_Ministerstwa_Gospodarki.pdf+ emigracja+zarobkowa+w+Polsce&hl = pl&ct = clnk&cd = 3&gl = pl

ACCEPTANCE OF SOCIAL MARKETING CONCEPTS BY SELECTED ROMANIAN LIBRARIANS: CULTURE AND CONTEXT

Hermina G. B. Anghelescu, James Lukenbill,
W. Bernard Lukenbill and Irene Owens

ABSTRACT

Social marketing is based on general marketing principles and strategies aimed at selling products and services to consumers with the purpose of changing an existing action; changing individual or group behavior, attitudes or beliefs; and reinforcing desired behaviors. The purpose of the study is to assess the acceptance of social marketing by librarians in post-Communist Romania within the context of this country's efforts to adopt democratic values into its social system. The study also uses the social marketing concept as an idea that requires change in attitudes and behaviors about the nature of librarianship. In so doing, it can be used as means of understanding the willingness of Romanian librarians to accept change. During the Communist regime, the librarians acted as tools that supported the dissemination of the totalitarian government's views.

Advances in Library Administration and Organization, Volume 27, 123–150
Copyright © 2009 by Emerald Group Publishing Limited
ISSN: 0732-0671/doi:10.1108/S0732-0671(2009)0000027012

Fifteen years after the collapse of Communism they continue the struggle to implement principles of participatory management. However, visible changes in Romanian librarians' mentalities, attitudes, and behaviors are still to come. A group of 74 librarians in attendance at a conference responded to a survey questionnaire based on the Social Marketing Scale (SMS) designed to determine the participants' acceptance and willingness to support social marketing within their institutions. Results reveal that on the surface, social marketing was rejected by the sample group studied. The study suggests that, if social marketing is to play a role in Romanian librarianship, Romanian librarians must first accept the concept that libraries are important institutions and that libraries play a vital role in a democratic society. Once Romanian society begins to perceive the library as an information agency, knowledge and experience in social marketing must be gained so that the administrative and institutional will to pursue social marketing can be encouraged. Romanian libraries continue the process of redefining themselves within the country's transition to a civil society.

Developing countries in the former Soviet-bloc region have received little attention by Western researchers of libraries. This study attempts to broaden this limited knowledge concerning librarianship in Eastern Europe by offering some insight into the culture of Romanian libraries and the Romanian librarians' readiness for change as they faced and continue to face the transition from an autocratic cultural and governmental system to a more open and democratic society with Romania's admission to the European Union as of 1 January 2007. The study uses "social marketing" as one means of ascertaining the degree to which Romanian librarians are willing to accept change.

OVERVIEW OF SOCIAL MARKETING CONCEPTS

Within the past few decades, social marketing has become extremely important to many professional, government, and social organizations in the West. The concept has assumed special importance in health fields where the dissemination of good health, disease information, and education are vital to both individuals and to society in general. For example, Population Services International, located in Washington, D.C. and London, published a series of research reports entitled, "Social Marketing and Communication for Health." Recent studies from this organization have focused on studying the effectiveness of social marketing campaigns on the prevention of HIV and AIDS in African countries (Population Services International, 2002). Social marketing is based on general marketing principles and strategies that are used to sell products and services to consumers. As in marketing, the process involves the planning and execution of concepts, determining prices, planning promotion campaigns, and the distribution of ideas, goods, and services. Although social marketing borrows from marketing principles, it is designed specifically to influence social behaviors – not to benefit the marketer, but to benefit the target audience and society in general. Like marketing, social marketing has a "product" to sell, and that product can range from encouraging the use of physical products (e.g., eyeglasses for the improvement of health) to improving the images of social and educational institutions (e.g., libraries). Social marketing may also include promotion of ideas such as freedom of information and the role of information in a democratic society. Social marketing has three basic aims (1) to change an existing action; (2) to change individual or group behavior, attitudes, or beliefs; and (3) to reinforce desired behaviors. It is generally recognized that, for social marketing campaigns to be successful, the campaign must offer a viable product or service, that people or potential clients or customers must first perceive that they have a genuine problem, and that the product offering is a good solution for that problem (Weinreich, 2002).

A central core of social marketing is the requirement to understand the consumers' perceptions of the problem and the product, how important the product is to them, and what actions they are willing to take to accept the product. Once this is understood, social marketing strategies must be planned that will provide the potential consumer with information so that informed decisions can be made about the product. In most social marketing campaigns an assumption is made that the product to be promoted will be of benefit to both the individual and to society as a whole.

As in marketing, promotion strategies are important in social marketing and can consist of advertising, public relations, promotions, media advocacy, personal selling, and entertainment presentations. As in any type of marketing, the focus is on informing customers about the product and creating and sustaining demand for the product (Weinreich, 2002). Like any marketing campaign, social marketing must be based on a firm understanding of social and cultural norms and expectations existing within a given society, and all strategies and information messages must respect such factors.

In addition, social marketing entails social responsibility – the idea that organizations and institutions are part of a larger society and are accountable to society for their actions. "The well being of society at large should also be recognized in an organization's marketing decisions. In fact, some marketing experts stress the societal marketing concept, in the view that an organization should discover and satisfy the needs of its consumers in a way that also provides for society's well being" (Berkowitz, 2000).

SOCIAL CONDITIONS OF ROMANIAN LIBRARIES AFTER THE FALL OF COMMUNISM

The fall of Communism in Eastern Europe in the last years of the 20th century ushered in a new political and social reality for the Eastern bloc. All countries that were aligned with the former Soviet Union in Eastern Europe suddenly faced a citizenship with unprecedented levels of expectations for change and improvement. Communism in Romania fell in December 1989 with the destruction of the Ceauşescu government. The country and all of its institutions faced monumental tasks of rebuilding a nation and culture according to democratic principles conducive to the concepts of a more open society.

During the cold war period, libraries in the Eastern bloc did not promote free access to information. On the contrary, drastic censorship principles restricted access to certain collections deemed harmful by the authorities. Formal library education in Romania ended in the mid-1970s when the Communist government decided that such training was not necessary and that library education could be conducted informally by libraries through on-the-job work experiences reinforced by previous education in various disciplines. This had the effect of preventing newer concepts of library service and the dissemination of information about library management from reaching library staff in all types of libraries across Romania.

Library education was reinstated in 1990 at the University of Bucharest. In the following years, other universities began to offer library science courses as part of minor study programs in librarianship. There is a current need, however, for adequately trained faculty members capable of intro-ducing the students to the latest trends and developments in library services in general and information science in particular.

Fifteen years after the demise of Communism, the country continues to struggle for the implementation of democratic practices and values within its institutions that for almost half a century operated on the principles of authoritarian management and controlled flow of information. After the fall of Communism, libraries of all kinds have been undergoing a slow metamorphosis in an effort to modernize their activities and integrate Western practices into their daily operations and services. This process has been more difficult than anticipated and has resulted in modest changes.

The timid progress of modernization of library services in post-1990 Romania is caused by a series of factors at the macro (societal) and micro (institutional) level. The macro level has been confronted with the legacy of the Communist system that had been in place since the end of World War II. The Communist regime was characterized by a hierarchical system where major decisions were taken at the very top and propagated further down through its institutions. Participatory management was an unfamiliar concept in all kinds of institutions, libraries included. At the micro level, employees had almost no part in the decision-making process in the institutions where they worked. They only followed the decisions made by those higher in the governance structure of these institutions. Often novel ideas were regarded as harmful and destabilizing. Library directors, who were often political appointees with no library training whatsoever, turned their libraries into propaganda tools that supported the dissemination of the official ideology (Anghelescu, 2000).

PERCEPTIONS OF ROMANIAN LIBRARIES

In the aftermath of World War II, Romanian libraries, as all libraries in the Eastern bloc, adopted the Soviet model of librarianship in which library collections were dominated by Marxist-Leninist literature, and access to information was under heavy government control. During almost half a century of Communist domination, libraries of all kinds – public, academic, school, and special – served as indoctrination institutions ensuring the dissemination of the propaganda of the Communist Party. Their primary goal was the political indoctrination of the nation. Romanian libraries that had collections of rare books and old periodicals made no effort to attract new users or to diversify their services. Librarians acted as custodians, in the true sense of the word, and guarded the collections from unwelcome users who were required to submit their credentials before being granted permission to access certain materials (Anghelescu, 2001). Today, with the exception of small local branches of public libraries, Romanian libraries continue to use a closed stacks system, thus preventing their clients from the benefit of browsing. The dismantling of the Communist-style subordination of public libraries to the Ministry of Culture and of school libraries to the Ministry of

Education by placing libraries under the tutelage of the local authority led to the disappearance of many public and school libraries in the country. The number of public, school, and special libraries has been decreasing steadily since the demise of Communism (Anuarul statistic al României, 2006) as libraries have been confronted with financial austerity. Only the number of academic libraries has grown due to the establishment of private universities after 1990. However, the quality of the collections and services provided by these newly established libraries is questionable (Anghelescu, 2003). Table 1 illustrates the dynamics of the Romanian library network during the 1990–2004 period.

A provocative article suggestively titled, "The Collapse of Romanian Libraries" by Mircea Regneală, the president of the Federation of Romanian Library Associations and the director of the Central University Library in Bucharest, the most prominent academic library in Romania, deplored the decay of the Romanian library system and denounced the government's continuing neglect of the library sector (Regneală, 2004). In an editorial in the February 2005 issue of *Biblioteca*, Emil Vasilescu, the editor-in-chief states

The situation of Romanian libraries has been visibly deteriorating. The causes are camouflaged, well hidden from the public opinion. It is clear that national bodies with

Table 1. Romanian Library Network, 1990–2006.

	Total	National Libraries	Academic Libraries	Special Libraries	Public Libraries	School Libraries
1990	16.665	2	48	2.128	4.458	10.029
1991	15.749	2	46	1.619	3.836	10.246
1992	13.999	2	60	1.326	2.883	9.728
1993	13.608	6	64	1.282	2.917	9.339
1994	13.866	7	75	1.309	2.933	9.542
1995	13.581	7	71	1.270	2.904	9.329
1996	13.808	7	75	1.277	2.902	9.547
1997	13.849	3	78	1.265	2.915	9.588
1998	13.821	3	82	1.222	2.915	9.599
1999	13.785	3	85	1.163	2.919	9.615
2000	13.422	3	91	1.052	2.870	9.408
2001	13.442	3	99	1.005	2.902	9.443
2002	13.377	3	99	986	2.902	9.388
2003	13.169	4	101	954	2.906	9.204
2004	12.574	4	110	890	2.908	8.662
2005	12.455	4	106	846	2.914	8.585
2006	12.081	4	106	789	2.925	8.257

responsibilities in the library field, mainly the Ministries [of Education and of Culture], have been ignoring the difficulties libraries have been facing, have overseen the information needs of millions of users. This process of "estrangement" of the national authorities has occurred at a time when the public's need for information is ever more acute. Despite the decreasing number of libraries, the use of public library space has been in ever higher demand. (Vasilescu, 2005)

It is equally important to address the general public's perception of libraries in Romania. Traditionally, major libraries have been regarded as repositories of the nation's cultural heritage and treasures, with collections that included church manuscripts, archives of the nation's most famous writers, scientists, and political thinkers, the first imprints in the country's territory, as well as other valuable collections to be used mostly for scholarly research. During the Communist period, a network consisting of some 21,340 libraries of various kinds operated throughout Romania, a country of 21 million inhabitants (Mărunțelu, 1995). Most of these libraries were creations of the Communist regime and were established to support the government in power. The general population viewed them as centers of dissemination of political and ideological literature and deliberately avoided them to avoid further indoctrination. In public libraries leisure reading literature was popular and circulated well. Romanian public libraries never played the role they played in the Anglo-Saxon world as community information centers, as institutions one could use to obtain quick solutions for daily information needs (Anghelescu, 2006).

The prevailing management policy for libraries as determined by the Communist government was that libraries served the party and the government by assisting in promoting the development of an ordered, socialist society. In accordance with this management mandate, information acquired and disseminated by libraries was highly controlled and a rigid system of censorship was in place to see that only information that adhered to existing Communist theory and practice was permitted in library collections. This exclusion also affected professional concepts. Many professional ideas about the management and operation of libraries originating in the West (e.g., the marketing of libraries, in general, and of the services they provide, in particular) were not seen as relevant and therefore not encouraged by library managers.

With the beginning of the great industrial expansion of the late 19th century and early 20th century most Western capitalist, industrialized countries, embraced the idea of marketing and the selling of goods and services as central to capitalism and creation of profit. Along with the expansion of commercialism in the early 20th century, libraries in the English-speaking as well as the Scandinavian countries had begun to use marketing strategies and public relations to promote the role and services of libraries within the framework of their governmental, social, and economic structures. The staff of Romanian libraries undoubtedly understood the concept of applying capitalist marketing strategies in promoting government services (e.g., library services); however, considering the Communist control of the press and all other forms of information delivery up through 1989, the practice was not widely adopted among Eastern European libraries into the 1990s.

PROBLEM STATEMENT

This study has two major purposes (1) to develop and test a survey instrument for measuring the acceptance of social marketing by librarians and (2) to determine on an exploratory level the degree of acceptance of the concept of social marketing as applied to libraries in Romania, and in so doing, offer a preliminary assessment of their willingness to accept new concepts for change.

THEORETICAL FRAMEWORK

The theoretical base of this study draws on concepts suggested in Rogers' (1983) classic explanation of the adoption and dissemination of innovation in so far as it can help in the development of a survey instrument and perhaps explain at a rudimentary level what might be occurring in Romania. According to Rogers, when new ideas or innovations are introduced into a social order, they follow a standard process of dissemination and adoption or rejection. Rogers maintains that behaviors or attributes of individuals within the social framework or environment can act as predictors of how and whether acceptance or rejection of the innovation will occur. Based on his general rationale, this study assumed that social marketing concepts are new and innovative ideas for Romanian librarians and that selected charac-teristics of both adopters and nonadopters might be present in this study population. Rogers' complete theory is not totally applicable in this study because of the limited number of librarians sampled. Nevertheless, the general theoretical base for developing the survey instrument was based on Rogers' rationale for the diffusion of innovation.

Personal predictors are a set of concepts that Rogers sees as important for an idea to be accepted and diffused. Based on Rogers, and as used in this investigation, personal predictors are characteristics of individuals that can serve as indicators of how likely they are to accept a new concept once it is introduced. For this study, personal predictors included characteristics of gender and age; educational attainment; professional cosmopolitanism (e.g., professional involvement, professional reading, attendance at conferences, travel abroad); administrative placement within the hierarchy indicative of authority; and levels of decision-making authority within their positions. The test instrument consisted of a series of demographic questions designed to ascertain personal predicator qualities (Rogers, 1983).

Because the study also sought to obtain information regarding the level of acceptance of the idea of social marketing for libraries within Romania, several questions based on Rogers' rationale were likewise included. A description of the instrument is included later in this discussion along with an analysis of it as a reliable instrument for measuring social marketing acceptance within librarianship and other related fields.

LITERATURE REVIEW

The concept of marketing within Romanian libraries was first introduced in library literature in 1993 with publications in *Biblioteca*, one of the few Romanian library journals with a nation-wide circulation. The articles published were mere abstracts of longer studies by Western authors with no original contribution or application to Romanian libraries (Fülöp, 1993; Sincai, 1993; Vacariu, 1993; Vasilescu, 1993). Most of this literature was at a theoretical level that offered little practical application. The examples of library marketing practices in other countries came mainly from the United States, Canada, France, Belgium, and Hungary with more emphasis on the final results and less analysis of the marketing strategies involved in achieving certain results. Later Anghelescu (1997), Moldoveanu (1997), Moldoveanu and Ioan-Franc (1997), Vintilă (1997), Ciorcan (1998), Petrescu (1998), Lupu (1999), Fartat (2001), and Niţă (2005) published brief articles on marketing, discussing both theoretical and applied strategies and approaches. Dragoş (2002) introduced the concept of interactive marketing applied to the cultural field, with focus on cultural institutions such as libraries, theaters, and lyric theaters. The volume *Marketing şi cultură* [Marketing and Culture] is the only groundbreaking monograph on this topic in Romania. In their introduction, the co-authors state that "This book is devoted to a theme which represents a novelty in our literature: the marketing of cultural services, the strategy of attracting and directing human and economic resources to the cultural domain" (Moldoveanu & Ioan-Franc, 1997). However, marketing research in Romanian libraries is still to come.

There are indications of international interest in marketing in Romania in general. Dan-Lascu, Manrai, and Manrai's (1993) article, "Marketing in Romania: The Challenges of the Transition from a Centrally-planned Economy to a Consumer-oriented Economy" describes the contrast between the state of marketing in Romania before and after the fall of Communism. The authors looked specifically at the use of the marketing mix (price, product, place, and promotion). This study is an indicator of interest in, and application of, marketing concepts for Romania as a whole. More specific to libraries, however, is the fact that the interest in marketing may be more far-reaching. In the program review of the International Federation of Library Associations (IFLA), Romania was one of the countries that applied for the IFLA International Marketing Award (2003–2004). Applicants for this award were judged on the following criteria: (1) strategic approach to marketing communications, (2) creativity and innovation, (3) potential for generating widespread public visibility and support for libraries, (4) effectiveness illustrated by efforts to emphasize the organization's communication and marketing goals, and (5) commitment to ongoing marketing and public relations activities.

METHODOLOGY AND DATA FOR ATTITUDINAL MEASUREMENTS

Data for the study were obtained by using a specially constructed instrument for this study called the "Social Marketing Scale" (SMS). It was first developed and reviewed in English, and then translated into Romanian. This scale used both demographic and attitudinal questions to determine how Romanian librarians would accept the concept of social marketing being applied to their libraries 12 years after the fall of Communism. Although SMS was not pretested with a Romanian population, it was reviewed and amended by experts on contemporary modern Romanian culture. The SMS questionnaire translated into Romanian was distributed to a group of 74 Romanian librarians who were attending a five-day library conference.

The SMS consisted of six demographic questions that asked respondents to give their gender, age, work assignment, level of education, professional involvements and activities, and work responsibilities within their home libraries. These questions were asked to both describe the respondent groups and to act as personal predictors of acceptance or rejection of social marketing as a tool for Romanian libraries. As previously stated predictor categories used in this study were suggested by and modified from Rogers' list of adopter characteristics (Rogers, 1983, pp. 241–270). The adopter characteristics (personal predictors) centered on (1) personal characteristics (gender, age); (2) educational attainment; (3) professional cosmopolitism (e.g., professional involvement professional reading, attendance at conferences, travel abroad); (4) administrative placement within the hierarchy indicative of authority; and (5) levels of decision-making authority given to respondents commensurate with their positions.

As shown in Table 2, 10 questions were asked regarding respondents' acceptance and acceptance or willingness to support social marketing within Romanian librarianship. Responses were measured on a Likert scale (5 = definitely agree; 4 = probably agree; 3 = unsure; 2 = probably do not agree; and 1 = absolutely do not agree).

SAMPLING PROCEDURES

In Romania, survey research of librarians is not well developed and the prospect of having available a large sample of librarians was highly unlikely. To overcome this difficulty, a convenience sample was used. Convenience sampling is used in exploratory research where the expense of the research must be considered and where unique populations are often hard to reach and study. Convenience sampling offers a means of obtaining inexpensive, but important approximations of truth (StatPac Inc., 2002).

DESCRIPTION OF THE SAMPLE CONFERENCE

The conference was held in Timişoara, Romania in August 2003 at the Eugen Todoran Central University Library, with instruction provided by groups of librarians and library instructors from two American Library Association (ALA) accredited graduate library science education programs in the United States: the Graduate School of Library and Information Science (now the School of Information) at the University of Texas at Austin and the Library and Information Science Program at Wayne State University in Detroit. One section of the conference was centered on social marketing as used by institutions in the West, particularly the United States.

Table 2.   SMS Questions Asked to Measure Attitudes.

1. Do you feel that social marketing should be directed at changing social behavior regarding attitudes and feelings that people have about the role of libraries in Romanian society?

2. Do you feel that social marketing plans as developed and executed by Romanian libraries would be beneficial and helpful in improving Romanian society?

3. Do you feel the library in which you are currently employed would be willing to design and manage a social marketing campaign that was aimed at increasing the public use of the library and its resources?

4. At the present time do you feel the library administration and staff of your library have the background and knowledge to *design* and manage a social marketing campaign designed to increase the use of the library and its resources?

5. If *you* responded negatively to question 4 (If *you selected* 3, 2, or 1), please check your reasons for your answers based on [the following] list provided. Select only three (3) of *the most compelling* answers: lack of knowledge and experience; social marketing would not be accepted in the current culture and society of Romania; lack of money and other resources to engage in social marketing; the political and government support will not be available to support social marketing; others as noted.

6. If you answered positively to question no. 4, please check your reasons for your answers based on the list provided. Please select three (3) of the most compelling answers: social marketing can increase the visibility of the library in Romanian society and culture; the concept is easily understood and can be applied by librarians in Romanian society without much difficulty; although money is tight, resources could be found to support social marketing for libraries; political and government support for social marketing would encourage the development of social marketing for libraries; others as indicated.

7. Do you feel the administration has the will and energy to engage in a social marketing campaign at the present time?
    (5. definitely agree 4. probably agree 3. unsure 2. probably do not agree 1. absolutely do not agree)

8. I would be willing to help with a social marketing campaign in my library.
    (5. definitely agree 4. probably agree 3. unsure 2. probably do not agree 1. absolutely do not agree)

9. If you answered positively to no. 8, please provide reasons for your answers based on the list provided. Select only 3 of the most compelling: would find it exciting and intellectually rewarding; would consider it a professional challenge for something that would benefit Romanian libraries and society; feel that we must do all that we can to bring better understanding to Romanians about the role that libraries play in society; social marketing is an approach which will help make Romania become more competitive economically; other as provided.

10. If you answered negatively to question 8, provide reasons for your answers based on the list provided: would find this task too involved to undertake personally and I would not learn much from it; the library as a part of society would not benefit from it; the Romanian public understands the role of libraries well enough; socially marketing would not help Romania to become more competitive economically; others as provided.

Western-style conferences are not the norm in Romania. This conference was a specialized conference developed to serve the needs for training library staff at all levels from several regions of Romania. The selection of the regional libraries was based on needs as assessed by Romanian library leaders in consultation with the director of the host institution. Participants were invited and selected mainly by managers of libraries in the region. A small number of other participants attended at the invitation of the conference director. Expenses for most participants were paid by their libraries. This was undoubtedly the first library conference attended by many of the participants.

RESEARCH QUESTIONS

This study focused on three research questions

- Whether Romanian librarians in this convenience sample would support the concept of social marketing in Romanian libraries;
- Whether gender, age, work assignments, levels of education, professional activities and involvement, and work responsibilities within the structure of participants' home library would be reliable personal predictors for how Romanian librarians represented in this group might accept social marketing concepts as a useful tool for strengthening and changing the role of librarians within Romanian society; and
- Whether the current measurement instrument met sociometric standards well enough to use within different and varied cultural contexts and subject disciplines.

DESCRIPTION OF PARTICIPANTS

Table 3 describes the participants. Not all questions in this category or in other categories of the instrument were answered by all respondents. Missing data are indicated as appropriate.

Gender, Age, Positions Held

Response data by participants showed 64 females (93%) and five males (7%). In terms of age, 46 (68%) gave their birth dates as between 1959 and

Table 3. Description of Respondents[a].

Gender N = 69		
Female	64	(93%)
Male	5	(7%)

Age N = 68		
1979 – 59	46	(68%)
1958–38	21	(31%)
1937–17	1	(1%)

Education N = 67		
Secondary	45	(67%)
Mid-level university degree	16	(24%)
High-level university degree	3	(4.5%)
Other	3	(4.5%)

Positions Held N = 71		
Professional	46	(65%)
Clerical/support	12	(17%)
Mid-level management	6	(8.5%)
Other	6	(8.5%)
Top Administration	1	(1%)

Cosmopolitanism N = 156 responses		
Read domestic library journals	56	(36%)
Attend domestic library meetings	52	(33%)
Read foreign language journals/books	31	(20%)
Travel abroad	11	(7%)
Attend foreign library meetings	6	(4%)

Policy-making activities N = 123		
Following policy set by others	41	(33%)
Comfortable helping to set policy	35	(29%)
Required to make policy decisions	30	(24%)
Feel more comfortable following policy set by others	17	(14%)

[a]Some categories reflect missing data.

1979; 21 (31%) between 1938 and 1958; and 1 (1%) between 1917 and 1937. Of these, 71 indicated the following types of positions held in their home libraries: 46 (65%) professional level positions; 12 (17%) clerical and support staff; 6 (8%) mid-level management; 6 (8%) other types of positions; and 1(1%) top-level administrative position.

Education

Sixty-seven subjects reported the following highest levels of educational attainment: 45 (67%) secondary-level (high school), 16 (24%) mid-level college degrees (equivalent of a bachelor's degree), 3 (4.5%) high-level degrees (equivalent of a master's degree), and 3 (4.5%) other types of education.

Professional Activities and Responsibilities: Cosmopolitanism

To gauge the degree of cosmopolitanism exhibited by participants as defined by professional involvement such as professional reading, attendance at conferences, and travel abroad, subjects were asked to indicate the level at which they participate or had participated in several activities. Participants were allowed to indicate multiple activities. One hundred-fifty-six (156) participants indicated the following activities: 56 read domestic library journals (36%); 52 had attended domestic library meetings (33%); 31 read foreign language journals and books (20%); 11 had traveled abroad (7%); and 6 had attended foreign library meetings (4%).

It is significant to note the high percentage of Romanian librarians indicated that they could read foreign languages: 31 (42% of the 74 librarians surveyed). Many Romanian librarians have degrees in foreign languages. Beginning in the mid-1970s, in the absence of a work force with formal library education after the library school at the University of Bucharest was closed, libraries hired graduates with degrees in comparative literature, foreign languages, history, and the social sciences.

Policy Making as a Professional Responsibility

As an indication of the extent to which participants may make or influence policy, including adaptation and dissemination of new ideas and concepts within their library environments, subjects were asked to indicate the nature of their professional responsibilities in relation to making policy. Multiple responses were allowed. The following 123 responses were reported: I follow policies set by others – 41 (33%); I feel more comfortable helping to set policy – 35 (29%); my position requires me to make decisions – 30 (24%); and, I feel more comfortable following policy set by others – 17 (14%).

DESCRIPTION OF INSTRUMENTATION

As discussed earlier, the SMS is a 10-item instrument designed to measure the acceptance of social marketing by library staffs. The instrument contains six Likert-type items with possible responses from 1 to 5, with 5 being positive toward the concept of social marketing (I definitely agree), and 1 being negative toward the concept (I absolutely do not agree). The instrument also contains five multiple response items which ask respondents to give the reasons for their responses.

Assigning each subject a total score, which is a simple unweighted sum of all the Likert-style items, was used in scoring the instrument. Internal consistency as measured by Cronbach's Coefficient α was high for a pilot instrument of this length ($\alpha = .67$) and exceeds the .60 thresholds that are generally accepted in the literature as the minimum acceptable level of reliability. When the α was measured by deleting items from the scale and recalculating the alpha it was evident that none of the items were damaging to the overall α. This analysis suggests that the reliability of the measure could be improved by including more Likert-type items.

A Pearson correlation analysis was also performed and yielded many significant correlations at the .05 level. Table 4 displays the results of this analysis. The largest correlation between variables was that between Appropriate Knowledge and Administrative Will ($r = .53$, $p < .0001$). This may suggest that at least for this sample, the link between having the appropriate knowledge to engage in social marketing activities and the administrative will to engage in the activities is a close one.

VALIDITY OF THE FINDINGS

The factorial validity of the instrument was measured by performing a factor analysis using squared multiple correlations in the principal diagonal and a Promax rotational technique to increase interpretability. SAS Proc Factor was used for the analysis (SAS/STAT, 1989). One factor was

Table 4. Pearson Correlation Coefficients of Relationships to Selected Measurements.

Prob > |r| under H0: $\rho = 0$ Number of Observations

	Q1	Q2	Q3	Q4	Q7	Q8
Q1 Social marketing directed at behavior	1.00000 71	0.39132 0.0012 66	0.2843 0.0163 71	−0.06593 0.5989 66	0.10082 0.4063 70	0.14522 0.2484 65
Q2 Helpful and beneficial	0.39132 0.0012 66	1.00000 68	0.30745 0.0108 68	0.19437 0.1122 68	0.11616 0.3492 67	0.0927 0.4556 67
Q3 Increase public use	0.2843 0.0163 71	0.30745 0.0108 68	1.00000 73	0.47841 <.0001 68	0.4354 0.0001 72	0.40605 0.0007 67
Q4 Appropriate knowledge	−0.06593 0.5989 66	0.19437 0.1122 68	0.47841 <.0001 68	1.00000 68	0.53016 <.0001 67	0.1919 0.1198 67
Q7 Administrative will	0.10082 0.4063 70	0.11616 0.3492 67	0.4354 0.0001 72	0.53016 <.0001 67	1.00000 72	0.21717 0.0799 66
Q8 Willingness to help	0.14522 0.2484 65	0.0927 0.4556 67	0.40605 0.0007 67	0.1919 0.1198 67	0.21717 0.0799 66	1.00000 67

Note: For responses to Q5, Q6, Q9, and Q10, see Appendix.

Table 5. Importance of Selected Measurement Items to Factor 1.

Rotated Factor Pattern (Standardized Regression Coefficients)

		Factor 1	Factor 2
Q1	Social marketing directed at behavior	-0.06692	0.58672
Q2	Helpful and beneficial	0.08654	0.52096
Q3	Increase public use	0.67451	0.19450
Q4	Appropriate knowledge	0.71247	-0.10771
Q7	Administrative will	0.68630	-0.07221
Q8	Willingness to help	0.32553	0.14415

Note: For responses to Q5, Q6, Q9, and Q10, see Appendix.

Table 6. Unweighted Sum of Responses to Selected Measurement Items.

Analysis Variable: Total Score

N	Mean	Standard Deviation	Minimum	Maximum
73	10.9315068	3.4654195	3	19

retained using the eigenvalue greater than one rule and screen-plot assessment. This factor accounts for 92% of the common variance of the items. Table 5 displays the relative importance of each of the items to this Factor (Factor 1). According to this analysis, the first factor appears to be heavily weighted toward measuring the attitudes of the participants toward their knowledge of social marketing, the administrative will of the bureaucracy, and the institutional will of the participants' library or institution to implementing social-marketing-based campaigns to enhance the standing of libraries in Romanian culture.

FINDINGS

Seventy four total responses were recorded from the Likert-style instruments. The unweighted sum of these responses is displayed in Table 6. Significant variance was evident in the subject's responses with a minimum response of 3.0 to a maximum of 19 out of a possible score of 30. Table 7 displays the responses to the individual items.

Table 7.   Variance of Subject Responses to Selected Measurement Items.

		N	Mean	Standard Deviation	Minimum	Maximum
Q1	Social Marketing Directed at Behavior	71	1.3943662	0.9020433	1	5
Q2	Helpful and Beneficial	68	1.4852941	0.7429800	1	5
Q3	Increase Public Use	73	2.0410959	1.0598527	1	5
Q4	Appropriate Knowledge	68	2.7647059	1.0091765	1	5
Q7	Administrative Will	72	2.3472222	0.9951958	1	5
Q8	Willing to Help	67	1.3731343	0.6705001	1	5

Note: For responses to Q5, Q6, Q9, and Q10, see Appendix.

Analysis of variance was used to examine the total score by a variety of standard demographic variables (predictors) such as age, sex, level of work responsibility, and educational level. None of these comparisons were significant at the .05 level. The most likely reasons for this are that the sample was too small and lacked the homogeneity needed to measure such attributes. For example, using a larger and more homogeneous sample group, Raper (1987) found support for Rogers' adopters and nonadopters characteristics (i.e., predictor characteristics) in her national innovation and diffusion study of 165 library administrators in 14 Thai governmental university libraries.

Mean scores clearly indicate that this group of library staff members (see Appendix), did not accept social marketing. Overall, this sample of library staff clearly rejected the idea of social marketing as a viable activity for the promotion of libraries within Romanian society. For example, negative feelings were revealed in questions 5 and 10. Of the 72 responses to question 5, 27 indicated that librarians lacked the knowledge to undertake such activities (35%); 26 that libraries as institutions lacked the resources (35%); 11 that there would be a lack of and/or problems with government support for social marketing (15%); and 8 that social marketing was not accepted within Romanian society (11%). Question 10, which also asked for reasons for not supporting social marketing, received 7 responses. Among these were that the tasks would be too involved on a personal level ($N = 1$, 14%); that the Romanian public understands the role of the library well enough ($N = 3$, 43%); and that social marketing conducted by librarians would not increase Romanian economic competitiveness ($N = 3$, 43%). However, question 6, which asked for these same reasons for not supporting social marketing presented as positive choices, received fewer responses.

By explanation, the reasons garnered only two responses and both noted that social marketing would increase Romanian economic competitiveness. Similarly, question 8 which also sought positive responses, generated only three responses, and these centered around the ideas that social marketing was exciting and intellectually rewarding; that it would be professionally challenging; and that it would increase Romanian economic competitiveness.

Table 7 displays the results of a Pearson correlation analysis that revealed several significant findings at the .05 or greater level. The largest correlation between variables was that between *appropriate knowledge* (Q4) and *administrative will* (Q7) ($r = .53$, $p < 0001$). This may suggest that at least for this sample the link between having the appropriate knowledge to engage in social marketing activities and the administrative will to undertake such activities is close one.

USEFULNESS OF THE INSTRUMENT FOR FURTHER RESEARCH

Because the SMS measurement instrument's internal consistency as measured by Cronbach's Coefficient α tested high for a pilot instrument of this length ($\alpha = .67$) and exceeds the acceptable threshold of .60, it appears that the instrument can be used for further social marketing studies with both librarians and other professional groups. As mentioned earlier, for future use the reliability of the SMS instrument might be improved by including more Likert-type items, especially items which relate to personality attitudes such as conservativeness and acceptance of change.

DISCUSSION

On the surface, this sample group rejected social marketing. Nevertheless, other factors must be considered as well. Although we cannot say that the study revealed negative or positive influences on the acceptance of social marketing for this study group, we nevertheless must consider the saliency that certain factors raise in this study and which might provide further evidence of how social marketing concepts are perceived by this group. These factors included knowledge about social marketing, both administrative and institutional; willingness to engage in social marketing; and the helpfulness and the beneficial aspects of social marketing applied to Romanian society.

The Romanian public is not used to expressing opinions openly. Freedom of expression continues to be only a desideratum in many work places. After half a century of repression of freedom of speech, people still feel reluctant to make their views known, even when completing a survey where their confidentiality will be protected. Fear from negative repercussions is still high. Responding to surveys is an unfamiliar procedure to a significant part of the population. Those who do respond to questionnaires avoid answering open-ended questions. Many Romanians do not feel comfortable when commenting in writing about the institution where they work, even if the surveys are anonymous.

In an earlier study of a similar group of Romanian libraries, Owens and Anghelescu (1999) found that change was difficult for Romanian librarians to accept in terms of adopting new concepts or methods of service, programming, and management. The old concept of libraries as institutions geared toward the preservation of cultural values without much attention paid to service and accessibility of information was a concept that appears to be much ingrained into the professional thinking of Romanian librarians.

There are significant differences between the American and Romanian education system. High school is followed by four years of study at the university level. Students graduate with a *licentiature*, a degree that would be the equivalent of a bachelor's degree in the United States. In Romania, such a degree can be continued at the doctoral level, with no master's degree required to precede doctoral studies. The 1990s marked the beginning of higher education at the master's level for certain disciplines. This distinction explains the small number of participants holding an advanced degree.

The near absence of any substantive attention to marketing in Romanian libraries should not be interpreted as a lack of relevance of marketing for these libraries, or as a single isolated challenge for the effective management of these libraries. Ion Stoica (1997) identifies several problems in the management of libraries where marketing strategies might be very applicable. The need to apply POSCORB (planning, organizing, staffing, coordinating/controlling, reporting and budgeting) is one such example.

Lyndall Urwick, an Englishman, and Luther Gulick, an American, in a 1937 paper to President Franklin Roosevelt introduced POSCORB in the United States as the functions of a manager. These functions have remained a mainstay in traditional management literature and in practice (Kotter, 1990). By definition, marketing is a part of the first P (planning; now more aptly designated as strategic planning due to the assumption that an organization in today's Information age is a dynamic and changing environment). The approach of linking strategic planning and marketing together was begun as one of the planning strategies utilized in the United States during World War II, and continued due to the economic growth that followed. Another influence to this combined approach was the Harvard Business School's method of emphasizing overall corporate strategy by defining strategic planning as an entity that combined production, finance, and marketing (Porter, 1987). Since that time numerous sources have used this same approach including Marketing/Planning library and Information Services (1999), Planning and Marketing (2000), Using Future Trends to Inform Planning/Marketing (1995), Planning through Marketing (1991), Marketing with a Capital S: Strategic Planning for Knowledge Based Services (1998), and Marketing/Planning for Maximum Effectiveness (1991). Also helpful to this process is Darlene Weingand's diagram of the marketing/planning process (1998).

Just as a case for marketing can be made as a useful instrument for the management of Romanian libraries based on POSCORB, there are reasons to use a type of marketing – social marketing – in Romanian libraries as well. In addition to the need for Romanian libraries to use POSCORB, Stoica (1997) states that "The managers of today, in many cases, do not have the knowledge, skills, and patterns of behavior that is any different from those that the leaders of yesterday possessed, and they continue the traditional empiricism and the rudimentary practices of the managerial tradition." Stoica's reference to "patterns of behavior" is a core tenet of social marketing, a change whose results could benefit the librarians, the library, and the society at large. Combined with these problems is the cost that the application of strategic planning and marketing brings; that cost is change. Change management is a universal issue and a challenge to all libraries, no matter the place or the frequency with which change occurs (Brand, 2000; Fyffe & Kobulnicky, 1999; Tucker, 2000).

Problems in Romanian library management are not limited to the need for application of the classical acronym, POSCORB. There is also a need to address issues of access on several levels; physical, bibliographical, and intellectual, for example. But it is the problem of intellectual access that draws attention to the role of the library in Romanian society as well as the role of librarians in a more democratic society (Anghelescu; 2001; Harden, 1989; Mowat, 1990). Social marketing is a useful entity in defining and redefining roles and in helping to shape a new image of both librarians and libraries in general.

If social marketing is to play a role in Romanian librarianship as a method for producing change, Romanian libraries must first accept the concept that libraries are important to the full development of Romania as a vital and democratic society. As mentioned, previous research by Owens and Anghelescu (1999) indicate that Romanian librarians do not consider libraries vital to the society and therefore their visibility is not important. The continuing decline of the number of libraries is an indication that local authorities, which are the funding agencies for public libraries, prefer to annihilate them rather than support them financially. Many local authorities perceive libraries as a financial burden, rather than centers aimed at serving the information needs of the local community. They prefer to direct the funding to other local projects (e.g., road pavement) which, in their view, are to the benefit of the entire community, not to the benefit of the few who use the library. As this attitude changes, social marketing can play a role in helping libraries become more visible and supported within Romanian society. Once this is accepted, knowledge and experience in social marketing must be gained, and the administrative and institutional willingness to pursue social marketing must be found and nurtured, and implemented with requisite evaluation for desired results.

Individuals play significant roles in helping to integrate new ideas into a social order. Rogers' characteristics of those who are likely to accept and promote new ideas are important. It appears that the sample investigated in this study was not homogenous and large enough to isolate such factors. Additional research and a different sampling technique may produce characteristics that can serve to identify individuals most likely to help introduce new concepts into Romanian librarianship, including social marketing. Adopting and fostering of new work strategies in institutional activities implies elimination of old mentalities, attitudes, and behaviors of the staff that work in those institutions. Such a change cannot occur over-night. It is difficult, if not impossible, to see visible attempts to replace ingrained mentalities, such as unwillingness to share information, with new attitudes such as customer-oriented services.

Changing mentalities is a slow process that might take generations. A continuing modernization of library school curricula aimed at introducing not only new technologies but also new work ethics and principles coupled with the customer-oriented work philosophy would produce library science graduates capable of bringing about change in libraries.

As students graduate from library science programs and are exposed to Western practices by attending conferences and participating in exchanges of experience abroad, they are likely to act as change agents by bringing new ideas back home and implementing them in their libraries, if allowed by the upper management. Change at the micro/institutional level will bring about change at the macro/societal level. Libraries represent pivotal elements in the transition of Eastern European societies from Communist dictatorships to open democracies. Change is equally needed at the policy-making level. Politicians who view libraries only as book repositories and put them on the lowest tier on their priority list are in great need of attitudinal change themselves. The entire library network in Romania is government-funded. Within the context of scarce library budgets brought about by an inflation-ridden economy, libraries need to identify new strategies to make their services better known to a wider audience. If Romanian legislators and the general public change their perception of libraries and, as library administrators engage in efforts to change the fashion, these institutions will operate and provide diversified services to attract new clientele; Romanian libraries will be able to contribute to the advancement of the society as a whole. Romania's recent integration into the European Union undoubtedly will impose new standards for library science education and for library operations and activities in order to bring them to par with their Western European counterparts (Anghelescu, 2005). Foreign aid is being used to modernize library services in Romania. Projects funded by the World Bank and the Bill and Melinda Gates Foundation (IREX, 2007; IREX, 2009) will bring new information technologies along with training for librarians so that they can serve as mediators to information, as they do in developed countries. The penetration of computers in the library sector in Romania and elsewhere will induce behavioral and attitudinal changes both in those engaged in facilitating access to information and in those seeking information, the public at large.

FUTURE SURVEY RESEARCH

Continued research is needed in the social and cultural as well as political aspect of Romania librarians and librarianship as this profession moves into a democratic society. Unfortunately, the nature of Romanian library culture and society does not presently lend itself to Western-style research where large populations of groups are available, easily identified, and accessible. With regard to this study (as well as future studies), it is highly unlikely that a completely homogeneous sample of librarians that would increase the accuracy of these findings will be available to library researchers in the near future. Such characteristics imply that small studies such as this, based largely on convenience sampling will be the research norm for a considerable time. Collectively, as these small studies are conducted and published, information about Romanian library behavior will emerge that will not only increase our overall understanding of Romanian library culture, but will help us better understand how librarians as a collective group face challenges of adaptation and change no matter where they are located geographically.

Social marketing is a relatively new concept in librarianship in general. Therefore library-based social marketing research conducted in developed Western societies is also needed. Informed comparisons about acceptance of new concepts such as social marketing which have the potential for leading to change can then be critically assessed against similar research findings from other developing countries like Romania.

CONCLUSION

Libraries everywhere in the world face the problem of having to continually define and explain their roles to the public. Influenced by marketing, many not-for-profit institutions such as libraries have learned that to be successful they must earn the trust and respect of their primary client groups or customers. Social marketing offers an avenue to not only explain the goals and mission of libraries, but also to actually influence and change customers' attitudes and behaviors in positive ways about the service and roles offered by libraries in democratic societies. Romania, in its attempt to modernize its library system faces many problems and challenges, and social marketing can provide an exciting opportunity in this process through the positive attention it gives to social, institutional, professional, and individual improvement.

REFERENCES

Anghelescu, H. G. B. (1997). Marketingul de bibliotecă si arhivă [Library and Archives Marketing]. In: H. G. B. Anghelescu (Ed.), *Biblioteci, arhive & centre de informare în secolul XXI: Lucrarile Conferintei. Brasov, 18-22 August 1997, Târgu Mureş, 25–28 August 1997* (pp. 77–83). Brasov: Editura Universitatii Transilvania, 1997.
Anghelescu, H. G. B. (2000). *Public libraries in modern and contemporary Romania: Legacy of French patterns and Soviet influences, 1830–1990.* Unpublished Ph.D. dissertation, University of Texas at Austin.

Anghelescu, H. G. B. (2001). Romanian libraries recover after the cold war: The Communist legacy and the road ahead. In: H. G. B. Anghelescu & P. Martine (Eds), *Books, libraries, reading & publishing in the cold war* (pp. 233–252). Washington, DC: Library of Congress.

Anghelescu, H. G. B. (2003). Academic and special libraries in Romania. In: M. A. Drake (Ed.), *Encyclopedia of library and information science* (Vol. 1, pp. 44–49). New York: Marcel Dekker.

Anghelescu, H. G. B. (2005). European integration: Are Romanian libraries ready? *Libraries & Culture, 40*(3), 435–454.

Anghelescu, H. G. B. (2006). Public libraries in Romania. In: M. A. Drake (Ed.), *Encyclopedia of library and information science*. New York: Marcel Dekker, online update. Available at http://www2.dekker.com/sdek/ftinterface?content = t713172967vnxs10000 100000127&ftform = 3&page = 1. Accessed on 4 July 2006.

Anuarul statistic al României [Romanian Statistical Yearbook]. (2006). Bucureşti: Institutul Naşional de Statistică.

Berkowitz, E. N. (2000). *Marketing*. Boston, MA: McGraw Hill.

Brand, M. (2000). University libraries as agents of change. *Collection Management, 24*, 5–14.

Ciorcan, M. (1998). *Marketing si publicitate in biblioteca [Library marketing and publicity]*. Bucharest: Ministry of Culture.

De Stricker, U. (1998). Marketing with a capital S: Strategic planning for knowledge based services. *Information Outlook, 2*(2), 28–32.

Dragoş, L. I. (2002). Marketingul interactiv in domeniul cultural [Interactive marketing in the cultural field] part I and II. *Biblioteca, 8*, 241–242; *Biblioteca, 9*, 273–275.

Fartat, I. (2001). Marketing in biblioteca comunala [Marketing in rural libraries]. *Biblioteca, 1*, 5–6.

Fülöp, M. (1993). Reconsiderarea activitatii bibliotecare in conditiile aparitiei marketingului [Reconsidering library activities within the context of marketing]. *Biblioteca, 9–10*, 29–30.

Fyffe, R. C., & Kobulnicky, P. J. (1999). Negotiating the soul of the library: Change management in information access and local collection development at the University of Connecticut. *Journal of Library Administration, 28*(4), 17–35.

Harden, B. (1989). Romanian library topples Ceausescu's literary monuments. *Washington Post, 29*, p. a26.

IFLA International Marketing Award. (2003–2004). Program overview. Available at http://www.ifla.org/III/grants/3m-award.htm . Retrieved on 6/7/06.

IREX. (2007). Global Libraries in Romania. Planning grant. Available at http://www.irex.org/programs/global_libraries/IREX_GL_Romania.pdf. Accessed on 1 May 2009.

IREX. (2009). Biblionet—global libraries Romania. Program overview. Available at http://www.irex.org/programs/global_libraries/index.asp . Accessed on 1 May 2009.

Kotter, J. P. (1990). *A force for change: How leadership differs from management*. New York: Free Press.

Lascu, D.-N., Manrai, L. A., & Manrai, A. K. (1993). Marketing in Romania: The challenges of the transition from a centrally-planned economy to a consumer-oriented economy. *European Journal of Marketing, 27*(11/12), 102–120.

Lupu, V. (1999). Marketing si management in biblioteca [Library marketing and management]. *Biblioteca, 3*, 83–84.

Mărunţelu, I. (1995). Biblioteca romana si avatarurile tranzitiei [Romanian libraries and hardships of transition]. *Biblioteca, 6–8*, 196–198.

Moldoveanu, M., & Ioan-Franc, V. (1997). *Marketing si cultura [Marketing and culture]*. Bucharest: Expert.

Moldoveanu, M. (1997). Viziunea de marketing in activitatea bibliotecilor [Marketing vision in library activities]. *Biblioteca, 3*, 65–66.

Mowat, I. R. M. (1990). Romanian library development: Past, future and future. *Library Review, 39*(4), 41–45.

Niţă, A. (2005). Marketing in bibliotecile universitare [Marketing in academic libraries]. *Biblioteca, 10*, 305–306.

Owens, I., & Anghelescu, H. G. B. (1999). Plowing in rocky land: Organizational culture, managed change, and quality improvement in selected Romanian post-Communist libraries. *The International Information and Library Review, 31*, 197–224.

Petrescu, V. (1998). Consideratii asupra implementarii marketingului in activitatea bibliotecara [Considerations on marketing implementation in library activities]. *Biblioteca, 3*, 80–819, 273–274.

Population Services International. (2002). Annotated catalogue of recent social marketing research and evaluation. Social Marketing and Communication for Health series. Washington, D.C. and London: PSI. PSI materials available at www.psi.org

Porter, M. (1987). Corporate strategy: The state of strategic thinking. *The Economist*, Vol. 17, Issue May 23, pp. 17, 22.

Raper, P. (1987). *Computers in Thai university libraries: A study of the innovation and diffusion process*. Unpublished Ph.D. dissertation, University of Texas at Austin.

Regneală, M. (2004). Colapsul bibliotecilor romanesti [The Collapse of Romanian libraries], *Revista 22*, Vol. xiv, No. 745, 15–21 June, 2004. Available at http://www.revista22.ro/html/index.php?nr = 2004-06-17&art = 949. Accessed 5 July 2006.

Rogers, E. M. (1983). *Diffusion of innovations* (3rd ed.). New York: Free Press.

SAS/STAT (1989). *Users' guide: Version 6*, 4th ed., vol. 1. Cary, N.C.: SAS Institute.

Sincai, A. (1993). Consideratii asupra marketingului bibliotecar in contextul tranzitiei [Considerations on library marketing within the context of transition]. *Biblioteca, 9–10*, 27–28.

StatPac Inc. (2002). Sampling methods. Available at http://www.statpac.com/surveys/sampling.htm. Accessed on 11 November 2002.

Stoica, I. (1997). More about management in Romanian libraries. *Library Management, 18*(7), 335–339.

Tucker, J. M. (2000). Managing change and changing management in academic libraries. *The Serials Librarian, 37*(4), 123–132.

Vacariu, E. (1993). Biblioteca si marketingul educational [Libraries and educational marketing]. *Biblioteca, 3–4*, 10–11.

Vasilescu, E. (1993). Marketingul in biblioteci [Library marketing]. *Biblioteca, 9–10*, 26–27.

Vasilescu, E. (2005). Semnale pentru schimbarile ce va sa vina [Signs for future changes]. *Biblioteca, 2*, 33–34.

Vintilă, C. (1997). Marketingul de biblioteca [Library marketing]. *Biblioteca, 8*, 229.

Weinreich, N. K. (2002). What is social marketing? Available at http://www.social-marketing.com/whatis.html. Retrieved on February 16, 2002. (note: Weinreich's presentation is based on Kotler, P. & Anderson, A. R. (1994). *Strategic marketing for non-profit organizations* (5th ed.)). Patterson, NJ: Prentice-Hall.

APPENDIX. ATTITUDES ABOUT SOCIAL MARKETING FOR SELECTED ROMANIAN LIBRARIANS

Measurements		N	Mean	Standard deviation
Q1	Social marketing directed at behavior and attitudes	71	1.40	0.90
Q2	Helpful and beneficial in improving Romanian society	68	1.55	0.74
Q3	Current place of library employment would be willing to design and manage a social marketing campaign aimed at increasing use of libraries and their resources	73	2.04	1.20
Q4	Administration and staff have appropriate knowledge	68	2.76	1.01
Q5	Positive responses to Q4	N = 2		
	Social marketing will increase visibility of libraries	1		
	Money could be found for social marketing	1		
Q6	Negative responses to Q4	N = 74		
	Lack of knowledge and experience	27	36%	
	Lack of Resources	26	35%	
	Lack of political and governmental support	11	15%	
	Not acceptable due to culture	8	11%	
	Other	2	3%	
Q7	Administration has will to develop and execute a social marketing campaign	72	2.34	1.00
Q8	Personally willing to help in social marketing campaign	67	1.40	0.67
Q9	Positive responses to Q8	N = 3		
	Exciting and intellectually challenging	1	33.3%	
	Professionally challenging	1	33.3%	
	Might bring better understanding of libraries to public	1	33.3%	
Q10	Negative responses to Q8	N = 7		
	Public understands libraries well enough	3	43%	
	Social marketing would not increase economic competitiveness	3	43%	
	Personally I find the tasks too involved	1	14%	

IMPLEMENTING ORGANIZATIONAL CHANGE IN THE REGIONAL PUBLIC LIBRARY IN PRISHTINA, KOSOVO

Svetlana Breca

ABSTRACT

The purpose of this chapter is to show how organizational change could be applied to local public libraries in a post-war country, in this case Kosovo. After decades under the communist system and a decade of conflict and political instability, Kosovo gained its independence in February 2008. Local libraries in Kosovo, fully developed under the previous communist system, almost collapsed in the post-communist period, which was characterized by conflicts that finally ended with the NATO bombing in 1999. They are now trying to catch up to western styles of work and development, trying to function within a region still governed by the UN, secured by NATO forces, and dealing with library users who have increased significantly their expectations of library services.

My work includes close cooperation with the libraries in Kosovo. I am familiar with their organizational structure and development. I would like to see libraries in Kosovo as open, user-friendly institutions, rich in books, and

Advances in Library Administration and Organization, Volume 27, 151–159
ISSN: 0732-0671/doi:10.1108/S0732-0671(2009)0000027013

electronic resources. I would like to see our local public libraries as institutions that serve as community centers, reaching out to the community with different services, cultural programs, and language courses. Currently, employees who work in libraries in Kosovo do little more than circulate books, and perform administrative and clerical duties. There are no programs, initiatives, or activities to attract readers.

In this chapter, I present my ideas about creating an environment within which library managers and staff will learn, be motivated, and will work together to better serve the community.

A SHORT HISTORY

The Prishtina Municipal Public Library has been located in the central part of the town for as long as I can remember. It has a charming little garden that makes me feel nostalgic, evoking pleasant memories from the time when I used this Public Library's services as a high school student. Twenty years ago, this Public Library was used by Albanians and Serbs equally. At that time, Kosovo was a Province of Serbia and even though Albanians were in the majority, Serbs held the authority in all matters. In 1990, a period of constant political turmoil began. At that time, the Public Library was controlled by Serbs and many Albanian staff were fired or forced into retirement. After the NATO bombing of Kosovo in 1999 when Serbian rule in Kosovo ended, Albanians took control over the Public Library in a new Kosovo that had a smaller Serbian population that no longer enjoyed its former unquestioned authority. Kosovo was then ruled by the UN Mission for Kosovo (UNMIK), which still maintains oversight in the newly independent Kosovo. Now, the Public Library is under the direct administration of the Ministry of Culture, which is part of the newly established Republic of Kosovo.

THE PRESENT SITUATION

Now, the Public Library has 25 employees, including a Director and a Manager of the Public Library. It has six sections: book processing, research and development, children's books, books for adults, heritage preservation, and reading rooms. The Public Library has about 80,000 books, magazines, daily newspapers, and a few videos, films, and CDs for children. Members (6,200) had been registered in the Public Library in 2005, when the first version of this paper was written. Now, the total number of registered patrons is approximately 7,200.

The Director of the Public Library communicates directly with the Ministry of Culture and the Municipal Office, both of which share the final say on professional, financial, and administrative issues. The Manager deals with professional issues and is responsible for the work of all sections and all Library Staff. Communication between staff and the Director goes through the Manager. Professional issues are discussed once in every three months at a general staff meeting, where plans and projects are discussed and reports submitted to the Manager. If the staff wish to propose any new initiatives at that time, they must report to the Director to seek final approval. The Director conveys all of his decisions to the staff through the Manager as well. Once a year all the Library Staff are invited to a meeting with both the Director and the Manager. The Manager announces this meeting by calling each staff by phone because there is no e-mail system for official library use.

The Director is informed about the work of the Library Staff from their quarterly reports and, from time to time, he makes brief appearances in the staff workspaces. Library Staff are always free to make recommendations, but final decisions depend only on the Director. The Public Library Mission, according to the Library Staff, is to serve Kosovo readers, to provide information, and to increase cultural awareness.

New technology is being adopted very slowly by the Public Library. The Public Library does not have its own server and there is no IT manager. Furthermore, the Public Library does not have its own domain, web site, or e-mail system. There are no electronic databases available and no web-based research is being conducted by Library Staff. The few librarians who do use e-mail have to use private yahoo or hotmail accounts.

The Public Library did offer a short training course on basics of computer use, but this was not sufficient. Most of the Library Staff do not speak English and have no experience using computers. Staff who do speak English usually learn from each other. However, those who do not speak English resist learning anything about computers, preserving traditional paper-based practices.

No system of awards exists within the Public Library. Staff believe that this is because the Public Library does not have the financial means for such a system. At the same time, many staff believe that any system of awards would only create divisions among employees rather than providing motivation. Staff say that the main reason for lack of motivation is low salary. Library Staff do complain about their low salaries to the Manager, but they do not voice these complaints to the Director. They say that they "lack the courage to do so."

Lack of resources for staff salaries and library operations is a constant topic of conversation among Library Staff. They do not see any viable solution and, thus, passively wait for "better times." They are aware that other local institutions have received support for their operations, but they claim that they do not know how this was accomplished.

Library Staff are aware that there are many international organizations to which they could apply for donations and support, but they express strong doubts about the outcome of any such application. In fact, this pessimism among the staff comes ultimately from the top. The Director has never tried to submit any project to any international organization or local private firm. Lack of initiative also follows that neither the Management nor the Library Staff know how to write a project proposal.

REVISED PUBLIC LIBRARY MISSION

The Public Library remains in a difficult transitional period, as are all local public institutions in Kosovo. Under the current circumstances, the Public Library no longer has a clear mission. However, the Public Library should be responsible for high-quality library services, collections, and information resources designed to meet the professional, intellectual, creative and personal needs of the community. Friendly, professional and well-trained staff should respond to the needs of users and offer the benefits and pleasures of learning and discovery through the library's services.

Developing a clear strategic mission and concrete goals for the Public Library should be the first order of business. A new mission statement should be drafted, discussed, and revised in response to the needs and requirements of Public Library users, the current environment in which the Public Library functions, and current technological changes.

MY RECOMMENDATIONS

Communication, Trust, and Change

Some time ago, I read an interesting article about building trust. I remember, in particular, one specific thought that you should "say what you do, do what you say, prove what you do, and improve what you do."

In Kosovo, I have always understood this recommendation to be about the fundamentals of trust-building. I further recall from the same article a vivid image of trust-building: Imagine a tree and that you are trying to throw a thick rope over one of its branches. This is how you can do it: You put a tennis ball on a very small string, and throw this first over the branch, followed by a thicker rope and then again an even thicker rope ... This is the way trust is built and in this way you become a part of one united family. This is the way I would try, if given the opportunity, to build relationships among the Library Staff in order to implement changes that would help develop their organization into a true learning organization.

According to Easterby-Smith, Burgoyne, and Araujo (1999): "Trust, as a cognitive state is the willingness to place resources at others' disposal; this willingness is based on an expectation that they will not be used in a way that will leave the truster worse off. Several decades ago social psychologists showed that trust was an essential prerequisite to persuading others to change their views (Hovland et al., 1953, p. 158)."

Communication between the management and the staff in the Public Library is one of the elements required to dispel the general atmosphere of fear and "lack of courage" by the staff to ask questions and initiate discussion of basic issues. To build a communication environment of trust, the Public Library Management should invest more time in developing quality relationships. When they do succeed in establishing such a communication environment, all will be able to engage in creative dialogue within it. Margaret Wheatley (1996, p. 4) in an interview with Scott London said: "If you are trying to create a healthy organization, one that can sustain itself over time, simply legislating and dictating behavior and outcome doesn't work at all." Employees should be included in the decision-making process. They should have the right to meet and discuss their own concerns, ideas, and proposed initiatives among themselves and, especially, with the Director.

The management should address such critical issues as staff salaries with more creativity in order to find solutions to fundamental problems. There are private companies, foundations, and international organizations that could help the Public Library. Furthermore, the management could provide staff with free or low-cost incentives. For example, the Public Library could easily obtain free theater tickets for Staff. It could also build cooperative agreeements with the local School for English Language to provide free language instruction to Library Staff.

According to Peter M. Senge (1990) in *The Fifth Discipline*, leaders can "work relentlessly to foster a climate in which the principles of personal mastery are practiced in daily life. That means building an organization where it is safe for people to create visions, where inquiry and commitment to the truth are the norm, and where challenging the status quo is expected – especially when the status quo is expected-especially when the status quo includes obscuring aspects of current reality that people seek to avoid" (p. 172).

If Library Staff become a part of change, they can influence change. In general, Library Staff resist those changes they fear the most and these, by and large, are those they feel they have no control over. In the Public Library those who speak English the least resist the use of computers than the most. If, however, they were encouraged to learn English and assisted by technical staff in developing an on-site computer training program that would meet their own specific needs, it is clear that general resistance to change among Library Staff would be considerably weakened.

Training for Change

From the Library Staff I have learned that they do not make a clear distinction between establishing a good professional relationship with their users and asking them questions about their private lives – "Do I know you from somewhere? Where do you work? Do you have any job openings in your institution? Are you married? How many children do you have?" A professional relationship with users, where librarians learn more about the fields of study and topics of interest to their users, should make possible the development of collections and services according to the needs of the users. Levitt (2004) says in his article "Marketing Myopia": "The view that an industry is a customer-satisfying process, not a goods-producing process, is vital for all business people to understand. An industry begins with the customer and his or her needs, not with a patent, a raw material, or a selling skill" (p. 14). If the Public Library would follow this path, it would serve the public better and it would be what the community expects it to be – an institution that provides strong support to all levels of the educational process in Kosovo.

First, the Public Library should establish a program for retired librarians in order to transfer knowledge from the experienced employees to the new employees. The Public Library should bring retired librarians back on a part-time basis and organize a mentorship program. This is what I would recommend in order to preserve the professional and tacit knowledge that is precious to every organization.

Benjamin Franklin said: "An investment in knowledge pays the best interest." There are different possibilities for organizing training for the Library Staff. The management should think about submitting a formal request to the Ministry of Culture or the Ministry of Education and also to international organizations in Kosovo to propose training programs and seminars, where librarians can learn about new technology and new developments in library science. In making such proposals, librarians should decide their own needs for professional education and the specific skills required for local development. They should also appeal to a wide range of sources for assistance in organizing and financing training. One obvious possibility is to invite volunteers from international organizations with a local presence to come and teach the Library Staff on basics of computer use, English, and other skills. In fact, there are many professionals and foreigners working in Kosovo who would be interested and willing to volunteer a few hours a week in the Public Library. The Director and the Public Library staff should take the initiative and show more creativity in finding outside resources to develop organizational knowledge and skills to overcome a pervasive pessimism in the Public Library.

New Partnerships and New Projects

Senge (1990) says: "Organizations learn only through individuals who learn. Individual learning does not guarantee organizational learning. But without it no organizational learning occurs" (p. 139).

Library Staff should be trained to write project proposals and learn how to find the appropriate international and local organizations that might support them. In this way, the Public Library can get much-needed funding for cultural programs, online databases, and the reconstruction of Public Library facilities. Goh (2003) says: "A continuous learning organization is an organization where employees are constantly encouraged to gain new knowledge, try new approaches to solving problems, obtain feedback, and learn new behaviors as a result of the experimentation" (p. 218).

The Library Staff should be taught how to plan and implement projects, organize media events, publicize the completion of projects, and create opportunities for potential sponsors to market their products or services at Public Library organized events. In this way, the Public Library would build good strong relationships with sponsors and would find new ways to identify other institutions and potential sponsors for future projects. Permanent relationship with international and local organizations which have programs and financial means to support libraries and educational and cultural activities would make it possible for Library Staff to build new kinds of professional contacts and to be invited to other seminars and training programs in the region and abroad. As they began to enjoy success in individual projects and as they saw their own ideas and initiatives realized in the public sphere, the Library Staff would dispel the present aura of pessimism and find new sources of motivation for future development.

CONCLUSION

If my specific recommendations for change were accepted, I expect Library Staff would be more enthusiastic and committed to their work. To the extent that they became a part of the process of change they would feel motivated to contribute to the change. They would be ready to respond to changes in the future because they would know how to direct change.

The model for change I would recommend would provide the basis for Library Staff to build a learning organization. They should cherish the same vision and work as a team. My specific recommendations could help to build a decentralized and nonhierarchical organization within which staff are learning and developing continuously.

The theory of learning organizations I would recommend is based on Senge's model of change and his five components for the building of organizations that can truly learn: System's Thinking, Personal Mastery, Mental Models, Building Shared Vision, and Team Learning.

Senge (1990) in his book *The Fifth Discipline* calls: "... systems thinking the fifth discipline because it is the conceptual cornerstone that underlies all of the five learning disciplines of this book. All are concerned with a shift of mind from seeing parts to seeing wholes, from seeing people as helpless reactors to seeing them as active participants in shaping their reality, from reacting to the present to creating the future" (p. 54).

The Public Library management and the Library Staff should focus on what they work to determine should be important for their organization. Senge (1990) says: "But as people in an organization begin to learn how existing policies and actions are creating their current reality, a new more fertile soil for vision develops. A new source of confidence develops, rooted in deeper understanding of the forces shaping current reality and where there is leverage for influencing those forces. I'll always remember a manager emerging from an extended "microworld" session at one of the companies in our research program. When asked what he had learned, he replied: 'I discovered that the reality we have is only one of several possible realities'" (p. 216). The staff of the Public Library should and could create another, more constructive reality where they all will have "freedom to create the result they truly desire. It is the heart of the learning organization, because the impulse to generative learning is the desire to create something new, something that has value and meaning to people" (Senge, 1990, p. 261).

REFERENCES

Easterby-Smith, M., Burgoyne, J. G., & Araujo, L. (1999). *Organizational learning and the learning organization: Developments in theory and practice.* London: SAGE.

Goh, S. C. (2003). Improving organizational learning capability: Lessons from two case studies. *The Learning Organization, 10*(4).

Levitt, T. (2004). Marketing myopia. *Harvard Business Review,* (July–August).

Senge, P. M. (1990). *The fifth discipline: The art & practice of the learning organization.* USA: Doubleday.

Wheatley, M. (1996). The new science of leadership: An interview with Margaret Wheatley. *Radio series insight & outlook, hosted by Scott London,* November 1996. Retrieved October 23, 2005, from http://www.scottlondon.com/insight/scripts/wheatley.html

LIBRARIES AND ECOLOGY IN POST-SOVIET RUSSIA

Ellen M. Knutson

ABSTRACT

In this case study of the ecological programs of the Bryansk Regional Public Library System, I used qualitative research methods including observation, interviews, and archival research. I collected data from 2002 to 2007 with the bulk of the data gathered in the summer and fall of 2006. The libraries in Bryansk have been working with ecological information and education since the meltdown at the Chernobyl nuclear power plant in 1986 and started a systematic program of ecological education in 1995. The types of ecological education activities that the libraries engage in range from the more traditional library activities such as developing collections, hosting seminars, and working with partners to much more hand-on activities such as taking field trips to nature preserves with library users and actually cleaning up the local stream or planting trees. Through these activities, libraries have become active participants in the ecological community in Bryansk.

The questions about ecology should be viewed not only as the protection of nature, but also to include wider questions of human habitat, ecological culture and ecology of the soul.

Olga Y. Kulikova
Deputy Director, BONUB

Advances in Library Administration and Organization, Volume 27, 161–191
Copyright © 2009 by Emerald Group Publishing Limited
ISSN: 0732-0671/doi:10.1108/S0732-0671(2009)0000027014

Вопросы экологии рассматриваются не только с точки зрения охраны окружающий среды, но и гораздо шире, включая в себя экологию среды обитания человека, экологию культуры и экологию души.

Ольга Ю. Куликова
заместитель директора БОНУБ

From the polluted Angara River flowing out of the southern end of Lake Baikal in the east to the meltdown of the fourth reactor at the Chernobyl nuclear power plant in the west, ecological problems and crises are prevalent throughout Russia and the former Soviet Union. However, some of the world's most ecologically clean areas are also located within the borders of Russia. Therefore, the spatial proximity to an ecological "hot spot" influences individuals,' not to mention politicians,' views on the need for environmental protection (Massa & Tynkkynen, 2001). One such ecological hot spot is the Bryansk region. Located in Western Russia, sharing borders with Ukraine and Belarus, the Bryansk region was contaminated with radioactive fallout from the explosion at Chernobyl in April 1986, and, like the rest of Russia, it struggles with other ecological problems.

A complicating factor to the ecological situation in Bryansk and elsewhere in Russia is that the Soviet government had a history of not being forthcoming with information, thus, a culture of distrust with regard to official information has long prevailed among much of the population. This distrust continued in the post-Soviet era and still exists today. People in the Chernobyl region have never received full and trustworthy information about the effects of the disaster (Somova, 2006; UNDP & UNICEF, 2002). The focus of this chapter is to examine the ecological information and education projects of the F. I. Tyutchev Regional Research Library in Bryansk, Russia (BONUB)[1] and the other public libraries in the region as they address this information need. Beyond simply providing information and ecological education, the librarians are also working to offer solutions to ecological problems, including the human social and psychological problems caused by poor environmental conditions. Additionally, they are working to instill an appreciation of nature in the population of Bryansk and to highlight both the cultural artifacts that have been created and those that have been destroyed. In this way, they hope to help people reconcile their thoughts and emotions about the ecological situation, especially in regard to the Chernobyl catastrophe.

Faced with the challenges accompanying a radical shift in the political and economic landscapes, libraries had an opportunity to play a new role in the community in the post-Soviet era. They were no longer expected to be an ideological arm of the Communist Party of the Soviet Union (CPSU), and this fact alone has affected all aspects of Russian librarianship

(Kimmage, 1992; Kislovskaya, 1999). The priorities of individual libraries depended more on the decisions of the local library administration than on the dictates of a federal agency. One of the goals assigned a high priority by the libraries in Bryansk is to increase ecological awareness in the population and to improve the overall ecological situation in the region by providing ecological information and developing ecological educational programs. The idea of democratization, which came to the forefront in Russian thinking during *perestroika*, opened up new forms and avenues of work for librarians. Yet, there was not a complete break with the past. In Bryansk, there are many examples of librarians who made the most of the new situation, who chose to be innovative and to repurpose old Soviet institutional structures and roles for new ends. What makes this story all the more interesting is that the Bryansk Public Library System has been under immense strain caused by poor financing, aging buildings and collections, a changing demographic of users, and changes in the political and economic system in Russia. Despite these challenges, librarians in the Bryansk region have reinvented themselves as social actors and built concrete programs that address the civic and social needs of their communities.

BRYANSK REGION PUBLIC LIBRARY SYSTEM

Bryansk is one of Russia's 84 regions and is divided into 27 districts.[2] In Bryansk, as in the other Russian regions, there is a main regional library that manages the region's public libraries, including centralized district and city libraries and their branches. In the Bryansk Region, there are 732 public libraries (BONUB, 2006a). Until 2006, the system included 1 regional library, 27 central district libraries, and 4 city libraries. Each of the district and city libraries had anywhere from 4 to 45 branches.[3] Although BONUB directly manages only the public libraries, it has good relationships and shares projects with all libraries in the Bryansk Region, including special, school, and academic libraries. Not only is BONUB the largest of the 732 public libraries in the region, but it also serves as the methodological center for the all the public libraries in the region (BONUB, 2001). In this capacity, BONUB provides training and support for other libraries, including activities such as training seminars, individual consultations – over email, by phone, or in person – and maintenance of a professional collection focusing on the state of librarianship. The locus of the training work is the Scientific/Research Methods Office (*Nauchno-Metodicheskii Otdel*). During Soviet times, the methods office served a controlling function, ensuring that librarians followed the dictates of the CPSU. In Bryansk, after the breakup of the Soviet Union, this office was transformed into a place where innovative ideas could take root and then be disseminated throughout the public library system. This office does not have a counterpart in US libraries. In addition to staff training, this office provides research and statistics about the library and consultations with other libraries. The issues discussed in individual consultations range from collection development to building social partnerships and from technological training to designing library programs and user services.

METHODS

The data used in this chapter were culled from a larger dissertation project (refer Knutson, 2008) that included three research trips to Bryansk. In addition to BONUB, I have visited 13 other libraries. In all, I visited 11 towns and villages in 6 of the 27 districts in the Bryansk region. During my on-site research, I was able to interview librarians who have knowledge of the activities of other libraries in the system as well as knowledge of the regional library itself. I also conducted interviews with librarians, library users, local government officials, and directors of non-governmental organizations (NGOs), including two environmental NGOs, and observed library training seminars and library discussion clubs as well as the typical day-to-day operations of the library. In addition, I carried out archival research to gather documentary evidence such as annual project reports about activities throughout the system. Table 1 gives an overview of the number and type of data collection strategies I used over the six-year period.

Interviews form the core of the data presented in this chapter. The interview data are supported and fleshed out with library reports and reports from the ecological information track at the Crimea Conference (an international library conference attended largely by Russian librarians) and an international professional development workshop for librarians called *eko-shkola*,[4] which had ecological information as its theme and was hosted by BONUB.

ECOLOGICAL INFORMATION AND EDUCATION IN THE LIBRARY

The regional library in Bryansk (BONUB) has been collecting ecological information and addressing ecological inquiries from its patrons since the

Table 1.   Overview of Types of Data Collected.

	2002	2003	Summer 2006	Fall 2006	2007	Total
Libraries visited	6	NA	5 (4 new)	5 (3 new)	NA	13
NGOs or other cultural institutions visited	2	NA	3 (2 new)	1 (new)	NA	5
Cities/towns visited	2	NA	5 (4 new)	6 (5 new)	NA	11
Conferences/seminars attended	1	NA	1	2	NA	4
Interviews	18 (I)	NA	10 (I) 1 (G)	11 (I) 1 (G) 2 (E)	16 (E)	39 (I) 2 (G) 18 (E)
Participants	13	NA	13 (11 new)	17 (14 new)	5	38
Questionnaires	1	1	2	NA	NA	4
	$n = 7$	$n = 12$	$n = 24$ and 19			$n = 62$
Archival documents	2 (AR) 5 (PR) 13 (B)	1 (AR)	9 (AR) 7 (DR) 40 (PR) 1 (SR) 16 (B)	7 (AR) 12 (DR) 21 (PR) 9 (SR) 12 (B)	1 (R) 2 (PR) 1 (SR)	20 (AR) 19 (DR) 68 (PR) 11 (SR) 41 (B)

Notes: I, Individual; G, group; E, e-mail; AR, annual report; DR, district report; PR, program report; SR, statistical report; B, brochure.

Chernobyl catastrophe in 1986. It was only in the mid-1990s, however, that they have become systematic about this activity and put a priority on working in this area. The meltdown at Chernobyl and its continuing effects in the region are significant components of the ecological information and education projects. Still, these projects have a broader mission that I will discuss before focusing on the activities put in place to address the Chernobyl catastrophe and its aftermath. In 2004, BONUB became the first Regional Ecological Information Center in Russia, giving it official status as a methodological center for ecological information. This was an acknowledgment of BONUB's leadership in this area from United Nations Educational, Scientific and Cultural Organization's (UNESCO) "Information For All" program and the Library Division of the Ministry of Culture. BONUB would like to see the ecological information centers they have created for Bryansk serve as models for a nationwide network of ecological information centers similar to the nationwide network of Public Centers for Legal Information that are largely housed in public libraries (IFAP Russia, 2005). It is important to note that, for the librarians in Bryansk, the problems of ecology are thought of broadly and include the social and psychological impact of ecological problems on humans. This holistic approach means that the ecological programs are not just about nature but also include things such as helping to resettle people displaced by the Chernobyl catastrophe. In 2006, BONUB's priorities for the ecological educational activities of the library were defined as the following:

• creating a resource base and providing access to ecological information;
• creating social partnerships and providing information support for the regional ecological community[5]; and
• maintaining methodological practices and exchanging practical experiences with libraries in Bryansk (BONUB, 2006b).

To expand access to ecological information, the libraries have used new information technologies to the extent they are able to do so. About 40 percent of the libraries with ecological information centers are connected to the Internet, which allows them to obtain bibliographic information from online public access catalogs (OPACs) of other libraries, electronic journals, and information from websites of public service organizations and NGOs working on ecology. The central district libraries have access to databases and print materials concerning legal information on ecology, and librarians have created lists of corresponding subjects. Libraries publish booklets, information leaflets, and bookmarks that contain information about ecological activities and issues, as well as pictures of natural areas in the region, and URLs of ecological websites and other bibliographic information. This type of self-publishing is useful because it fills the information gap left by a lack of the funds required to purchase all the necessary publications on ecological issues. These print materials are also essential to the librarians serving readers in the 60 percent of libraries without Internet access.

In addition to their own publishing endeavors, the librarians work with local newspapers to publish stories about the ecological situation in Bryansk. Nina Ladniuk, former head of BONUB's methods office, gave an example of this: "A newspaper columnist is a member of the [library's] garden club which discusses environmental issues. Sessions of the club take place twice a month, and we have lectures by scholars and specialists. When he [the reporter] is interested in the issues discussed at the club, he publishes something on the topic" (Interview 020219NVL). In the early work of the Ecological Information Center at BONUB, the staff relied heavily on the knowledge of local specialists who presented lectures and served on roundtables to supplement the information found in their print collection.

The Ecological Resonance Project was conceived after Ladniuk attended a conference on ecology. At the conclusion of that conference, she said that she recognized the undeniable fact that the environmental situation was not good and that the library had to play a role in addressing the problem (Interview 020219NVL). Beginning in 1995, this became the library's first systematic ecological project. The original five-year project was later expanded and extended to cover the years 2000–2005. The stated purpose of the project, as set by the library administration and the head of the Ecological Information Center, is "The formation of ecological conscious-ness of the population by professional, systematic educational activity" (BONUB, 2005, p. 4). The basic activities are four-fold: (1) to inform government officials about ecological problems, (2) to provide information support for nature preservationists, in particular "to help with concrete preservation work," (3) to provide information support for scientists and ecologists, and (4) to provide for the mass distribution of ecological knowledge to the population (BONUB, 2005, p. 4).

The various factors that contribute to the current poor environmental situation in Bryansk are numerous and mirror ecological problems throughout Russia, such as forest fires, pollution from industrial processing, lack of potable water, processing of household and industrial waste, and the reduction of agricultural areas. These factors also include things more specific to the Bryansk Region, such as radiation from the Chernobyl catastrophe and the location of a large chemical weapons arsenal in the Pochep district. Each of these ecological problems can cause adverse health effects for the population. Also, as part of this project, librarians have concerned themselves with the demographic issue of a birthrate that does not equal the death rate in the region. In some villages, this demographic issue is pronounced because young people have been more likely to move out of polluted regions in favor of environmentally cleaner areas, whereas the elderly have had more of an attachment to their home villages and remained there. The project is based on the contention that the ecological concerns listed earlier *require* the library to provide such ecological education and information support. The underlying assumption that the library should be playing an active role in addressing societal concerns is a motivating force for the librarians in Bryansk.

Throughout the Ecological Resonance Project, there is a strong emphasis on the role of the library in influencing ecological policy in the region. This relates to the first direction of work, to inform decision makers. The list of activities devoted to this particular goal includes creating analytic reviews and bibliographies of ecological information and presenting new literature and creating exhibits. Project activities address the following:

• Aspects of the rehabilitation of the area with radioactive pollution as a result of the failure of the Chernobyl nuclear plant

- The experience of the population who live and work in the areas polluted by radioactive material
- Industrial waste and ways to recycle the waste
- Construction and the environment
- Economics of wildlife preservation
- Quality of the environment and health of people
- Ecological education
- Preservation of biodiversity (BONUB, 2005).

The project also includes activities geared to teachers, students, and preschool children. With the first two groups, the focus is on consultations and bibliographic support for their needs and general help with ecological literacy. The work with preschool children is focused on instilling an appreciation of nature (plants and animals) through the use of fairy tales. Librarians also work with kindergartens to help teachers acquaint children with nature. In my interviews and interactions with librarians, they also talked about taking children on field trips to visit natural areas in their communities – in essence to develop an appreciation of the local river by going to explore the nature surrounding the river.

Larisa Merkeshkina, a senior librarian at the ecological information center in BONUB, said, "For example, in the countryside, librarians may take children to the forest, to the river, so they see the pollution and assist in clean-up activities. They [librarians] solve small problems" (Interview 061024LVM). She went on to describe the bigger problem – the lack of an "ecological culture" – and the educational programs of the library that help to instill ecological culture in young people as well as others in the population. By ecological culture, the librarians mean an understanding and an appreciation of the environment and all living things, and they argue that, by creating ecological culture, the ecological literacy of people is increased.

The libraries strive to apply new techniques to promote the study of ecological conditions in the Bryansk region and to stimulate the public to think about problems of ecology. As an example, librarians conduct bibliographic research on the problems of ecology and make use of a technique they call "press monitoring." They review the regional press (newspapers and magazines) for information relating to the ecology and then analyze those accounts and integrate them into a picture of the ecological landscape at the regional level. This monitoring of research often results in information digests, which include either physical or digital copies of the articles organized and indexed, and bibliographies created by the librarians (BONUB, 2006b). Through the monitoring process, the librarians believe they are making a place for the library in the general system of ecological education.

The BONUB ecological information center also conducts training for and has consultations with other librarians in the region. Merkeshkina described the methodological work in this way: "We organize workshops for librarians, and the seminars take place in our library or in other libraries. Sometimes we visit small libraries to hold consultations. We often receive invitations to participate in events. And we exchange information over email, and it is also a way to do consultations." She continued by giving more details about what constitutes a consultation: "We present how to work with information, how to establish social partnerships, how to organize deliberative forums, how and what information should be collected about environmental problems in Bryansk. We collect the contact information of NGOs in the field" (Interview 061024LVM).

Library-sponsored ecological activities occur in many libraries throughout the region. Excursions to nature preserves, most notably to the Bryansk Forest Preserve (*Brianskii Les*) in the Suzemka district, have become staples in the ecological education activities of several libraries. Both the Suzemka Central Library and the Navlia Central Library participate in a project called "The March of Parks." This is a very popular activity. In addition to the excursion to the forest preserve, children reenact fairy tales with ecological themes, and the librarians use competitions and quizzes as education tools to teach about ecology. Moreover, they invite people to roundtable discussions and offer consultations by doctors, librarians, journalists, and students. Cultural and sporting events round out the activities (Golub, 2006; Khokhlenko, 2006). In Navlia, they also have had book exhibitions on the theme that the earth is threatened with ecological catastrophe and that man is both a cause and a solution. The library sponsors five clubs that discuss ecological issues, and it has created information lists of new books around the themes "Ecology and Law/Rights," "Radiation in Bryansk," and "Radiation Hygiene" (the precautions one can take to protect one's self from radiation) (Khokhlenko, 2006). In Suzemka's central library, the librarians prepared a biology lesson "Water is Life." Rural librarians in the district held actions where they cleaned up a stream. Additionally, as part of March of Parks, they cleaned the streets and planted trees and bushes (Golub, 2006).

Libraries are using deliberative public forums[6] as part of their ecological education work. Although the libraries host deliberative forums on various topics, ecology is by far the most popular. I asked Natasha Lekanova, a senior librarian at BONUB who trains other librarians to moderate forums, why there had been so many ecology forums. Her response was that

> People are concerned about Chernobyl and the state of the [Bryansk] forest. If they were not worried, there would not be such forums. Librarians keep calling me and saying:
>
> "Natasha, help us do a forum."
>
> "What topic?"
>
> "Ecology."
>
> It is our life, our health. There are other topics, drugs, etc., but, by popular demand, they are all trumped by ecology. (Interview 061030NVL)

During the International Forum on Ecological Culture and Information for Sustainable Development, which took place at BONUB in 2004, libraries throughout the region participated in conducting forums using the issue guide "Ecology of Bryansk: Yesterday, Today, and Tomorrow." There were 14 forums involving a total of more than 500 people. Each used one of three different approaches (Lekanova, 2004). Eleven of the forum moderators (all librarians) sent reports on the forums to BONUB. The reports listed some basic information such as date and number and type of participants in the forums and then had a description of the nature of the discussion that ensued around the three approaches. Some included librarians' analyses on the overall success and effectiveness of the forum. The issue guide used for the forums outlined the three approaches to be used as a starting point for the public discussion.

Approach 1 – Education: To form ecological culture. It is necessary to overcome the ecological illiteracy and the barbarous attitude about nature by means of education and educational methods.

Approach 2 – Management: To supervise, coordinate, finance. It is necessary to direct efforts of the authorities to enact essential, capable laws, to control and coordinate environmental protection activities and to finance ecological programs.

Approach 3 – Initiative: To activate the role of the public. It is necessary to promote participation in civic initiatives and the activities of ecological public organizations and movements (Ekologiia Brianshchiny, 1996, p. 3).

In each of these approaches, participants discussed the positive and negative consequences of applying such an approach. The feeling about education was that it was necessary, but that it was a long-term solution and the ecological problems required more immediate action. The second approach put much of the burden on the State, which people seemed comfortable with, except for the fact that they thought there was too much corruption in government for the government to actually manage the ecological situation. Additionally, participants worried that the officials themselves lacked ecological culture. The third approach raised skepticism about the influence people can have over the bigger issues relating to ecology, but people agreed that they can have small positive effects.

The forums allowed participants to discuss issues with representatives of government as well as with specialists in the field and together discuss new approaches to addressing the problems. Although many people felt the forums were a good experience that let them express their opinions and thought that the library should hold more forums on a regular basis, there were some participants who were more skeptical (e.g., "There were no specific results, talk and that is all." and "The authorities avoid dialog with people."). But it did seem that the positive responses outweighed the negative. In several forums, participants came up with concrete actions and proposals. In Kletnia, a representative from a neighborhood association (*ulichkom*) recommended that a public ecological committee be formed to coordinate the ecological education in the district. Forestry specialists suggested to school representatives that children could do some forest activities during their summer camp, such as building feeders for the wild animals. Participants from Bryansk strongly felt that there needed to be an independent public council for environmental protection. The ideas and proposals that were expressed in the forums were reported in the media (newspaper, TV, and radio) and shared with local administrators.

From the library's point of view, the forums gave people a sense of responsibility for solving the problems. "We are confident that the organization and holding of such forums is a contribution to the development of citizenship, and support for democratic principles, and the participation of citizens in public life" (Lekanova, 2004, p. 33).

Lekanova (2004) further reported that the forums began a new stage in the formation of environmental ethics for the region. In these forums, people had the opportunity to voice their opinions and work toward finding common ground from which to begin to address the ecological issues in Bryansk. To hold the ecological forums, the libraries cooperated with many partners including government, NGOs, educational institutions, social organizations, and the mass media.

COOPERATION WITH THE ECOLOGICAL COMMUNITY

Creating strong partnerships is essential to the libraries' continued work in ecological education. The partners with which the libraries work range from individual scientists and ecologists to the mass media and from citizen groups to government agencies. Partnerships are important on a number of levels. They provide additional resources, both human and financial, for the library projects. For example, NGOs are able to apply for more grants than state-supported institutions such as libraries. As part of the partnership, the NGO may share grant money to support collection development or fund a seminar that would take place in the library. The library will then support the NGO by giving them information on how to apply for grants and offering space for meetings. The central library in Suzemka received a computer from the Bryansk Forest Preserve to create a database on natural resources in the district. However, once that project got started the library decided to expand the database to also include more information about local history, thereby meeting a greater demand for local studies information (Golub, 2006). Kulikova (2004) reports that BONUB fostered a partnership with the Regional Nature Protection Agency (GUPR), which resulted in financial support from GUPR. The benefit of partnerships goes beyond providing additional resources; partnerships also add legitimacy and authority to the libraries' work. The libraries then use this authority to solidify and strengthen their role in the community. In these partnerships, BONUB often plays a convening role, bringing together the NGOs, scientists, and mass media to discuss ecological problems and to deepen their understanding of their role in the environment.

   BONUB has created partnerships with environmental NGOs, and, as part of my study, I met with people from two such organizations: *Erika* (the name of an endangered plant in the Bryansk Region) and *Radimichi*. The mission of *Erika* is to create educational videos about the environment and serve as a resource center for other NGOs. They supply the videos to other groups and organizations that wish to use them in their educational work. According to Aleksey Chizhevskii, the director and ecology professor, there are about 150 NGOs working in the region. *Erika* was founded in 1995 through foreign grants from the Soros Foundation, USAID, and the Dutch Embassy. In 2002, for the first time, *Erika* received funds from the Russian government. Chizhevskii discussed why ecological information and education is important.

   My students asked me "Why do you explain ecological collapse? We cannot change anything." This question surprised me. At that time, I wanted to understand what each of us can do to solve ecological problems. [At *Erika*] we have come a long way in our activities, and we learned that we *can* change things. And we would like to give this opportunity to other people. We try to give not only materials but we show the experience of people who have changed things. To show that it is realistic. (Interview 020213AC)

The biggest part of *Erika*'s work is consulting and providing information support to other NGOs. They have many education programs, some of which were held at BONUB. They have found that to be effective in their education work, it is important to find partners. Chizhevskii went on to say that "In the beginning, we decided to do a program by ourselves. We worked directly with the community, but it was not effective. We found it more effective to work through partners: libraries, museums, schools, universities. This works well. We create special instructional tools for how to work with the information and how to use our materials" (Interview 020213AC). Chizhevskii's discussion of partnerships illustrates that the benefit and necessity of partners is not just on the library's side. Indeed, Laura Henry's (2005) study of the environmental movement in Russia found that many grassroots NGOs utilized Soviet-era cultural institutions, such as libraries, to support their activities through use of their space and resource sharing.

Radimichi is an organization that works specifically with people affected by the Chernobyl catastrophe. It is located in the Novozybkov district that is severely contaminated with radioactive pollution. Novozybkov was one of the seven districts from which the government required residents to move because of the level of radiation. There were 47 settlements in the district plus one neighborhood within the city of Novozybkov, which were determined to be unsafe. *Radimichi* began initially as a student club in 1987, but it has expanded tremendously. The staff and volunteers at *Radimichi* hold summer camps for children and conduct special activities for children with disabilities. They work with elderly people who were left behind when the young people left many of the contaminated areas. In their work with young adults, they created a tourist club that takes them to explore natural places and introduces them to ecological work with the goal of offering an alternative to using alcohol and drugs as a means of escape. Pavel Vdovichenko, the founder and director of *Radimichi*, was a history teacher during Soviet times. When perestroika happened, he realized that he had been lied to and that he was, in turn, lying to children. He decided not to lie any longer. After the meltdown at Chernobyl, he felt that he had to do something to help the sufferers. But when asked why he stayed in Novozybkov even though it is the district in Russia most affected by Chernobyl, he answered, "I'm not a hero, I just did not have the money to go somewhere else." Clearly proud of the achievements and partnerships created by *Radimichi*, Vdovichenko stated that "The UN Mission visited our Novozybkov camp and our offices and said the organization is unique. When the mission came and understood how we work, they changed their minds about the ability of Russia to have a volunteer movement" (Interview 020213PV).

At BONUB, to foster connections between individuals and organizations as well as the connection between the library and ecological community, librarians have created a database of everyone in the region who in some way is connected to the ecological community. The database includes individual ecologists, environmental groups, research organizations, all levels of government agencies, and more. For each entry, they include contact information and what their area of specialization is in the field of ecology. The purpose of the database is to identify possible networks of people and organizations who might undertake a given ecological project. Additionally, when new books arrive in the Ecological Information Center, the librarians will use this database to identify people who might potentially have an interest in new books as they are added to the collection so that they can alert them when it arrives at the library.

The relationship with *Radimichi* is certainly not the only connection between Chernobyl and the ecological work of the library. Without a doubt, the effects of the Chernobyl catastrophe play a central role in the ecology of the Bryansk region and is a focus of much of the ecological education work; therefore, I will devote the next section to a brief discussion of the meltdown at the Chernobyl nuclear power plant and its human and environmental consequences.

CHERNOBYL

Infringements on the natural balance, any pollution leading to the ruin of whole kinds of plants and animals, to deterioration of health of the population, are the bitter fruits of human activity.

V.F. Motylev
Deputy Head GUPR, Bryansk

Нарушения природного равновесия, любые загрязнения приводящие к гибели целых видов растений и животных, ухудшению здоровья населения, - горькие плоды деятельности самого человека.

В.Ф. Мотылев
заместитель начальника ГУПР
по Брянской области

On April 26, 1986, the fourth reactor at the Chernobyl nuclear power plant failed. The subsequent meltdown and clean-up activities have had, and continue to have, far-reaching effects on the surrounding area, including regions in three countries: Ukraine, Belarus, and Russia. Within Russia, the Bryansk region sustained the greatest amount of radioactive contamination. Even now, 22 years later, the population lives with low levels of radiation and uncertainty about its effects.

As the date indicates, Gorbachev was General Secretary of the CPSU when the Chernobyl catastrophe occurred. Although he had already instituted some policies to open up the press, he obscured the fact that a disaster had occurred. It took him 18 days before he fully admitted the failure, after scientists in the West had already surmised that the radiation readings they were monitoring had to have come from such a meltdown. The resulting illness and dislocation that affected so many was related to the social and political structure in the Soviet Union and, later, in the independent countries of Ukraine, Russia, and Belarus (Petryna, 2002).

The major release of radiation continued for 10 days after the explosion and included iodine, cesium, strontium, and plutonium isotopes.[7] There were three main radionuclides that had severe health consequences, each with a different half-life. The initial damage was largely due to radioiodine (I-131); the longer term effects were due to radiocesium (Cs-137) and radiostrontium (Sr-90). The ingestion of I-131 was the cause of an outbreak of thyroid problems, namely, cancer, and was the problem for which Gorbachev's decision to downplay the catastrophe proved to be most detrimental. Giving the affected population doses of commonly available potassium iodine tablets would have been an effective antidote to I-131. Such tablets were given to the plant workers, and, in a nonsystematic way, to their families in the town of Prypiat and that significantly lowered the number of thyroid cancer cases in this population. However, this remedy was not made available to all affected populations. As noted earlier, I-131 has a short half-life, eight days, and therefore, it was not responsible for longer term health and environmental concerns.

Radiocesium (Cs-137) and radiostrontium (Sr-90) are the two main culprits for longer term concerns. The main concern is the prevalence of these two radionuclides in agricultural products, especially milk and meat, and in forest foods such as berries, mushrooms, and the animals that consume them (International Atomic Energy Agency & Chernobyl Forum Expert Group, 2006). The route for Cs-137 and Sr-90 to appear in agricultural products is through absorption into soil from which they are transferred to the plants through root uptake. The plants, in turn, are eaten by animals, and the radionuclides are absorbed in the digestive tracts and bound to animal proteins, mainly meat and milk. The main route for human ingestion is by eating the contaminated plants directly or by eating the animals that consumed the plants. The presence of Cs-137 in milk and meat remains the primary contributor to the internal dose of radiation in humans (International Atomic Energy Agency & Chernobyl Forum Expert Group, 2006).

There are remediation actions that can reduce the amount of radiation absorbed by plants and animals. Livestock can be fed clean fodder and kept from grazing on contaminated grass. This works well with larger farms and was the main technique used on the collective farms during Soviet times. It is not as viable for small subsistence farmers, nor for a peasant who has one cow and lets it graze on unimproved land. Moreover, it did not help prevent I-131 from finding its way into milk. Because of the initial lack of information, by the time the remediation techniques were put into place, I-131 was past its half-life. Fertilizing with potassium or lime helps reduce root uptake. Plants prefer to absorb these nutrients (potassium and lime) that are chemically analogous to Cs-137 and Sr-90, respectively. This countermeasure is made more effective when combined with deeper plowing to bring uncontaminated soil to the root layer. Even if an animal continues to eat contaminated feed, it can be fed binding agents that reduce the radionuclide transfer across the digestive tract. "Prussian Blue" is a common, well-tested binder that has been used to reduce Cs-137 absorption by 90 percent. However, fertilization, plowing, and feeding cesium binders to animals are not viable techniques for remediation in forests. The main remediation for forest foods is to encourage people not to eat mushrooms, berries, and wild animals from infected forests. Though it is possible to cook the food long enough to kill the radiation, this also removes most nutrients – not to mention flavor (Chernobyl Forum & International Atomic Energy Agency, 2005; Smith & Beresford, 2005; International Atomic Energy Agency and Chernobyl Forum Expert Group, 2006).

Remediation efforts, while taken seriously, also fluctuated with the strength of the economy. The presence of Cs-137 in plants, milk, and meat tested in the Bryansk Region has not been on a steady decline. There was an increase in the mid-1990s that was likely due to the poor economic situation in Russia that led to a major devaluation of the ruble in 1998 (Anspaugh et al., 2005). Bryansk is one the last remaining regions to continue to have Cs-137 activity concentration in food products above national and international action levels (100 Bq). The other regions are Gomel and Mogilev in Belarus and Zhytomir and Rovno in Ukraine (International Atomic Energy Agency & Chernobyl Forum Expert Group, 2006). The daily online newspaper, *Briansk.ru*, ran a story on 3 March 2008 about the levels of contamination of Cs-137 and Sr-90 found in food products. Novozybkov and Zlynka remain the areas that have the largest number of contaminated food products making their way to market. Based on the levels of radiation after the catastrophe, many people were forced to evacuate. Owing to the ease in which it can be measured, and its radiological significance, Cs-137 was chosen by government officials to determine levels of radioactive contamination. Soil contaminated with $37\,kBq/m^2$ was set at the minimum contamination level. At this level, the average annual radiation dose for humans is 1 mSv (Chernobyl Forum & International Atomic Energy Agency, 2005, p. 57). In the immediate aftermath, within the first 10 days after the explosion, 116,000 people were evacuated from the 30 km radius of the reactor. People were forced to migrate when the radiation level created the average annual human dose in excess of 5 mSv and could choose to migrate (with state support) when the average annual dose exceeded 1 mSv. Some people have argued that this level was set too low as the average annual dose of ionizing radiation to humans worldwide from natural sources is estimated to be 2.4 mSv (Chernobyl Forum & International Atomic Energy Agency, 2005). During the subsequent years, more than 200,000 people were relocated. Relocation policies have not been fully carried out, in large part, due to insufficient funds. In Bryansk, they have only been able to build 62 percent of the needed housing for people who wish to leave contaminated areas (UNDP & UNICEF, 2002). Nevertheless, this mass migration put strain on people and communities. Libraries in the Bryansk region began to adapt their services to aid those who had been affected.

LIBRARY RESPONSE TO CHERNOBYL CATASTROPHE

Libraries in the region, especially in the affected areas, responded at once by having conversations, giving instructions and recommendations about safety measures for living in the radiation zones. The official published information was absent; it had to be reconstructed little by little through the creation of topical collections. Many were paralyzed by the question-"How do we survive?" And everyone who had become an involuntary hostage of the radioactive cloud, in each household, tried to find the answer.

Natalia Aleksandrovna Somova
Head, Culture Department, Bryansk

Библиотеки области, особенно пострадавших районов сразу откликнулись в своей работе на новый вызов времени – памятки, беседы - рекомендаций о мерах предосторожности в условиях проживания в радиационных зонах. Официальная опубликованная информация отсутствовала, ее собирали по крупицам, формировали тематические подборки. Главный вопрос тогда застыл в глазах многих - «Как с этим жить?». И каждый, из тех, кто стал невольным заложником радиоактивного облака, на своем бытовом уровне пытался найти ответ.

Наталья Александровна Сомова
Начальник управления культуры
Брянской области

The libraries began working to help people understand what happened at the Chernobyl nuclear power plant and its consequences following the explosion. However, their early work was not organized into systematic projects or programs. Rather, the librarians in Bryansk provided what information they could to their patrons. Alla Minenko, a librarian at BONUB, wrote that "People went to libraries and asked the librarians as if they were the main experts on all questions connected with radiation and its influence" (Minenko, 2006, para. 7). The librarians, however, were hindered by the same lack of official information that the general population faced. Books on the topic of radiation and ecology contained in existing library collections were scientific treatments. Information aimed at the general public was lacking. Librarians tried to remedy this situation by gathering information from newspapers and magazines. Ladniuk said of her ecological collection: "Back then, I had nothing. I was just cutting out articles" (Interview 020219NVL).

The first large event relating to the consequences of the meltdown at Chernobyl was held in the Zlynka Central Library at the end of 1987. Zlynka is in extreme southwestern Bryansk and is one of the districts that was severely affected by radiation from Chernobyl. The event was a showing and discussion of the documentary film, *Echo of Chernobyl*. In recent years, the theme of Chernobyl continues to be prevalent in the information actions of libraries in the Bryansk region. For example, branch number 5 in the Bryansk district led a discussion for readers, both young and old, concerning ecology and health after the Chernobyl failure. In several rural libraries in Novozybkov, there were meetings where village residents and library users could interact with heads of the local administration, ecologists, and doctors. They called these meetings *Chernobyl: Days of Tests*. In rural libraries in the Unecha district, in addition to providing printed resources, they organized practical ecological activities. One such practical action was *Pure Courtyard*[8] where they held conversations about how to care for the home environment (BONUB, 2006b).

The role of libraries in helping to resettle people who were forced to migrate to a new environment is also a focal point of the ecological work. The mass movement of people away from areas contaminated by radiation raised many issues for communities, both the ones people left and the communities they joined. Not the least of these were social-psychological issues caused by relocation. In Russia, they say that, if you move a tree without its roots, it dies. While people are not trees, it is also difficult for them to leave their roots behind. Where people resettled, the village libraries worked to preserve the historical memory of those lost roots and to provide a continuity of traditions in which the old and new organically combined. Village life is more like an extended family in which everyone knows all about the comings and goings of everyone else, and the lack of this intimacy often made the transplants feel even more like outsiders. The director of BONUB in her presentation at the Crimea Conference said that the task of the library is to find ways to acclimate the new people to village life and also to help those already living in the village meet and understand the new residents (Dediulia, 2006).[9] Work with the existing residents is important because they often hold misconceptions about those who have come from the contaminated areas, including the impression that these people introduced communicable diseases into their new surroundings (UNDP & UNICEF 2002).

Fig. 1 shows the districts in Bryansk from which people were evacuated (marked with an O) due to Cs-137 contamination and those to which people were relocated (marked with a Π). Residents of over 127 settlements were relocated to one of the "clean" districts in Bryansk or to other regions in the Russian Federation.

DOMANICHI VILLAGE LIBRARY

One village that took in people from the contaminated areas is Domanichi. It is located in the Pochep district, southwest of the city and district of Bryansk. The population of Domanichi is less than 700 people, but it hosts immigrants from many countries of the former Soviet Union as well as people who were displaced because of Chernobyl. The library there is just a small one-room building (Fig. 2). Inside, between the open book shelving, the walls are covered with artwork by local artists. One small area is

O: Resettlement from District
Zona otseleniia iz raionov

Π: Resettlement to District
Zona kompleksnogo pereseleniia raiony

Fig. 1. Map of Bryansk Region Evacuation and Relocation Districts.

Fig. 2. Exterior of Domanichi Village Library.

dedicated to folk crafts and historical domestic items; it is really a mini-local history museum within the library.

When I was there in October, 2006, there was a display celebrating all of the nationalities in the village. The collection was separated into three areas: the general collection, the children's collection, and a new collection of which they are very proud. This collection is also a general collection, but it consists of all new books given to the library because it won a competition among rural libraries to become a "model rural library."[10] The librarian in Domanichi, Lilian Dubinchina, told me she wanted to keep this new collection separate so that people could find it easily, because it had become the most popular set of books in the library. The library also received a computer, photocopier, and digital camera, and therefore, the staff had been busy visually documenting all of the library activities. It does not yet have an Internet connection, but Dubinchina is working with some library users to plan a website for the library (Interview 061031LD).

The library has provided a venue for the creation of social groups. Working with her patrons, Dubinchina helped form a sewing circle for elderly women. Most of these women came from the Chernobyl region and used the sewing circle to preserve the quilting techniques and traditions they brought with them. There is also a group of computer enthusiasts unsurprisingly made up of teenage boys who are meeting there. That group has created its own journal called "*Yunyi Khaiker*" (Young Hiker) in which they publish – using the library's computer and photocopier—tips on how to use computers, various software packages, and games. After publishing several issues, Dubinchina asked if she could include a column about the library and services it offers aimed at young people. The teens agreed that it would be a good idea (Interview 061031ANT).

Dubinchina herself had migrated to Domanichi from Tajikistan, and the head of the Culture Department in the Pochep district said that Dubinchina's experience as an immigrant means she knows the problems and needs of more recent immigrants and is able to make the library a great cultural center for the exchange of customs and experiences. She described the library as a cozy, clean place where people could come to relax, to talk, and to get information. She thought that, for the uprooted people, this was particularly important. "Moving is always difficult, especially if you're forced to move. We organize events that bring people from Domanichi and Chernobyl together ... [this helped] people from the city who had a hard time adapting to the rural environment. Understanding what you can grow, what you can do, what kind of work you can find. They still have problems" (Interview 061031LD). Around the 20th anniversary of the Chernobyl disaster, they held a conference in the library where people could come and meet with officials and get their questions answered. "The conference addressed concrete issues, and there was movement forward. We tried to bring the power (*vlast*) to the people. So the little man could ask the big man ... and could get the answer right then. You could get to the qualified person and find the answer during the meeting" (Interview 061031LD). She reiterated that even when people do not come into the library to find reading material, the library is *the* place where people come to talk, to relax, to meet their neighbors, and to find solutions to their problems.

ZABORSKO-NIKOLSKAIA SLOBODA VILLAGE LIBRARY

Zhukovka is another district that took in forced migrants from the Chernobyl region. Many of the residents of the Zabore village in the Krasnaia Gora district who were forced to migrate due to the radiation from Chernobyl found a new home in the village of Nikolskaia Sloboda in the Zhukovka district. This village is now called the village of Zaborsko-Nikolskaia Sloboda in recognition of the incorporation of the new immigrants. The library and resource center for the displaced people is located within the village school and works closely with the psychological rehabilitation center, which was opened on 24 November 1994 with support from UNESCO and other funding agencies from Germany and Canada. Nearly 87 percent of the library's users were forced migrants. Thus, the library's work is focused on their needs. Environmental and health concerns are the top priorities for the library. Library staff work with all age groups; 22 percent of the library users are under the age of 15, 32 percent are aged 15–30, 36 percent are aged 30–55, and the remaining 10 percent are pensioners. The work with children and youth revolves around games and organized excursions to the forest as well as book talks. For the adults, the librarian has organized many discussion clubs, including talks from health workers on medicinal plants and home care. The library, together with other organizations in the village, helps to make the transition to the immigrants' new life as smooth as possible. At the library, "each visitor finds comfort, a kind attitude, and a good book" (Bychkova & Rubeko, 2006, para. 11). The librarian, however, does not just serve patrons within the walls of the library. She makes trips to dairies and farms to hold conversations about healthy living and the healing properties of plants (Bychkova & Rubeko, 2006; Iz zhizn Zaborsko-Nikolskoi Slobody, 2006).

COOPERATION BETWEEN LIBRARIES (RUSSIA, BELARUS, AND UKRAINE)

The geographic proximity of the Bryansk region in Russia, the Chernigov region in Ukraine, and the Gomel region in Belarus lends itself to easy contact and cooperation among institutions in the regions. Although the libraries have had a cooperative project since the early 1970s,[11] the failure at the Chernobyl nuclear power plant united them in a way that even the breakup of the Soviet Union could not destroy. They were bound together through a collective memory of the tragedy, and this collective memory and struggle to understand what it meant in many respects strengthened the cooperative bonds between the libraries in this border region. Natalia Somova (2006), head of the culture department in Bryansk, noted that this cooperation was not led by politicians, but by those actually working in the cultural field.

Maria Mushkina, a librarian who works with ecological information at the Novozybkov Central District Library, emphasized the relationship between the regions. While discussing their work with information about Chernobyl, she said, "We are at the crossroads of three nations and are working on international cooperation on the subject so that it can be passed among the nations and be systematized" (Interview 061020MM). Mushkina also discussed the need to follow the problem of Chernobyl as reported in the local, regional, and national newspapers so they could put together a digest. This digest is compiled primarily on paper because most of the library patrons do not have access to computers and are more comfortable working with print sources. However, the librarians have also utilized PowerPoint to organize an electronic version of the articles. This is an interesting utilization of the software. Essentially, they have made use of the external and internal hyperlinking capabilities of PowerPoint and created a database-like information product. They also continue to work to preserve and present the memory of the Chernobyl catastrophe by organizing educational activities for students. According to Mushkina, the work with ecological information includes outreach and working with local media. She stated, "We are raising the consciousness of the people so that they know that the library is there and that they can get information from us" (Interview 061020MM).

At the regional library level, two recent cooperative projects focused on the libraries that were closed due to the failure at Chernobyl. In April 2006, there was a virtual conference, conducted over the Internet, marking the 20th anniversary of the catastrophe called *From the History of the Lost*

[Casualty] Libraries.[12] Later, there was a follow-up meeting at the Churovichi Village Library in the Klimovo district of Bryansk called State of the Lost [Casualty] Libraries: 20 years after the Chernobyl Tragedy. This conference was an expansion of the activity of libraries with a discussion of the international cooperation. It led to the creation of a uniform cultural and information space relating to the study of the consequences of the Chernobyl accident and dealt with information about problems of forced migration. Participants in both conferences were from the three neighboring regions in Russia, Ukraine, and Belarus, with the majority coming from Bryansk.

As a result of the meltdown at the Chernobyl nuclear power plant, villages that had existed for hundreds of years were labeled too contaminated to live in, and, in these villages, there were, of course, libraries. According to official accounts, five libraries were closed due to the radioactive pollution caused by the failure at Chernobyl. All five were village libraries: Zabore and Barsuki rural libraries in the Krasnaia Gora district, Sviatsk rural library in the Novozybkov district, Kamenka rural library in the Zlynka district, and Novosergeevka rural library in the Klimovo district (Minenko, 2006). However, more than 35 libraries have closed in the western districts of Bryansk. While not officially, or perhaps even directly, attributable to the Chernobyl disaster, that event certainly was a factor. Many people moved away from the areas affected by Chernobyl, and, when enough people moved away, the cultural institutions faltered.

The conferences mentioned earlier are illustrations of how many of the librarians in the regions affected by Chernobyl have taken on the task of preserving the memory of these lost libraries. When examining the reports of the conference, it becomes clear that they are also remembering and documenting what could potentially have easily been forgotten. For example, one paper that is based on the diary of the village librarian discussed how the library had served the workers of two collective farms. This paper offered detail about the library's users and their taste in books (Zaborskaia selskaia, 2006). In addition to this paper, someone created a list of documents, located in the archives that regulate the closing of libraries (Spisok dokumentov, 2006). Also, information was collected about the villages themselves and the type of information that might have been in the village library's local history collection (Polenok & Lukianenko, 2006; Selo Barsuki, 2006). There are stories of how whole collective farms were moved, along with the farm workers, but without their library collections, which were thought to be too radioactive to move, even when measurements of the radiation showed it to be no different from books from other districts

(Degtereva, 2006). And there are laments that the library closures were not reflected in the local newspapers (Bondareva & Poletaeva, 2006). Papers like this last one point to what is perhaps the librarian's worst fear: that her library will close and that no one will care. Many of the libraries in the Bryansk region are working so that this will not be the case, especially in regard to ecological education. Situating themselves in the midst of many ecological activities, they endeavor to be central to the community.

CONCLUSION

Kulikova and Merkeshkina (2006) conclude their paper for the lost libraries conference in this way: "Today, libraries are free to choose and define their priorities for development. For us this priority is ecological education and minimization of the consequences of the Chernobyl failure." This quote is telling for two reasons: (1) it references a time when libraries were not free to set their own priorities and (2) it is an indication of the active stance librarians at BONUB choose to take in the work of ecological education. Coupled with the idea that ecological questions encompass social and psychological questions, BONUB set out a broad and varied agenda for the library. Clearly, the library is working to position itself as a civic institution that helps society address vital social problems, and for them, ecology is at the top of the list.

A problem the libraries face is the population's distrust of official information, especially as it relates to Chernobyl. Natalia Somova, the head of the Culture Department for the Bryansk Region, notes that to this day the library still must piece together information on Chernobyl. She considers the official information to be policy-driven and not complete. However, she does argue that the library is the appropriate infrastructure through which to disseminate the ecological information requested by the population, with the subtext that the government should show more support for libraries because they are working in this area (Somova, 2006).

Several of the librarians I spoke to expressed frustration about not having good measures of the outcomes of their work. But they also pointed to things they considered to be measures of success. For example, BONUB is now a contributor to the official government report on the status of the environment in Bryansk, and indeed, the report contains a section devoted specifically to the ecological work of the library. The librarians at BONUB feel that this kind of official recognition raises their status and authority in the community. Another indication of success was mentioned by the director of the Suzemka Central Library. She cited a study that showed an increase in the number of people who are concerned about the environment. In 1994, 22 percent of respondents answered positively to the question "In your opinion, is it necessary to protect natural areas in Bryansk?" In 2004, 90 percent of the responses were positive. She thought this was an indication that, although ecological education is complex and many-sided, they had instilled a feeling of responsibility for nature in many different people (Golub, 2006). Although the libraries have not been involved with every ecological activity that would have contributed to the increased awareness of the poor ecological situation in the region, they have certainly been active participants. Thus, the credit that the director of the Suzemka Central District Library ascribes to the library is appropriate. The other types of activities listed in the annual government report on the status of the environment include conferences hosted by the universities, activities of the forest preserve, and regional competitions for students or professionals (e.g., a competition about best practices in forest management) (Ministerstvo prirodnykh, 1999, 2000, 2003). It should also be mentioned that there is a strong likelihood that the libraries contributed indirectly to these activities by contributing information.

In the scholarship on environmental activities in Russia, little is said of the role that libraries can and do play. The only mention I found was in Henry's (2005) chapter on environmental movements in *Russian Civil Society*. She writes, "Grassroots environmentalists frequently use Soviet-era educational or cultural institutions – such as schools, libraries, small museums, dormitories, kindergartens, houses of children's creativity, former Pioneer summer camps, or nature preserves (*zapovedniki*) – as the site for their group's activities" (p. 219). I have shown that in the case of Bryansk, the libraries are more than just "sites of activities"; rather, they are active partners. It is true that they make use of their physical space to offer meeting rooms, but they also provide a range of information resources and services, making the librarians full participants in the region's ecological community.

NOTES

1. In Russian, the library's name is *Brianskaia Oblastnaia Nauchnaia Universalnaia Biblioteka imeni F.I. Tiutcheva*, which translates directly as Bryansk Regional Scientific Universal Library named for F. I. Tyutchev. Here, "scientific" indicates the

scholarly nature of the collection rather than a focus on the sciences, and "universal" indicates that they collect material on a variety of topics. For the remainder of the chapter, I will refer to the library by its Russian acronym, BONUB. Fyodor Ivanovich Tyutchev (1803–1873) was one of the great Romantic poets of Russia. He was born in the Bryansk region.

2. As of March 2008, Russia's 84 administrative divisions are 47 oblasts, 21 republics, 8 krays, 5 autonomous okrugs, 2 federal cities, and 1 autonomous oblast. Bryansk is an oblast. Beginning in 2005, several administrative divisions merged to form larger territories, and additional mergers are planned. For clarification, I should note that the city of Bryansk is located in the Bryansk district of the Bryansk region.

3. In 2006, Federal Law 131 came into effect, which further decentralized local control and funding of municipal institutions, including libraries. As a result, many of the libraries that had been branches of the district systems became autonomous libraries.

4. These types of workshops are part of the library education system in Russia. Diplomas from such workshops are required for promotion and advancement in the profession.

5. The ecological community includes groups such as scientists, official bodies, and environmental activists.

6. Deliberation is a method of interaction and communication that can help make the area between agreement and disagreement more visible. It is a procedure for communication in which the choices are weighed with the goal of making a decision. Deliberation is not a debate. Its goal is not to win or to prove your opponents wrong. In an ideal deliberation, all sides of an issue are brought out. Complex issues are never just two-sided, as is often portrayed in a debate (you are either for abortion or against it). Another example of how deliberation differs from debate is that in a deliberation, participants weigh the various choices looking for consequences and tradeoffs before making a decision. No decision comes without consequences, both positive and negative. Therefore, in a deliberation, even the negative aspect of a preferred choice is considered, whereas, in a debate, the negative consequences are minimized if acknowledged at all. Thus, in a deliberation you might hear someone say, "I would be willing to do X even if it means Y."

7. The total release of radionuclides is estimated at 14 EBq (1 EBq = 1018 Bq) including 1.8 EBq of I-131, .085 EBq of Cs-137, .01 EBq of Sr-90, and .003 EBq of plutonium isotopes. Becquerels (Bq) and Curies (Ci) are the measurements for radiation in the environment. In humans, the effective dose of radiation is measured in millisieverts (mSv).

8. Many people in the region live in apartment building with shared courtyards.

9. The conversations around the role of library in this instance are not unlike conversations that happened in the United States around library service to immigrants (see Jones 1999).

10. This competition was funded by the Soros Foundation as part of the project "The Library: A Center for Information and Education for Migrants and Refugees in a New Living Condition."

11. The cooperative project between the three regional libraries is outlined in the website http://www.scilib.debryansk.ru/project.php?id = 24. The main areas of

188   ELLEN M. KNUTSON

cooperation are the preservation and consolidation of the general information space,
the preservation of the book as emblems of national culture, the work of libraries in
the multicultural environment, to support the humanitarian and educational
missions of libraries working in an information society and in the new economic
policy.

12. The materials from this virtual conference are available in the website http://
www.scilib.debryansk.ru/project/chernobyl (in Russian).

ACKNOWLEDGMENT

This research was supported by the Charles F. Kettering Foundation in
Dayton, Ohio.

REFERENCES

Anspaugh, L. R., et al. (2005). Environmental consequences of the Chernobyl accident and
    their remediation: Twenty years of experience. Paper presented at International
    Conference: Chernobyl – Looking Back to Go Forward, Towards a United Nations
    Consensus on the Effects of the Accident and the Future, 6–7 September, 2005, Vienna.
    Available at http://www-ns.iaea.org/meetings/rw-summaries/chernobyl-conference-2005.
    htm. Retrieved on April, 25 2007.
Bondareva, E. M., & Poletaeva, T. M. (2006). Iz istorii poselka Novosergeevka i ego biblioteki
    [From the history of Novosergeevka village and its library]. Paper presented at Iz Istorii
    Pogibshikh Bibliotek, Bryansk, Russia. Available at http://www.scilib.debryansk.ru/
    project/chernobyl/klimovo.html. Retrieved on May 21, 2007.
BONUB. (2001). Informatsionnyi otchet 2001. Gosudarstvennye biblioteki Brianskoi oblasti v
    2001 godu [Information report 2001. State libraries in the Bryansk Region in 2001].
    Bryansk, Russia: BONUB.
BONUB. (2005). Programma "ekologicheskii rezonans": Rabota bibliotek Brianskoi oblasti
    sovmestno s prirodookhrannymi organizatsiiami v pomoshch ekologicheskomu prosvesh-
    cheniiu, obrazovaniiu i konkretnoi prirodookhrannoi deiatelnosti, 2000–2005 gg [Program
    "ecological resonance": Collaboration of Bryansk Region libraries with environmental
    organizations to help ecological education and concrete preservation activities, 2000–2005].
    Bryansk, Russia: BONUB.
BONUB. (2006a). Informatsionnyi otchet o rabote Brianskoi oblastnoi biblioteki za 2005 god
    [Information report on the work of Bryansk regional libraries 2005]. Bryansk, Russia:
    BONUB.
BONUB. (2006b). Deiatelnost bibliotek Brianskoi oblasti po ekologicheskomu prosveshcheniiu
    naseleniia v 2006 godu [Work of the libraries in Bryansk Region for the ecological
    education of the population in 2006] (Available at http://www.eco.scilib.debryansk.ru/
    5library/eco_prosv_2006.html. Retrieved on May 15, 2007). BONUB.
Briansk.ru. (2008). V Novozybkovskom raione bolshe vsego radiatsionno zagriaznennykh
    produktov [Novozybkov has the most radioactive contaminated products]. Briansk.ru,

March 3, Available at http://briansk.ru/society/200833/109766.html. Retrieved on March 3, 2008.

Bychkova V. G., & Rubeko, S.V. (2006). Rol biblioteki v zhizni vynuzhdennykh pereselentsev [Role of the library in the lives of internally displaced]. Paper presented at Iz Istorii Pogibshikh Bibliotek, Bryansk, Russia. Available at http://www.scilib.debryansk.ru/project/chernobyl/zhukovka.html. Retrieved on January 3, 2008.

Chernobyl Forum, & International Atomic Energy Agency. (2005). *Chernobyl's legacy: Health, environmental and socio-economic impacts and recommendations to the governments of Belarus, the Russian Federation and Ukraine* (Available at http://www.iaea.org/Publications/Booklets/Chernobyl/chernobyl.pdf. Retrieved on May 14, 2007). Vienna, Austria: IAEA.

Dediulia, S. S. (2006). Rol i znachenie bibliotek v minimizatsii posledstvii Chernobylskoi avarii [The role of libraries in minimizing the consequences of the Chernobyl disaster]. Paper presented at Crimea Conference, 10–18 June 2006, Sudak, Autonomous Republic of Crimea, Ukraine.

Degtereva, N. A. (2006). Chernobylia polynnaia trava [Chernobyl's wormwood grass]. Paper presented at Iz Istorii Pogibshikh Bibliotek, Bryansk, Russia. Available at http://www.scilib.debryansk.ru/project/chernobyl/degtereva.html. Retrieved on May 21, 2007.

Ekologiia Brianshchiny: Vchera, Segodnia, Zavtra? [Ecology of Bryansk: Yesterday, today, tomorrow?]. (1996). Bryansk: Russia.

Golub, E. N. (2006). Vozmozhnosti informatsionnogo partnerstva [The possibility of information partners]. Paper presented at Eko-Shkola, Suzemka, Russia.

Henry, L. A. (2005). Russian environmentalists and civil society. In: A. B. Evans, Jr., L. A. Henry & L. M. Sundstrom (Eds), *Russian civil society: A critical assessment.* Armonk, NY: M.E. Sharpe.

IFAP Russia. (2005). Programma UNESCO "Informatsiia dlia vsekh" v Brianske: Obzor [UNESCO "Information for all" program in Bryansk: A review]. Available at http://www.ifap.ru/pr/2005/050330a.htm. Retrieved on September 29, 2007.

International Atomic Energy Agency, & Chernobyl Forum Expert Group. (2006). Environmental consequences of the Chernobyl accident and their remediation: Twenty years of experience. Radiological assessment reports series, Vol. 1239. Vienna: International Atomic Energy Agency.

Iz zhizni Zaborsko-Nikolskoi Slobody [From the life of Zaborsko-Nikolskaia Sloboda]. (2006). Paper presented at Iz Istorii Pogibshikh Bibliotek, Bryansk, Russia. Available at http://www.scilib.debryansk.ru/project/chernobyl/zhukovka2.html. Retrieved on January 3, 2008.

Jones, P. A. (1999). *Libraries, immigrants, and the American experience.* Westport: Greenwood Press.

Khokhlenko, N. S. (2006). Vozmozhnosti informatsionnogo partnerstva [The possibility of information partners]. Paper presented at Eko-Shkola, Suzemka, Russia.

Kimmage, D. A. (Ed.) (1992). *Russian libraries in transition: An anthology of glasnost literature.* Jefferson: McFarland & Co.

Kislovskaya, G. (1999). Ten years of change in Russia and its effects on libraries. *Liber Quarterly: The Journal of European Research Libraries, 9*(3), 266–274.

Knutson, E. M. (2008). *Libraries, community and change in post-Soviet Russia: The case of the Bryansk Regional Public Library System.* Ph.D. dissertation, University of Illinois at Urbana-Champaign.

Kulikova, O. Y. (2004). Rol bibliotek v rasprostranenii ekologicheskoi informatsii i formirovanii ekologicheskoi kultury naseleniia Brianskoi oblasti. [Role of the library in the distribution of ecological information and the formation of ecological culture in the population of the Bryansk region]. *Vestik Ekologicheskogo Obrazovaniia v Rossii, 1,* 13–14.

Kulikova, O. Y., & Merkeshkina, L. V. (2006). Iz opyta raboty bibliotek Brianshchiny po radiatsionno-ekologicheskomu prosveshcheniiu naseleniia. [From the experience of the work of libraries in Bryansk on the radiation-ecological education of the population]. Paper presented at Iz Istorii Pogibshikh Bibliotek, Bryansk, Russia. Available at http://www.scilib.debryansk.ru/project/chernobyl/Kulikova_Merkeshkina.html. Retrieved on May 21, 2007.

Lekanova, N. V. (2004). Ekologiia Brianshchiny: Chto dumaiut grazhdane? [Ecology of Bryansk: What do citizens think?]. Bryansk, Russia: BONUB.

Massa, I., & Tynkkynen, V. P. (2001). *The struggle for Russian environmental policy.* Helsinki: Aleksanteri Institute.

Minenko, A. G. (2006). Svideteli proshlogo-pamati budushchego [Witness of the past-to the memories of the future]. Paper presented at Iz Istorii Pogibshikh Bibliotek, Bryansk, Russia. Available at http://www.scilib.debryansk.ru/project/chernobyl/minenko.html. Retrieved on May 21, 2007.

Ministerstvo prirodnykh resursov Rossiiskoi Federatsii, Glavnoe upravlenie prirodnykh resursov i okhrany okruzhaiushchei sredy MPR Rossii po Brianskoi Oblasti. (1999). *Doklad: O sostoianii okruzhaiushchei prirodnoi sredy po Brianskoi oblasti v 1998 godu* [Report: On the state of environment in the Bryansk Region 1998]. Bryansk, Russia.

Ministerstvo prirodnykh resursov Rossiiskoi Federatsii, Glavnoe upravlenie prirodnykh resursov i okhrany okruzhaiushchei sredy MPR Rossii po Brianskoi Oblasti. (2000). *Doklad: O sostoianii okruzhaiushchei prirodnoi sredy po Brianskoi oblasti v 1999 godu.* Bryansk, Russia.

Ministerstvo prirodnykh resursov Rossiiskoi Federatsii, Glavnoe upravlenie prirodnykh resursov i okhrany okruzhaiushchei sredy MPR Rossii po Brianskoi Oblasti. (2003). *Doklad: O sostoianii okruzhaiushchei prirodnoi sredy po Brianskoi oblasti v 2002 godu.* Bryansk, Russia.

Petryna, A. (2002). *Life exposed: Biological citizens after Chernobyl.* Princeton: Princeton University Press.

Polenok, S. M., & Lukianenko, S. M. (2006). Selo Zabore [Zabore village]. Paper presented at Iz Istorii Pogibshikh Bibliotek, Bryansk, Russia. Available at http://www.scilib. debryansk.ru/project/chernobyl/zaborje.html. Retrieved on May 21, 2007.

Selo Barsuki [Barsuki village]. (2006). Paper presented at Iz Istorii Pogibshikh Bibliotek, Bryansk, Russia. Available at http://www.scilib.debryansk.ru/project/chernobyl/barsuki. html. Retrieved on May 21, 2007.

Smith, J. T., & Beresford, N. A. (2005). *Chernobyl: Catastrophe and consequences.* Springer-praxis books in environmental sciences. New York: Springer.

Somova, N. A. (2006). Chernobyl kak novoe znanie, kak novaia realnost [Chernobyl as a new knowledge, new reality]. Paper presented at 2nd Interstate Seminar: Ecological Culture in the Interest of Sustainable Development, Bryansk, Russia.

Spisok dokumentov, reglamentiruiushchikh zakrytie bibliotek [List of documents regulating the library closures]. (2006). Paper presented at Iz Istorii Pogibshikh Bibliotek, Bryansk,

Russia. Available at http://www.scilib.debryansk.ru/project/chernobyl/dokumenty.html. Retrieved on May 21, 2007.

UNDP – United Nations Development Program & UNICEF. (2002). *The human consequences of the Chernobyl nuclear accident: A strategy for recovery* (Available at http://chernobyl.undp.org/english/docs/Strategy%20for%20Recover.pdf. Retrieved on May 14, 2007). UNDP.

Zaborskaia selskaia biblioteka. [Zabore village library]. (2006). Paper presented at Iz Istorii Pogibshikh Bibliotek, Bryansk, Russia. Available at http://www.scilib.debryansk.ru/project/chernobyl/kormilceva.html. Retrieved on May 21, 2007.

LIST OF INTERVIEWS

020213AC – Aleksey Chizhevskii (Director, Erika), personal interview with author, February 13, 2002.

020213PV – Pavel Vdovichenko (Director, Radimichi), personal interview with author, February 13, 2002.

020219NVL – Nina Ladniuk (Head, Research Methods Office, BONUB), personal interview with author, February 19, 2002.

061020MM – Maria Mushkina (Librarian, Novozybkov Central Library), personal interview with author, October 20, 2006.

061024LVM – Larisa Merkeshkina (Head, Ecological Information Center, BONUB), personal interview with author, October 24, 2006 (with email follow-up).

061030NVL – Natasha Lekanova (Senior Librarian, Methods Office, BONUB), personal interview with author, October 30, 2006.

061031ANT – Aleksandr Terebunov (Head, Pochep Culture Department), personal interview with author, October 31, 2006.

061031LD – Domanichi Village Library Group Interview (Lilian Dubinchina, Director, Domanichi Village Library, Elena Stepanovna, Librarian, Pochep Central District Library, Galina Mikhailovna, Department of Rural Administration, Mikhail Fisunov, Local News Reporter/Pochep Library User), personal interview with author, October 31, 2006.

INTERNET AS AN INFORMATION RESOURCE IN EURASIA ☆

Mark Skogen and Myles G. Smith

ABSTRACT

As more people become Internet users, the likelihood of free public Internet access at libraries or other institutions increases. However, demand alone does not drive governments to offer this public service. Governments in Eurasia face economic, reform, and freedom of information challenges. People in Eurasia face computer illiteracy, lack of affordable computers and Internet providers, missing relevant online content in their mother tongue in their local context, and disinterest in creating content or learning new technologies.

Today, Ukraine, Kazakhstan, and Georgia have made the most progress in promoting the Internet as an information resource in the public sphere. Moldova, Uzbekistan, Belarus, Azerbaijan, and Kyrgyzstan have made progress in some key areas, but government, political, market, economic, and geological impediments need to be addressed. Tajikistan and Turkmenistan have two of the lowest percentages of Internet users in the world, and they have barely begun to make the Internet a relevant public information resource.

☆The views expressed in this chapter are entirely the authors' and do not necessarily reflect the views of USAID, US Department of State, or IREX.

Advances in Library Administration and Organization, Volume 27, 193–219
ISSN: 0732-0671/doi:10.1108/S0732-0671(2009)0000027015

The next generation of leaders (those currently below 25 years of age) and increased government support of access, training, and content will raise rates of Internet adoption. As this unfolds, a mixture of government reform in its support of libraries and donor support could improve libraries' current abilities to meet the information needs of the citizens in Eurasia.

INTRODUCTION

The collapse of the Soviet Union left the successor states of Eurasia with inferior structural and institutional bases from which to develop information and communications technology (ICT) as an informational resource for their populations. Not all republics started this process from the same point, depending on the state in which Moscow left them. Some were less prepared, such as those that had been largely designated for agricultural or resource extraction, those facing civil or cross-border war, and those governments who did not serve with the people's or development interests in mind.

The rise of the Internet in the West took place during Eurasia's transition decade, where the Internet quickly became a resource of first choice for everyone from casual information seekers to serious researchers, resulting in today's ICT gap. Prosperous Western communities were able to offer basic computing courses widely in schools, libraries, and other public institutions, while prosperous families were able to afford a home computer. As is commonly true for technology adoption, the younger generations adopted earlier, but by the mid- to late-1990s, the Internet had become an important resource for public information relevant to all age groups.

The transition from a print to an online information generation happened seamlessly at places such as libraries in the West. They already had computer centers due to earlier efforts to digitize records and catalogs, and librarians and users were generally computer literate, or at least not technologically averse. As a result, approximately 99% of the US libraries provide free public Internet access in today's ever-expanding public information environment (Bertot, McClure, Jaeger, & Ryan, 2006, p. 1).

From the early 1990s in Eurasia, Internet adoption has been stinted by underdeveloped infrastructure, high costs associated with computers and Internet access, low computer literacy, lack of relevant language content online, and inadequate government support for ICT development programs, free markets, and free information. However, conditions have been improving in the past three years especially. The Internet is getting cheaper, Internet service provider (ISP) services are improving and expanding, more people are using the Internet regularly, governments and outside investors are spending money on infrastructure and connecting government institutions and schools, and governments are less restrictive on content.

Struggling to provide heating, electricity, and new books, libraries in Eurasia have been poorly positioned to provide Internet access to the public. Yet this has not been the greatest obstacle to a more widely adopted Internet. The Internet has largely remained irrelevant as a meaningful information resource, because it has not widely been culturally adopted, as it was in the West. As a small but important contribution to that effort, international donors and programs have been addressing the effort to increase access and training for computers and Internet.

INTERNET ACCESS AND TRAINING PROGRAM

The Internet Access and Training Program (IATP) started under funding from the US Information Agency and administration from the International Research and Exchanges Board (IREX, www.irex.org) in 1996. After 1999, funding continued under the US Department of State Bureau of Educational and Cultural Affairs (ECA, www.exchanges.state.gov). In 2007, the United States Agency for International Development (USAID, www.usaid.gov) took over the funding role. The program brought free Internet access and training to more than 160 cities in 11 countries of Eurasia. During its peak in 2005, IATP served more than 35,000 individuals every month. By November 2008, the program operated in 46 communities spanning 8 countries.

In addition to ensuring users have access to free flow of information, the program provides the public with the skills and resources necessary to utilize ICT to meet professional, educational, and institutional goals. Equally important, the program teaches users the skills necessary to create online content, websites, wikis, and blogs, to provide resources of relevance to citizens in their local languages, enhancing the public information environment and stimulating demand for the Internet as an information resource.

IATP centers are partnered with libraries, non-governmental organizations (NGOs), and universities, whose ideals of unrestricted open access to information match those of the program. Typically a center has between

6 and 14 workstations and an administrator to assist users and conduct regular courses free-of-charge for the public. Administrators specifically aim to bring in and teach those who have information to share, including journalists, librarians, NGO employees, teachers, government employees, and small business owners.

As it is impossible to evaluate outlying factors, users, and institutions, some generalizations are made in the chapter to describe the status of the Internet as an information resource in Eurasia. The authors designed scoring systems for this chapter, which are meant to objectively score and compare the countries. The role of public libraries are emphasized due to IATP's experience with libraries and the presumed role of the library as a public information source. The authors conclude with some brief recommendations.

For the purposes of this chapter, the authors use "Eurasia" to refer to the countries of Azerbaijan, Belarus, Georgia, Kazakhstan, Kyrgyzstan, Moldova, Tajikistan, Turkmenistan, Ukraine, and Uzbekistan.

EURASIAN LIBRARIES IN THE INTERNET DEVELOPMENT PROCESS

In a focus group conducted in the rural, poor small town of Garm, Tajikistan in October 2008, when discussing where a person usually obtains necessary information, the group nearly forgot to mention the library, because nobody visited it due to its "old books" (Bekenova, 2008). Nearly every community across Eurasia has a local library, but most libraries struggle to play a relevant role for the people in these communities. Few offer free Internet access other than those supported at one time by IATP or other development programs. Of the few libraries that do, it is generally those that have also invested in adequate staffing, training, and improving services for users. The correlation between better libraries and likelihood of free Internet at libraries exists, because the library director and her/his supportive local government figures understand the need to expand information offerings through libraries, and they see the Internet as a part of a thorough library modernization effort. Two libraries IATP worked with in Kazakhstan illustrate extreme examples of those ready to play a relevant role and those not.

The first is a regional central library located in northeastern Kazakhstan that hosted an IATP center for several years. Between 1999 and 2005, the committed library management initiated its own paid Internet center to coexist with the IATP center, established itself as a local ISP to generate funding for more initiatives, founded a network of more than a dozen village and town libraries, provided them with Internet access and training, started a legal advising center with a computer database of legislation, and ensured that many other services were offered to benefit the people in the city. Nearly four years after IATP stopped funding the center, the library continues to offer free IT courses and Internet access to the public, because the directors and every librarian employed there understand the value of Internet in the library and their role as librarians. Walking into the library doors, one might think that he/she is in any well-run library in the United States.

The feeling is completely different in the second library that is located in a western Kazakhstan oil city of a similar size with a less supportive culture. Not only did the library director need extra pushing from IATP staff to arrange a meeting with regional government officials to discuss the IATP center's importance for the region and library, but IATP staff needed to arrange and attend the meeting after the director failed to do so on her own. Although the northeastern Kazakhstan counterpart had been involved and informed regularly, the western Kazakhstan oblast representative did not even know the library hosted an Internet center. Nevertheless, he expressed support and promised financing to cover staff and Internet after IATP support ended. Unfortunately, the library director never heard from the official again, she did not pursue it strongly, and the library closed the doors of the Internet center a few weeks after IATP support ended. The very reason behind the failure of the Internet center also explains why there is so little foot traffic, there are so few initiatives and offerings, the staff is unhelpful, the local government is not involved, and people do not turn to the library for information and assistance.

Unfortunately, there are far more libraries in Eurasia resembling the library in western Kazakhstan than the well-run and well-supported library in the East, which makes national library modernization programs less likely.

To illustrate the lack of focus on customer service, one can look at what it is like to search for a book in a typical Eurasia library. Usually, books are referenced only in card catalogs and stored in basements away from browsing readers. If one does not know the book title or author, one is at the mercy of the librarian's knowledge and recommendation. Even if the library had a computer with a database of the collection, it is likely that users lack the skills to use it, rely on limited staff to use the sole computer with the database, or the database could only find an author and title, but not perform a complex subject search.

Many factors prevent the development of library services, such as those required by a well-run free Internet center, including a variable mixture of the following:

- Broken support systems for libraries, be they centralized systems under one ministry or a localized system, and no thorough library reform plans;
- Inadequate budget allotments in relatively wealthier countries and inability to make allotments in poorer countries for library salaries, training, and resources;
- Persistent corruption with little public accountability and fund misallocations;
- The need for new books and periodicals is as great as for Internet;
- Governments lack thorough plans to introduce free Internet access at libraries;
- Decision makers underestimate the Internet's benefits;
- The worse libraries are the more likely government and communities ignore them and their development;
- Lack of developed and free civil societies to advocate public improvements, and lack of government will or ability to implement such programs;
- Lack of demand from library users for Internet due to lack of understanding of its usefulness;
- Few efforts to create digital, searchable library catalog that is publicly available;
- Libraries do not communicate or share best practices;
- Legacy of bad cultural customer service and perception by some of a librarian's role as nothing more than a book guardian;
- The majority of library staff, while well intentioned, are of pre- or retirement age and less likely to acquire new skills. A librarian in an IATP focus group discussion mentioned low incentives dissuade her from learning to use the Internet (Bekenova, 2008);
- Inadequate infrastructure for hosting a public Internet center (a recent IREX assessment of library readiness produced for Global Libraries in Ukraine found 40% lack reliable electricity, 4% lack telephone service,

more than 50% lack heating systems, and 26% are in communities with no available broadband Internet service) (Cronin, Katz & Guard, 2008, p. 4).

Facing these challenges, donors seek to improve libraries, because libraries are places with a diverse mix of the population and open doors to all, where people would go for information. No donor program can solve the challenges without major government reform. Specific solutions for library development, government budgeting and priorities, and library staffing are best left for others to address. The authors use their expertise in understanding the state and use of the Internet in a Eurasian context to discuss the implications of this process on society.

The development of the Internet is at varying stages in Eurasia, which directly affects the impact it makes in a library. In some countries, Internet would only marginally increase a library's ability to provide better information to average citizens, taking into account the data presented in the next section. In others, it has already become a valuable information resource that is as or more worthy than new books in a library.

THE STATUS OF INTERNET IN EURASIA

As a way to measure the status of Internet as an information resource across Eurasia, it is necessary to consider a series of factors affecting its sustainable development. Reliable statistics and policy data spanning the region are not readily available, which lead the authors to develop and conduct their own pilot research to analyze the subject and present their findings for the purposes of this chapter. Some data are subjective and based on estimates from an expert in each country, who used common scoring methodology. Each category is rated on a scale of 1–4, 4 being the highest. Higher total scores indicate countries where the Internet is becoming a more useful, accessible, and unfettered resource in the public information environment. Lower scores imply the Internet is underdeveloped, restricted, or otherwise limited in access, and thus not a useful source of public information.

The scoring measures are relative;[1] criteria apply to countries with *developing* conditions for Internet, and most countries where Internet is developed already would score near a perfect 40. The definitions of each measure and the scale by which they were measured are summarized in the following tables.

Internet in 10 Eurasian Countries, November 2008

	Public access				Development programs				Content issues			
	Internet penetration	Access distribution	Private infrastructure	Public Internet cafés	Internet at schools	Internet at libraries	Government programs	Foreign donor programs	Relevant Web content	Official regulation	Online media	Total score
Azerbaijan	2	2.5	2	2	2	2	2.5	2	1.5	2.5	3	**24**
Belarus	3	3.5	1.5	2	3	2	1	1	3	2	2.5	**24.5**
Georgia	2	2	2	3	3	2	3	3	2.5	3	3.5	**29**
Kazakhstan	3	3	2	2	4	2	2.5	3	2.5	2.5	2.5	**29**
Kyrgyzstan	2	2.5	1.5	2.5	2	2	2	3	1	2	3	**23.5**
Moldova	3	2.5	2.5	2	3	2	2	3	2	2	2.5	**26.5**
Tajikistan	1.5	1.5	2.5	2.5	1.5	1	2	3	1.5	3	1.5	**20.5**
Turkmenistan	1	1.5	1	1	1.5		2	1.5	1	1	1	**13.5**
Ukraine	3	3.5	3	3.5	2	2.5	2	3	4	4	4	**34.5**
Uzbekistan	2	3	1.5	2.5	3	3	2	2.5	2.5	1.5	1.5	**25**
Average	2.25	2.55	1.95	2.3	2.5	1.95	2.1	2.4	2.15	2.35	2.5	**25.05**

Measure	Definitions and Comments	Average	Ratings	Scale/Indicator
Public Access				
Internet penetration	*Percentage of population who are considered Internet users. Ukraine, Kazakhstan, and Belarus sources boast the highest figures, nearing 35%.* Higher penetration correlates with ease of attaining a private connection, the cost of access, and/or higher incomes	2.25	1	0.1%–3%
			2	4%–12%
			3	13%–35%
			4	>35%
Access distribution	*Distribution of Internet access across the country, from capital cities to urban centers and rural areas. Belarus and Ukraine top the category.* Belarus is compact, flat, borders more digitized EU countries and lays astride a main Internet channel to Moscow	2.55	1	Limited access even in urban areas outside capital
			2	Dial-up available nearly everywhere
			3	DSL in urban centers; dial-up only elsewhere
			4	DSL available throughout country
Private sector infrastructure	*Extent to which private sector ISPs providing services to the public, often at lower rates and with higher standards of quality.* Each country started with a national Telecom, which meant the country relied on one state-owned monopoly to install	2	1	Government owns or controls all ISPs
			2	ISP monopolies in most of country
			3	Many ISPs in capital, few Independents in regions
			4	

(Continued)

Measure	Definitions and Comments	Average	Ratings	Scale/Indicator
	or upgrade telephone lines, offer fair dial-up prices, and allow competition and some Telecom structures are the only first-tier ISP in the country			Wide selection of Independent ISPs nationwide
Public Internet Cafés	*Extent to which private sector is providing public access points to the Internet.* Most countries have large numbers of Internet cafés in their capitals and cities with more than 25,000 people generally have at least one café or business offering paid public access. *Ukraine* again sets the pace with large numbers of Internet cafés in all urban areas. However, it is common for "Internet cafés" everywhere to cater to PC gamers and not offer Internet	2.3	1	Very limited and tightly restricted
			2	Somewhat limited or restricted
			3	Extensive in all urban areas, few restrictions
			4	Extensive in number, no restrictions
Development Programs				
Internet at schools	*Extent to which Internet is available at public education institutions.* Ministries of Education (MoE) will discuss computer to child ratios and other grand visions, but success at integrating Internet classrooms, usually only one per school has been	2.5	1	No Internet at public schools
			2	Internet at select public schools in urban areas
			3	Internet at 15% of public schools

limited to how much teachers integrate the Web's new resources and potential. Every MoE has a plan for Internet in schools, and *Kazakhstan* has most widely achieved the goal to provide Internet to public schools, including smaller towns

Internet at 30% public schools nationwide

Category	Description	Score		
Internet at libraries	*Extent to which Internet is available at public libraries.* No country has an outstandingly high score, and most libraries with free Internet exist, because they were started by foreign-aid programs, such as IATP. This measure was the lowest average for the region, based on our rubric. *Azerbaijan, Kazakhstan*, and other countries announced grand plans to digitize libraries across the country, with very limited results, other than scanning books	1.95	1	No Internet at libraries
			2	Internet at <5% of libraries, provided by foreign donors
			3	Internet at libraries in 50% of regions
			4	Internet available at libraries in all regions
Government programs	*Efforts of the host government to provide Internet at public institutions through its own development initiatives and policies.* Every country has an e-government initiative, but few countries have done more than	2.1	1	No useful or realistic ICT policy
			2	ICT policy exists but little results shown
			3	ICT policy implemented but limited in success

(Continued)

Measure	Definitions and Comments	Average	Ratings	Scale/Indicator
	oversee the creation of ministry, departmental, and state websites		4	ICT policy implemented and moderately successful
Foreign programs	*Extent to which foreign governments are providing Internet to the public through development programs, and the support of the host countries to those programs.* Generally, countries are willingly accept aid in the IT sphere, but political tensions with donor countries, corruption, interior political tensions, lack of competent government specialists, and concerns about ulterior motives have made some countries less amenable. *Georgia* and *Kazakhstan* have decent records of cost sharing foreign development programs on its territory, an ideal model for sustainability	2.4	1 2 3 4	Government restricts foreign programs Government gives vocal support but no other effort Government gives cost share to their best ability Government bankrolls foreign programs
Content Issues Relevant Web content	*Relevance of Internet content to population, considering language issues.* With less local content, people	2.15	1	Limited local content, foreign language skills limited

	have fewer reasons to get online. No single country has seen a major explosion of local content the way countries in the West have, especially using the national languages		2	Limited local content, advanced foreign language skills
			3	Decent local content, decent foreign language skills
			4	Large amount of content in locally spoken languages
Official regulation	*Extent of government intervention and restriction on Internet content.* Nearly every government has pressured ISPs to conveniently make Internet or certain websites unavailable for some period, but others have made it more systematic. *Ukraine* has the most permissive Internet environment in the region and received the highest grade	2.35	1	Significantly interfere with access to content
			2	Somewhat interfere with access to content
			3	Rarely interfere with access to content
			4	No content regulations
Internet media	Availability of varied, unbiased, quality media sources in locally relevant languages that are accessible to the population. Online media gauges the availability of varied, unbiased, accessible, and quality media sources on local issues from local journalists in relevant languages	3	1	No domestic Independent online media accessible
			2	Very limited number and access, poor quality, some bias
			3	Several sources, decent quality, unbiased and unfettered
			4	Many quality Independent sources in local languages

Public Access Issues

Access Distribution, Public Internet Cafés, and *Private Infrastructure* largely dictate a country's *Internet Penetration.* Internet use in the region has increased significantly in the past several years. Ukraine, Georgia, Belarus, and Kazakhstan enjoy the most reformed business environments and generally the highest scores in the public access grouping. Although Belarus is relatively authoritarian and restrictive, it enjoys high penetration and distribution rates due to the government policy of adopting ICT for its export-dependent economy and its favorable geography – flat, compact, and in Europe.

Places such as Kyrgyzstan, Tajikistan, Turkmenistan, and Georgia see parts of the country still inaccessible to dial-up due to underdeveloped telecommunications in rural, mountainous regions especially. Turkmenistan and Tajikistan have Internet penetration between 1 and 5%, ranking near the lowest in the world, but for very different reasons (worldinternetstats. com, 2008). From 2002 until his death in December 2006, the late Turkmen President Niyazov reversed Internet penetration trends and strictly limited access to the Internet. In Turkmenistan, the government operates the handful of Internet cafés and the only ISP that distributes a small number of expensive private accounts that provide slow access in a few cities. Tajikistan is poor, suffers regular electricity shortages, and is divided by mountains. However, the government has generally done what it can to support Internet development. IATP pays between four and six times more for Internet connectivity for its centers in Tajikistan than in Georgia and Ukraine, where average salaries are two or three times higher. One "Internet café" owner in Tajikistan explained to IATP researchers that they offered only games and stopped offering Internet, because it was one less bill to pay (Bekenova, 2008).

Over the past three years, the hourly price for dial-up has fallen by as much as 50% in Eurasia, with the exception of Turkmenistan, where dial-up was generally not available three years ago (Amansakhatov, et al., 2008). Turkmenistan's handful of government-owned Internet cafés dropped prices by more than 40% the day after the country's president noted that prices were too high, although this price (more than $2/hour) is still too high for most to afford. The prices for dial-up connections are 100% higher than in neighboring Uzbekistan, and accounts are still not sold freely to the public. In Kazakhstan, where the average monthly salary is about $300/month or nearly three times that of Turkmenistan, one hour of dial-up is as low as $.40/hour, and one hour at an Internet café would cost about $1

(Amansakhatov, et al., 2008). Internet is becoming more affordable to the growing middle classes in Eurasia, such as they exist, in urban areas of most countries. Unfortunately, the individuals who constitute information hubs in these countries, such as journalists, teachers, and librarians, are poorly compensated for their work and would be among the last to afford regular Internet access in all 10 of these countries.

Most Internet users are from urban areas. At least 95% of the Internet users in Turkmenistan are from the capital, Ashgabat (Amansakhatov, et al., 2008).

Finally, especially true outside the capital of Tajikistan, traditional and Islamic values limit women's participation in public life and education, further depressing the number of potential Internet users. Members of an IATP-led focus group in one small Tajik town suggested in October 2008 that men should not allow their wives to be corrupted by the Internet (Bekenova, 2008).

ICT Sector Development

Internet at schools and Internet at libraries are largely the result of projects founded under foreign donor programs and host government programs, encompassing the development of ICT by government programs and policies. With a few exceptions, the governments of the region are generally supportive of foreign assistance programs, but largely unable or unwilling to contribute their own resources.

The US, EU, NATO, private companies, World Bank, UN, Asia Development Bank, private foundations, and embassies have intervened by developing infrastructure, granting computers, donating software, establishing access points, providing training for end users and trainers, influencing government policy, running study tours, and more. In addition to IATP's mark, NATO's Virtual Silk Highway project has been one of the more successful projects in terms of long-term impact of bringing sustainable Internet to academic institutions through satellite connectivity and development of an ISP. The Bill & Melinda Gates Foundation recently initiated funding for a major five-year project with IREX to add Internet to libraries as a comprehensive effort to make libraries across Ukraine more relevant, starting in 2009.

Host governments have all issued grand statements about digitizing public institutions, e-government plans, and prioritizing the IT sector, and most have been met with limited success. Turkmenistan's president recently issued a decree that no new school be opened without computers and an Internet connection, although students in many schools report that computer rooms are locked by administrators who fear that use will lead to depreciation or by teachers who cannot use them. Georgia has instituted some of impressive capacity-building programs in e-governance. Kazakhstan's deep coffers allowed it to provide computers for high schools nationwide.

President Berdimukhamedov has embraced Internet in rhetoric and ordered the bureaucracy to expand access, which has been mired by lack of infrastructure, ISPs, experts prepared to provide Internet, and large majority of computer- and Internet-illiterate government employees. Without the policy and base of experts to make Internet development, governments have not succeeded. The NATO–EU Virtual Silk Highway has connected 59 Turkmen schools, universities, and institutes to the Internet in some capacity over the past three years (www.science.gov.tm, 2008).

Content Issues

Content regulation and *online media* are two important factors, along with overall Internet adoption, contributing to the level of *Relevant Web Content*. Countries free of government restrictions on media and Internet are free to create more content. Language is also an important determinant.

Nearly every country in the region has some record of denying content to information seekers. For example, democratic stalwart Georgia saw some ISPs block all websites from Russia in August and September 2008, and more advanced blocking techniques, including entries such as "South Ossetia" on Youtube.com. This not only prevented Georgians from reading Russian news accounts of the war but also kept many from using their personal .ru e-mail addresses, which are most common due to the lack of quality personal .ge providers. Ukraine has remained most open with several competing interest groups and power centers. Some countries with better scores have relaxed and removed blocks on websites. Kazakhstan is an example that has opened access.

Reporters without Borders (rsf.org 2008) sensationally declares Belarus, Turkmenistan, and Uzbekistan as "Internet Enemies," largely due to monitoring Internet browsing, filtering and blocking Web content, and imprisoning, harassing, or preventing those posting politically challenging materials. Traffic is known to be monitored by security services. "Opposition" websites have been and likely will continue to be blocked.

Even English-language sites with the potential to carry anti-government content, such as newspapers, YouTube, and Facebook are blocked at times. ISPs are responsible for blocking websites, and the secret service, the former KGB, puts pressure on each to seek out "offensive" materials. According to one ISP employee in Uzbekistan, the ISPs are not simply using URL address blocking. Some use so-called "smart technology" similar to the so-called "Great Firewall of China" (www.rsf.org, 2008).

Even in those less restrictive environments, Eurasia is far from seeing the Web influence an election the way the 2008 US presidential election was impacted, but there is some growth in Internet news readership, blogging, and YouTube viewing. YouTube videos of President Saakashvili chewing on his necktie, overwhelmed by emotion during the South Ossetia war, were an embarrassment for many Georgians despite their support for him.

Word-of-mouth is still a dominant news source, but likely online news could increase its word-of-mouth role in informing citizens. A teacher who has never used the Internet in rural Tajikistan shared that he tried to follow the war in Georgia through the media but had struggled because his access to information is limited. He relied on verbal reports from a friend, who knew how to use the Internet (Bekenova, 2008).

New Web 2.0 technology such as social networking sites and blogs is only beginning to find a niche for publishers and readers of alternative content. One group of students started an online discussion in Batumi, Georgia on Odnoklassniki.ru, one of the Russian-speaking world's most popular social networking websites. Russian media, which reaches most of Eurasia, offered a pro-Russia account of the conflict, whereas Georgian media contained its own bias. The online forum connected Georgian youth directly with 384 participants from Russia, Ukraine, Belarus, and Moldova. Students used the online forum in order to express their view on the military conflict, share firsthand information on the events that took place around them, and discuss the war and its consequences for the both countries. Without the Internet, these ordinary people would have had limited options for spreading information, photos, videos, and personal opinion. Evaluated more closely in a later section is the impact of local language content on Internet users in Eurasia.

INTERNET STUDY SCORING CONCLUSIONS

To conclude, one might look at the Eurasian countries' ability to navigate the broad list of factors examined here that have impeded or assisted in

Internet development and place them in one of three categories:

- *Toward Sustainable Internet Environments:* Ukraine, Kazakhstan, and Georgia have made the most progress in instilling the Internet as an information resource for the public sphere and should be expected to continue. Ukraine and Georgia have the most open, transparent, and democratic systems.
- *Measured Progress toward Sustainable Internet Environments:* Moldova, Uzbekistan, Belarus, Azerbaijan, and Kyrgyzstan have made progress in some of the key areas, but government, political, market, economic, and geological impediments need to be addressed. Azerbaijan has a stated policy of becoming an ICT hub for the Caucasus region, and it has more natural resources to prop up this goal, but the development is hindered by ineffective governance, corruption, and negligence of development outside Baku. Uzbeks benefit from affordable Internet, a decent Internet media, and educated society, but suffer from disastrous economic policies and unaccountable leadership. Kyrgyzstan has a core constituency of educated urbanites and a more open political environment, but is divided by terrain, clan, politics, and poverty. Belarus and Moldova enjoy the benefits of their locations along the borders with the EU and Internet connectivity prices are within reach of a larger segment of the population, but Belarus is hampered by authoritarianism and Moldova by its economy and tension with the breakaway region of Transnistria.
- *Unsustainable Internet Environments:* Tajikistan and Turkmenistan fall into the lowest category, though for different reasons. Tajikistan is the poorest nation in the former Soviet Union, burdened with the harshest terrain, and left with the worst infrastructure. Turkmenistan's entirely centralized system, low penetration, and low Internet relevance mean that there would still be great leaps to be undertaken to instill Internet as an information resource for the population. Without self-sustaining demand and advocates, the government has the power to continue to severely limit access, but it also possesses enough oil and gas revenue to make the major necessary investments for a relatively quick turnaround.

LOCALLY RELEVANT INTERNET

One of the most illuminating factors in the above analysis in determining the potential of the Internet to become an information resource is the relevance of the Internet to potential users.

Bilingual population segments in Eurasia, who know English or Russian, can find the content they need generally, but some countries are seeing a decline in foreign language knowledge. Owing to poor English instruction and learning environment, the number of English speakers in Eurasia is limited to students of English or younger people who managed to learn English through tutors, exposure to foreigners, time abroad, or a gift for learning. Most countries have maintained their Russian skills, but countries such as Georgia and Azerbaijan are not teaching their youth Russian.

A Google or Wikipedia search in Tajik will demonstrate that too few Tajiks are creating online content in the local Tajik language to support an increase in Tajik-speaking Web users. A teacher in Garm, Tajikistan, brought her students to the IATP center to browse information related to their studies, but she was quickly frustrated by her students' complaints. They only understood Tajik, and she needed to translate everything into Tajik, minimizing the students' ability to search and study on their own (Bekenova, 2008).

Google and Wikipedia are two of the most popular online resources in the world, and both have pages and content in relevant Eurasian languages. Search results in each language demonstrate a quantifiable and qualitative response to questions about the richness of local-language content. In general, the development of the usefulness of the Internet in a given language will generally mirror the quantity and relevance of hits returned by Google and the fullness and documentation of the topic's Wikipedia page.

One only needs to compare a few Google search results in order to understand the differences and thus compare on-the-ground relevance for the Internet in the languages of the 10 Eurasian republics. In Tajik or Turkmen, a search for the word "Seoul" returns few or no relevant results. In Georgian, Google returns 2,770 pages for "Seoul." In stark contrast to Eurasian national languages, Google.com in English returns millions of hits, images, current news, and useful links near the top of the results list. Russian search results on Google.ru are also generally useful.

English Wikipedia entries on a typical subject of study are usually several pages in length and contain dozens of images, scores of citations, and copious links to related articles. Many Eurasian national languages lack even basic information about a topic or suspiciously resemble old Soviet encyclopedia text.

The List of Wikipedias at http://meta.wikimedia.org/wiki/List_of_ Wikipedias orders Wikipedias by article count and provides a quantitative glimpse into local language content.

Of the 264 languages currently used for Wikipedia, the following local-language Wikipedias rank:

1. English
10. Russian
16. Ukrainian
18. Romanian (essentially the Moldovan language, but Moldovan has separate Wikipedia, which ranks 195)
49. Georgian
59. Azeri
72. Belarusian
87. Tajik
94. Uzbek
122. Kazakh
156. Turkmen
176. Kyrgyz
203. Karakalpak (spoken in Uzbekistan region).

For those using their national Eurasian languages, Moldovans and Ukrainians can probably find at least some useful information on nearly any typical research topic. Things get worse as one goes down this list. Some countries have nearly failed in the development of the Wikipedia as a source of information in the national language. At the same time, many of these countries would not have had a Wikipedia at all five years ago.

The gap that separates countries where Internet serves as a meaningful information resource and where it does not will not be easily closed. Content and usability will only get better everywhere; Web 2.0 will become Web 3.0, and countries that have done little to develop local-language Web 1.0 content face a problem not only of catching up but also of keeping up.

In addition to a language barrier, Eurasian countries are seeing problems of insufficient content about local conditions or context that is relevant to the people. For example, if one is seeking information about local business hours in Naryn, Kyrgyzstan, a phone call or two is more likely to yield an answer than a Google search in any language. People are less likely to turn to the Internet for answers online, because they are not there.

Generally, the more Internet users of one language a country has, the more creators of content it has. Governments can assist in breaking barriers to Internet adoption and thereby increase both users and content creators. Government, library, and education institutions can also drive content development, and user numbers increase by developing more and better online content and services.

More new content in a local language is not the only solution. Populations with more Russian speakers clearly have an advantage with content search, such as Kazakhstan, Belarus, and Ukraine, who are creating and consuming content of local interest. Nearly every country has ultranationalists who try to discourage Russian, and in some cases, they have come to power or passed legislation that has affected Russian used in education, government, and media. If Russian is maintained and not discouraged, it at least solves the need for a local-relevant Internet language.

Most countries are teaching English in schools, some from the first grade, but they need to improve teacher training, curricula, and offer more encounters with English, such as original language TV programming with subtitles instead of voice-over dubbing. Where English is widely spoken, as it is in Scandinavian countries, the Internet booms from users able to navigate in both languages. Countries such as Sweden outrank the United States on some Internet penetration figures.

The authors recognize the failure of this analysis to evaluate linguistic skills of Internet users or the percentage of Internet users and Russian-speaking users. Some results such as Kazakh's Wikipedia rating or failure to find many Kazakh-language websites likely reflect the correlation between Internet users in Kazakhstan who also know Russian, not the relevance of the Internet to people in Kazakhstan. Whether the growing use of Kazakh, but continued dominance of Russian, in Kazakhstan will affect Internet adoption can only be predicted with further analysis and study.

In addition, it is not clear how Wikipedia statistics are counted, since there are versions of Turkmen and Azeri that are spoken in Iraq and Iran, which use different alphabets that are not understood in Turkmenistan and Azerbaijan.

Nevertheless, the simple methodology of Google searching and perusing the List of Wikipedias does present a picture of local-language content availability.

CONCLUSIONS

Although the present situation provides a mixed picture for Internet as an information resource in Eurasia, Internet development is nearly inevitable. Standards of living are generally rising, infrastructure will improve, and technology will leap other barriers. Satellite access could solve lack of phone lines. The Great Firewall of China will constantly face grappling technology such as proxies. The Soviet Union created a culture that values education, literacy, and technology, but if older people of these countries lack the need or curiosity about technology and acquiring the skills necessary to use it, it is the younger generation that is already embracing it. More than half of IATP users are under the age of 25. Equal gender opportunity was also valued, and females in Muslim Uzbekistan are more likely to become Internet users than their counterparts in Afghanistan. Indeed, about half of IATP users in Uzbekistan are women.

Even those countries making limited progress toward sustainable Internet environments show enough strength in a combination of several sectors, including market deregulation, open political discourse, rapid economic growth, and exposure to international content from outside sources, to permit cautious optimism. Although progress will not be as fast as it should be, it will probably come.

However, there are risks that countries will face delayed development. Turkmenistan and Tajikistan are countries where there are too few users who would miss the Internet and strongly advocate for it, if it were taken away. A nervous government might choose to strangle information resources that would include Internet if it felt threatened. Given the common "president for life" democracies in Central Asia and Azerbaijan, a shaky transition could harm a country's or entire region's development. Other countries dependent on the world economy could face needs to reduce government expenditures on necessary infrastructure development and library and school programs if the ubiquitous gloomy economic predictions for the next few years are realized.

The work of programs such as IATP has contributed to solving the access, training, and content shortfalls in Eurasia that limit broader Internet adoption as a primary information resource. How closely citizens embrace the Internet will depend on a momentum of computer- and Internet-literacy. In order to monitor trends and success toward Internet adoption, the following factors will indicate the extent to which the Internet fills the public information needs of the citizens:

1. *Rate of generating more ICT users.* The Internet will be relevant once everyone from powerful government officials to unemployed villagers have the access and skills they currently lack.
2. *Rate of generating more Web content.* Once businessmen, journalists, librarians, students, teachers, governments, and NGO officials are

creating new Internet content with information they desire to share already, they will perpetuate a positive cycle that meets their needs and the needs of local Internet users.

3. *Rate of investment in people and resources at public information institutions.* The more governments invest in improving libraries, schools, universities, and public services, the more likely they are to include Internet as a part of these initiatives.

4. *Improvement of policy, planning, and environment.* Governments that do a better job with infrastructure development, ICT initiatives such as e-government, telecom and ISP deregulation, open business and trading environments, freedom of media and expression, and encouragement of civil society. This will create a better atmosphere in which Internet can become more affordable, accessible, and relevant.

To conclude, everyone needs information, but the degree to which information is needed and accessible or freely expressed varies. Improved democracy will increase but not guarantee a greater value on information. Once Eurasian cultures undergo more soul searching and reach a stage of development that is higher than basic survival, it will become clearer as to whether the cultures embrace the Information Age as much as the West has and what role the Internet will serve.

NOTE

1. The primary source for the index was an internal IREX assessment conducted by the authors and their colleagues on the ground in each country in October 2008. Their names and sources they used are found in the References list.

REFERENCES

Bekenova, E., Focus Group Moderator. (November 2008). Users of the Internet: Khamadoni Muzafarov, Iqbola Alijeva, Savriniso Khavizova, Bakhtjer Sirozov & Mansur Khajotov. Garm, Tajikistan, October 22, 2008. Internet Access and Training Program administered by IREX and funded by USAID.

Bekenova, E., Focus Group Moderator. (October 2008). Ten anonymous users of the Internet. Bishkek, Kyrgyzstan, September 8, 2008. Internet Access and Training Program administered by IREX and funded by USAID.

Bekenova, E., Focus Group Moderator. (November 2008). Users of the Internet: Amirali
    Siyovuim, Djalon Umarov, Aziz Izatzoda, Parvizi A., Davlatyor Mubarakkadamov,
    Bakhtiyor Nadjmiddilov, Zamira Kolonova, Sattor Davlatov, Khusenzod Sazdi,
    Rukiya Pirimsho & Mikhail Azranzade. Dushanbe, Tajikistan, October 20, 2008.
    Internet Access and Training Program administered by IREX and funded by
    USAID.
Bekenova, E., Focus Group Moderator. (November 2008). Non-users of the Internet:
    Mirzodavlat Shorafov, Kienurdin Shaev & Nuship Nallaev. Garm, Tajikistan, October
    22, 2008. Internet Access and Training Program administered by IREX and funded by
    USAID.
Bertot, J. C., McClure, C. R., Jaeger, P. T., & Ryan, J. (2006). *Public libraries and the Internet
    2006: Study results and findings*, September. For: The Bill and Melinda Gates
    Foundation and The American Library Association. Available at http://www.ii.fsu.edu/
    projectFiles/plinternet/2006/2006_plinternet.pdf
Cronin, R., Katz, A., & Guard, C. (2008). Assessment for country grant: Global Libraries
    Initiative, July. Ukraine. Submitted by IREX to The Bill & Melinda Gates
    Foundation.

References List for the Index on the Status of Internet in Eurasia

Amansakhatov, Azimova, Balmus, Bekenova, Davlatshoev, Mytkytsey, Naimov, Solodkov,
    Tevadze, & Zarukaeva (2008). A primary source for the index entitled "Status
    of Internet in Eurasia" was an internal assessment conducted by the authors and their
    colleagues at on the ground in each country in October 2008. Status of Internet
    Assessment. Additionally, this team and the authors participated in a Consulta-
    tive Meeting on the Establishment of a Network of Telecenters in Central Asia,
    in Baku, Azerbaijan in on May 6–7, 2008. Information gathered at this meeting
    of NGOs and government representatives in the ICT sector contributed to this
    study.
OpenNet Initiative CIS Country Profiles. Available at http://opennet.net/research/region/cis.
    Retrieved on November 5, 2009.
CIA World Factbook. Available at http://www.cia.gov/publications/the-world-factbook/geos/
    az.html/. Retrieved on October 20, 2008.
The Internet Coaching Library. *Internet world statistics: Usage and population statistics.*
    Available at www.internetworldstats.com. Retrieved on October 30, 2008.
Wikipedia.org List of Wikipedias. Available at meta.wikipedia.org/wiki/List_of_Wikipedias.
    Retrieved on November 11, 2008.
International Telecommunications Union. *ITU global view.* Available at www.itu.int/ITU-D/
    connect/gblview/index.html. Retrieved on November 2, 2008.
Reporters without Borders. *Internet enemies.* Available at www.rsf.org. Retrieved on November
    2, 2008.
Gallup.com. *Russian language enjoying a boost in post-soviet states*, August 1, 2008. Available
    at http://www.gallup.com/poll/109228/Russian-Language-Enjoying-Boost-PostSoviet-States.
    aspx. Retrieved on November 8, 2008.

Global Internet Policy Initiative. Available at www.internetpolicy.net. Retrieved on October 15, 2008.
Computer Industry Almanac. Available at www.c-i-a.com. Retrieved on October 12, 2008.

Azerbaijan

Law of Azerbaijan on Mass Media. Adopted on December 7, 1999.
Decree of the President of Azerbaijan no. 1146. On the Establishment of a National Strategy on ICT.
Day.az. Azerbaijani Internet: ISPs can provide VoIP services, January 29, 2007. Accessed October 28, 2008.

Belarus

Belarus Telecom High-Speed Internet Division. Available at http://Byfly.by/. Retrieved on October 19, 2008.
BelTelecom. Available at http://beltelecom.by/company/about/. Retrieved on October 19, 2008.
The Internet and Elections: The 2006 presidential election in Belarus. ONI Internet Watch. Available at http://www.opennetinitiative.net/belarus/. Retrieved on October 20, 2008.

Georgia

Magradze, M. (2008). Internet development tendencies in Georgia. *Georgian Journal of Economics and Business*, 3, 37–40.
Ministry of Education and Science. Available at http://www.dlf.ge/en/
http://www.idg-georgia.org.ge/statistics.html

Kazakhstan

UNESCO Cluster Office for Kazakhstan, Kyrgyzstan, Tajikistan and Uzbekistan, Communication and Information Themes. Available at www.unesco.kz/?sector = Communicationand Information&lang = . Retrieved on October 27, 2008.
Organization for Security and Cooperation in Europe. *Governing the Internet*. Available at www.osce.org/publications/rfm/2007/07/25667_918_en.pdf. Retrieved on October 28, 2008.
Organization for Security and Cooperation in Europe Centre in Astana, Media Development Department. Available at www.osce.org/astana/19100.html. Retrieved on October 28, 2008.
National Library of the Republic of Kazakhstan. Available at www.nlrk.kz. Retrieved on October 27, 2008.
KazakhTelecom. Available at http://portal.telecom.kz/

Kyrgyzstan

http://press-uz.info
KyrgyzTelecom.
Bekenova discussions with staff of the National Library of Kyrgyzstan. October 26, 2008.
24 Kyrgyzstan News Service. Available at www.24.kg
Center for Internet Policy Initiatives (CIPI) in Kyrgyzstan.

Moldova

National Regulatory Agency for Telecommunications and Informatics (ANRTI).
Staff discussions with Moldtelecom, Starnet, Sun Communications, and Moldova Business Survey.

Tajikistan

Staff discussions with Ministry of Communications and Transport, Center for Internet Policy
    Initiatives, (CIPI) in Tajikistan, TajikTelecom, Library of the National Academy of
    Sciences, American Councils, Firdavsi National Library, and Association of Tajikistani
    ISPs.
Aslitdinova, Alla on "Concept for Libraries' Electronic Resources Development." Concept
    paper submitted to the government, October 2006.
Resolution of the Government of Tajikistan No. 188, June 6, 2005. On the Implementation and
    Development of IT in the Tajik Language.
Asia Plus News Service. Available at www.asiaplus.tj

Turkmenistan

Supreme Council on Science and Technology under the President of Turkmenistan. Virtual Silk
    Highway Program. Available at www.science.gov.tm. Retrieved on October 25, 2008.
United Nations Development Program. InfoTuk Project. Discussions with staff from InfoTuk.
Staff discussions with Private telecommunications firm MTC.

Ukraine

Scribd.com. Ukrainian Internet market overview. Available at http://www.scribd.com/doc/
    11602723/Ukrainian-Internet-market-Overview. Retrieved on November 1, 2008.
Ukraine Telecom. Available at www.ukraine-telecom.com. Retrieved on October 27, 2008.
IREX. *Assessment of Ukrainian Libraries conducted in response to the Gates Foundation Global
    Libraries Program Request for Proposals for Ukraine*, June 2008.
IREX. *Assessment of Internet as an information resource in Crimea*, August 2008. Conducted at
    the request of the United States Agency for International Development.
www.c-i-a.com

Uzbekistan

UZInfoCom Center for Development of ICT. Available at www.uzinfocom.uz/services/ examination/. Retrieved on October 28, 2008.

ICT Development in 2007 in Uzbekistan. Available at www.aci.uz. Retrieved on October 28, 2008.

Uzbekistan Agency for Communications and Information. Available at www.aci.uz/ru/news/ uzaci/article/807/. Retrieved on October 22, 2008.

United Nations Development Project UzSciNet.net. Available at www.uzscinet.net. Retrieved on October 28, 2008.

Ferghana News Service. Available at www.Ferghana.ru. Retrieved on October 22, 2008.

WHY STUDY UP? THE ELITE APPROPRIATION OF SCIENCE, INSTITUTION, AND TOURISM AS A DEVELOPMENT AGENDA IN MARAMUREŞ, ROMANIA [☆]

Catherine Closet-Crane, Susan Dopp, Jacqueline Solis and James M. Nyce

ABSTRACT

This chapter argues that including "studying up" (Nader, 1969), a close attention to elites and hierarchy, into the Library and Information Science (LIS) research agenda will strengthen the research the LIS community carries out on information behavior and use. Looking at issues that interest Nader, (i.e., the role class and inequity play in social life), this chapter reviews and critiques LIS user studies. The chapter then illustrates the value this approach can have for LIS researchers.

[☆]An earlier version of this chapter "The Past Is Our Only Industry: The Legitimization of Cultural Tourism in Maramureş, Romania" was presented by Catherine Closet-Crane at Walls and Bridges: Refiguring "Socialist" and "Postsocialist" Spaces in a Deterritorializing World (2006 Soyuz Symposium), Bryant University, Smithfield, RI, March 3–5.

Advances in Library Administration and Organization, Volume 27, 221–238
Copyright © 2009 by Emerald Group Publishing Limited
All rights of reproduction in any form reserved
ISSN: 0732-0671/doi:10.1108/S0732-0671(2009)0000027016

Fieldwork recently carried out in Maramureş, Romania, suggests that the cooption of science (both its authority and institutions) at local levels has helped the elite legitimatize and profit from cultural tourism as a development strategy. This research also suggests that the differential (elite) access to and use of information and knowledge especially when tied to local institutions and practices of science have been neglected in the analysis of change in post socialist states.

INTRODUCTION

The number of user studies the library and information sceince (LIS) research community produces seems to increase every year. These studies differ from each other in methodology, theory employed, and in the set of users whose information needs, requirements, and behaviors are surveyed. Having said that, the user studies LIS researchers publish tend to fall into one of two categories. Of the two, the largest by number represents a cluster of different occupational groups. However, not all occupations have received equal attention. Nor have all workers been surveyed to the same extent. There is in fact a marked preference to study the information behavior of high status professionals (Andrews, Pearce, Ireson, & Love, 2005; Cole & Kuhlthau, 2000; Gorman, 1995; Haug, 1997; Leckie, Pettigrew & Sylvain, 1996, Sutton, 1994, among others). The second set of users, a smaller set, tends to be just the opposite. In this set, we can place underrepresented demographic classes (Chatman, 1999, 1991). We can also include here those whose work the middle class tends not to value (see particularly Chatman, 1996, 1992, 1990, 1987). It is also difficult to find any LIS research that looks carefully at the interaction that can occur between these two different groups of information users: This topic will be discussed however at some length here. There is still another set of users seldom seen as forming a class by itself; these we might call inadvertent or accidental users – ones whose information needs and behaviors are not "full time" (Radhika & Wiedenbeck, 1993). An example of accidental information use might be public library patron requests.

It seems that LIS researchers prefer to study high status (and by extension expert) work. What is not clear is whether the LIS research community is aware of the consequences this has had for what we know about information behavior and requirements/needs. It is also not clear, while we studied high status work and workers, that we have learned what we need to know about the role hierarchy plays in defining information needs, requirements, and behavior. In the LIS research community's discussions of information behavior and requirements, the focus has been on status and occupation more than on the significance that hierarchy per se has in determining information behavior. In short, there is a paradox at work here. Although the literature on users is biased in direction of high status professionals, little attention has been paid to the role hierarchy plays in defining information behavior and need within a society.

In particular, we have not acknowledged that the high status groups LIS research tends to be preoccupied with represent a category, the elite, and that they need to be treated and discussed as such. The result is that we know less than we should about the role important social and cultural categories such as class play in information behavior and requirements. (For a discussion of the role class plays here, see Sennett & Cobb, 1972.) Furthermore, when we do mention class and hierarchy, we tend to do so only in reference to low status, working class life and work. The inverse occurs when the middle class is discussed: The LIS literature tends to treat middle classness as the natural order of things. In short, the LIS literature seldom acknowledges that middle classness and that the information behaviors associated with it also results from a particular, historical determined set of sociological, read hierarchical, operations. For example, we would be hard pressed to find a single study published by a LIS researcher that explicitly links hierarchy and class position to information behavior with any analytic precision.

When LIS researchers do talk about class, they tend not to acknowledge that class by definition implies inequity or that the social order does not always operate in the best interests of all those who participate in it. Instead we talk about equity or participation. For examples of this, see discussions of equal access in system design that invoke ideas of social justice (Cogburn, 2004; van den Hoven, 1995; Smith, 2001). However, the best and most pervasive example of this tendency can be found in the LIS research and policy discussions that focus on the "digital divide" (e.g., Floridi, 2000; Di Maggio & Hargittai, 2001; Norris, 2001; Warschauer, 2003; Rogerson, 2004) or information poverty (Britz, 2004). Here, while we acknowledge "difference" we do so in ways that do not allow us to get analytic purchase on how and why class and hierarchy "matter" when it comes to information behavior and use.

To correct this (and to demonstrate why this is an important area of research), we will for the rest of this chapter discuss the value "studying up" (Nader, 1969) can have for LIS researchers. This is an important issue if only because there is strong empirical evidence that power and wealth are being concentrated more and more in the hands of a few. The same is true when it comes to knowledge and information.

To understand how information and knowledge actually "work" in society, it is necessary to acknowledge the link that exists between power, hierarchy, and knowledge. This is what Nader means by "studying up": This kind of intellectual project is a quite different one than what LIS researchers have so far undertaken in respect to highly valued occupations. Obviously, the best place to study this set of interactions is where it occurs most often and most obviously, and that is in the upper class and the elite. In fact, without being aware of it, because LIS researchers have not "studied up," it can be argued that the LIS research community has inadvertently served the class interests of the elite. This is because the research the LIS community has done on information/knowledge transfer has either ignored or mystified the central role hierarchy plays in defining how knowledge and information gets acquired, disseminated, and used in modern western societies.

There are at least two arguments for why LIS should take on this project. One is a political one. Given the LIS profession's long-standing commitment to access and equal opportunity in respect to information, we have an obligation to try to identify, understand, and "compensate" for those mechanisms that stand in the way of social equity. The second, while related to the first, has to do with science. Unless LIS researchers take into account all those social markers that constitute, inform, and drive modern complex societies, the maps we draw and the interrelations we posit between knowledge and information and other important features of society will be skewed and incomplete.

LITERATURE REVIEW

More than 10 years ago Pawley (1998) argued that the LIS research community has not paid much attention to either class or hierarchy. Regrettably, the situation has not changed, and this has weakened the kinds of statements we as LIS researchers can make about knowledge and information use in society. Pawley unfortunately did not focus on the consequence this has had for LIS user studies – perhaps the discipline's most important research genre. Referring to Michael Harris's (1996), "State, class, and cultural reproduction: Toward a theory of library service in the United States," Pawley criticizes his theoretical framework for "failing to distinguish a separate managerial perspective." Unfortunately, the argument she makes in her paper regarding pluralism and manageralism diverts the reader's attention away from the issue of class. In effect Pawley sabotages her own effort to bring class to the attention of the LIS research community. Nor did she propose any kind of research agenda that might help us sort out the differential effect(s) pluralism, manageralism or class might have on each other or on information use and behavior within society. This weakened her paper and the argument Pawley makes about the important role class plays in information behavior.

In Harris's 1986 essay, perhaps the first to introduce a class perspective to LIS studies, he first defines the "pluralist paradigm that guide[d] ... research" (p. 212) in LIS in the United States up to the time of writing, then critiques the limitations of "the pluralist paradigm" (p. 212), and finally proposes a theory of library service that incorporates a class perspective. Citing Stuart Hall (1982, cited in Harris, p. 217), and Vincent Mosco (1982, cited in Harris, p. 217), Harris introduces issues of class, power, and hierarchy to LIS studies and concludes:

> The pluralist perspective so widely and uncritically adopted by librarians has dictated long and broad structured silences relative to the ways in which social, economic, and cultural power relations shape the nature and extent of library service in America. (p. 221)

To remedy this, Harris proposes to draw "from a variety of disciplines and ... [proceed] analogically from problem solutions in the social sciences to similar, but unsolved problems in library science" (1989, p. 222). Reviewing theories of the state, ideological hegemony, and cultural reproduction, Harris refers to Milibrand's critique of the conception of the state as a neutral agent (Harris, 1986, p. 223), Carnoy's "class perspective analysis of the state" (p. 223), Gramsci's understanding of the relationship between culture and power and his concept of "ideological hegemony" (pp. 223–224), Williams' concept of "selective tradition" (p. 225), Gitlin's concept of "frames" (p. 226); Gandy, Bartlett, and Wilson's research on "the ways in which powerful political and economic forces can dramatically influence decisions on what is news and the character of that news" (p. 227), Kellner's division of the ideological landscape into four "ideological regions" or realms – economic, political, social and cultural – (p. 228), and Gans's hierarchical categorization of "five taste cultures: high, upper-middle, lower-middle, low, and quasifolk low cultures" and his synopsis of the critique of mass culture (p. 229). Harris also refers to Carey's definition of an "anticanonical" research tradition in the book scholarship in which "the equation linking the book and literacy with wisdom and progress is seen as part of a complex ideology that justified the technology of printing as it served the interests of those who controlled it" (p. 230); Lentriccia's definitions of "the will to power" and "the systematic act of tradition-making" which allows the reproduction of "social hierarchy and political domination by passing along a dominant culture" (p. 231); Larson's work on the sociology of the professions (p. 233); and finally Bourdieu's work on the "reproduction of culture" and his notion of "cultural capital" (pp. 237–238). Despite this extensive review of the literature, which Harris claims will inform a theory of library service in the United States, he does not give us in this paper anything that resembles a research or intellectual agenda. What Harris provides instead is some 26 propositions (aphorisms) about libraries, librarians, library users, library management, and the social order.

In short, although Harris does acknowledge that hierarchy "matters" when it comes to information use and behavior, he, like Pawley, does so in ways that do not allow us to get any firm analytic purchase on the important role hierarchy plays in this domain of social life. To correct this, we will demonstrate here the yield "studying up" (Nader, 1969) can have for LIS researchers and the LIS research literature.

In searching for other discussions of power and elites in regard to knowledge and information production, access, and use, we reviewed the LIS literature from the early 1990s through the present. Extensive database searches were carried out using alternative search terms such as class, middle class, upper class, social class and "classe sociale," ruling class, elite, intellectual elite, power elite, political elite, "nomenklatura," and establishment. These searches did not return many results; the few found were not particularly relevant given this paper's endpoints.

So we narrowed our search "universe" to user studies by occupational groups. What we found was that user studies of high status professionals dominate the recent LIS literature. After Leckie et al. (1996), research has been published on the information needs and seeking behavior of lawyers (Haruna & Mabawonku, 2001; Kuhlthau & Tama, 2001; Wilkinson, 2001; Otike, 1999), healthcare practitioners (Andrews et al., 2005; Owen & Fang, 2003; Gorman, 1995), clinical research coordinators (Wessel, Tannery, & Epstein, 2006), veterinarians (Wales, 2000), educators (Herman, 2004; MacMullen, Vaughan, & Moore, 2004; Quigley, Church, & Peterson, 2001; Bates, Wilde, & Siegfried, 1993; Grefsheim, Franklin, & Cunningham, 1991), finance and securities analysts (Kuhlthau, 1999; Spies, Clayton, & Noormohammadian, 2005), and executives and managers (Auster & Choo, 1991, 1993, 1994; Baldwin & Rice, 1997; Choo & Auster, 1991; Drucker, 1995; Ellis, Allen, & Wilson, 1999; Ginman, 1988; Katzer & Fletcher, 1992; Mackenzie, 2004; Mick, Lindsey, & Callahan, 1980; Rockart, 1979, 1982; Wolek, 1984, 1986; Zach, 2005).

However, although these user studies often included discussions of the relationship between information/knowledge production and use, little reference was made in any of them to class, hierarchy, or power. The most relevant articles came from the international LIS literature (Marshall & Brady, 2001; Frohmann, 1994; Van Der Linde, 1990). For example, Sturges (1998) directly acknowledges the link between information and power in his paper on Malawi. Sturges states:

> In fact, if the contention that information is power were reversed to say "Power is information" it might better reflect reality. From this perspective, only what is generated by power relations has the status of information, and only through the exercise of power is the effect of information achieved. This draws attention to the underlying political economy of information: the ways in which power defines information, delimits it, governs its availability, pre-structures its effect. (p. 186)

Sturges found that "the political economy of information can be seen in particularly stark outline in the context of developing countries" (p. 186), an argument that our research in rural Romania supports.

However, to find empirical-based discussions of the relationships between hierarchy, knowledge, and power, one has to turn to the social science literature and to journals and texts such as *Higher Education* (Kogan, 2005); *International Social Science Journal* (Stehr, 2003); *International Studies Quarterly* (Dimitrov, 2003); *Journal of Strategic Studies* (Lonsdale, 1999); *Medical Anthropology Quarterly* (Rasmussen, 2000); and *Knowledge, Space, Economy* (Allen, 2000).

Nevertheless no one since Nader has argued that "studying up" be given priority. Some social scientists have published on the same topic; for a recent review of this literature see Shore (2002). However, no one else has written as well as Nader on the issues "studying up" raises for how researchers understand the social world. It is clear that this research has to focus on the link(s) that exist between power, hierarchy, and knowledge, and although this has been pointed out again and again in the literature social scientists produce on the elite, still little research has been done on these issues (Herzfeld, 2000). This is largely because of the lack of interest social scientists, especially anthropologists, have shown in material and expressive instantiations of knowledge like information.

METHODOLOGY

This research, analysis, and write-up are informed by the Anglo-American tradition of ethnography (Whipple & Nyce, 2007). The methods used in the field included informal and formal interviews and participant observation.

A series of community surveys, document analysis, and a literature review (pre and post entry) were also done. Artifacts and printed material were collected for analysis; still photography and video recordings were used to record aspects of community life.

Context

Data were collected in rural areas of Maramureş, a northwest region of Romania bordering Ukraine, for 15 days in May 2005. (Nyce has also conducted fieldwork in Romania in summers 2003, 2004, 2007, and 2008.) Researchers included three cultural anthropologists from two American universities, and 14 graduate and undergraduate students in library/information science, classics, and anthropology from a number of American universities. Researchers focused on issues of information access and transfer, information technology and delivery paths, and information technology implementation choices. Individual and group interviews were recorded on audiotape and augmented by field notes. Transcriptions of the audiotapes and of field notes were prepared, shared, discussed, and analyzed by group members. Video recordings, photographs, artifacts, and printed material were also collected, discussed, and analyzed.

Participants

The participants in the interviews were predominantly rural villagers: farmers, storeowners, teachers, school principal, doctors, nurses, priests, artists, and artisans; the mayor and the chief of police of the commune (the local administrative district) were also interviewed. Field observations of local public libraries were done, and library personnel were interviewed. The researchers also visited two museums in an urban center and interviewed their directors. All interviewees agreed to participate and have their interviews audio taped.

Procedure

To collect qualitative information, researchers used data elicitation methods common in cultural anthropology. Interviews were conducted with the help of three translators: two males (a father and son) with family ties to the village who spoke English well enough to translate questions and responses; and one female, a guide who spoke English well. Two of the translators had received a university education in Romania; the younger male is still pursuing his studies. The woman was not a village member; she had a university degree in tourism and historical preservation. The researchers' host family was a "portal" to the community and helped identify and make contact with potential informants. To expand the pool of informants, researchers snowballed both informants and interview topics. The translators, especially the father and son, also gave us access to informants outside the community where we stayed. Nyce collected additional data in the village and region in December 2006 and Summer 2007.

Interviews typically lasted an hour and followed the pattern described below. Through an interpreter, one person (generally a faculty member) introduced the members of the interviewing group and described the project's research agenda. Participants were asked whether the interview could be recorded and were assured of the confidentiality of their responses. Often, translators would discuss their answers with participants before translating; they also frequently would just summarize or paraphrase what informants had told them unless researchers intervened.

Data Analysis

A first pass at field data found that many of the themes we collected data on fell into the following areas: information transfer among community members, debates about modernization and tradition, concern about upcoming accession to the European Union, and selection of appropriate rural development strategies. While reviewing the literature on the Maramureş, we found that much of the recent work that discusses these issues has been published in the geography and tourism literature (Hall, 2000, 2004; Muica, Roberts, & Turnock, 1998; Muica & Turnock, 2000; Ploaie & Turnock, 2001; Turnock, 2002). However, this literature tends to portray rural development issues in relatively unproblematic, (i.e., utilitarian), pragmatic terms and to argue that cultural tourism in "post socialist" states such as Romania is an effective way to "bootstrap" (leverage) rural populations into the "modern" world.

A second pass at field data led us to the issue of how local elites use both information agencies/institutions and information itself to define and set the economic development agenda for the Maramureş region. Although there has been much discussion of how elite in post socialistic states have profited from public assets, these analyses have paid little attention to "intangible" or intellectual assets such as scientific knowledge (see for example Walder, 2003). Some has been written on how the Romanian state prior to the 1989 revolution "deformed" science but this is another matter (Kligman, 1998; Turda, 2007a, 2007b). What we found in Maramureş is that local elites mirrored (co-opted) the same languages found in the geography/tourism literature, (e.g. a relatively naive neoliberal, free market discourse) and that of science to argue for one particular rural development strategy.

THE LEGITIMIZATION OF CULTURAL TOURISM: THE ECOLOGICAL SOCIETY OF MARAMUREŞ

Romania, as part of its Local Agenda 21 compliance planning, has embraced ecotourism as a form of sustainable development supported by the United Nations. Local Agenda 21 is the mandate given to local governments within the larger Agenda 21 sustainable development program, which was adopted at the 1992 Earth Summit in Rio de Janeiro. This emphasis on ecotourism is encouraged and supported at the regional and local levels by the United Nations Environment Programme (UNEP, 2003) and International Council for Local Environmental Initiatives (ICLEI)-Local Governments for Sustainability. ICLEI in particular serves an important role in the dissemination of knowledge and lessons learned regarding Local Agenda 21 implementation among its members, which includes Baia Mare, Romania, where groups such as the Ecological Society of Maramureş have incorporated the push for ecotourism as part of their ecology program.

The Ecological Society of Maramureş (Societatea Ecologista din Maramureş) is a non-governmental regional organization based in Baia Mare whose charge is to help protect biodiversity in the region. The Ecological Society membership (and collaborators with the Society) have included the local elite. Among its membership have been members of the Romanian Parliament, educators, and local professionals.

The group's stated objectives are education about environmental protection, identification and limitation of sources of pollution, and maintenance of relations with similar organizations; but the group also has an agenda of promoting tourism and the traditional customs of the region. One of the group's objectives is the organization of "symposia, competitions, expositions and other activities on themes of ecology, protection of flora and fauna, and the folklore and traditional customs of Maramureş"

(Societatea Ecologista din Maramureş, 2003). Additionally, the group's website lists areas of responsibility including consulting for the preparation of projects to implement eco-tourism and the development of ecologic tourism, eco-tourism, agrotourism, and forestry tourism. Services the group provide include the creation and implementation of tourist route signs, consulting for conservation and biodiversity projects, and the organization of conferences, one of which was devoted to cultural tourism (Primăria Municipiului Baia Mare, 2005; Societatea Ecologista din Maramureş, 2003). The Society has done consulting for the Ministry of Environment and Water Management with the Maramureş County Council and the local EPA for the Maramureş Natural Park project (GEF, 2005). The Society is a sub-contractor in a Global Environment Facility (GEF) grant, of which one goal is to make eco/cultural tourism one of the top three industries in Maramureş by the year 2008 (GEF, 2005). The Society has also published on its website a guide for behavior of persons working in tourism and a catalog listing the location of some 78 private ecological rural tourism facilities in Maramureş (Primăria Municipiului Baia Mare, 2005).

The Society's focus on ecotourism is especially noteworthy given that the area around the city in which the Society is located has had severe industrial pollution due to mine runoff (Guzelova & Wright, 2000; Monbiot, 2000; Purvis, 2001). It is also worth noting that small-scale farmers in rural regions of Maramureş have the option to receive state grants as an incentive to replace traditional fertilizers with more modern (chemical) alternatives produced by foreign agribusinesses. It seems these two areas would be likely areas of concern for an ecological society, but instead the group is concentrating much of its efforts on the development of cultural tourism.

For example, the Ecological Society of Maramureş together with the local government of the commune of Ocna Sugatag co-sponsored "The Festival of Local Traditions and Conservation of Biodiversity" in 2004. Among the presentations given by professors and academics during this three-day festival were "Tourism: Principal source of earnings for inhabitants: Authorization of farms and agrotouristic pensions," "Ecologic education: Determining factor in development of tourism," and "The socio-economic-scientific importance of natural monuments in Maramureş" (NGO.ro, 2004). The mayor of the Ocna Sugatag commune also presented, "The Historic Maramureşean Hearth," at this festival (NGO.ro).

In rural Maramureş, we observed first hand "the survival" of traditional ways of life, which is made possible not only because villagers hold on to their customs but because it is also encouraged through what appears to be a coordinated public/private effort at preserving tradition. Supported by state and regional policies as well as international NGOs (such as UNESCO, Open Society Institute and Soros Foundation and Swiss Arts Council), local politicians and cultural elites utilize a network of national, regional, and local institutions such as museums (for example, the National Museum Complex in Sibiu, the Museum of the Romanian Peasant in Bucharest, or the Ethnographic Museum and Village Museum of Sighetu Marmatiei), cultural foundations, family associations, and other types of organizations as agents for the marketing and commodification of Maramureş peasant life and traditional culture.

We discovered in our field work in Romania that one of the goals of maintaining this traditional life is to market traditional villages as cultural tourism destinations. Rural residents of Maramureş county have a desire to maintain their traditional customs and ways of life, and the "elite" have access to information that will allow them to promote this traditional life while profiting from it.

DISCUSSION

The people of Maramureş for the most part are small-scale, rural farmers. As such, even in today's "information age," they are vulnerable to the effects of differential access to information. The result can be, among others, inequities in accessing opportunities such as sources of funding, available land grants, or agriculture-related information. But all too quickly discussions like these can turn to issues of motivation, volition, and self-interest. In other words, it is too easy to take a "normative" or "psychological" turn here. Rather than go in this direction, we need to ask questions about how constraint, opportunity, and success can be defined and negotiated through local resources and social institutions. For example, the literature has paid little attention to how local traditions, institutions, and cultural resources (especially knowledge and information) can be appropriated by a region's elite to legitimate and justify a particular economic development strategy.

In the recent literature on Maramureş, local elites and their institutions are often treated as a monolith whose actions only either embrace or impede the hegemony of Western cultural and financial institutions. This misreads how the historio-cultural processes we call modernization and legitimation have played out in the region. In particular, it has obscured the role that the differential access to information and knowledge can have in framing which development strategy, regardless of its "objective" benefits, is seen as more credible or legitimate than another.

Here we have looked at the role of elite institutions in this process, including those, like scientific foundations, that common sense generally tells us have little to do with setting economic priorities for a region. We focused on local institutions and local practices because after the 1989 revolution these were reinvented and given new meaning and roles. In Maramureş, they were deployed to make an argument about what the future should "be" in reference to economic development.

What we observed in Maramureş suggests that, for local agents and actors, capitalism and socialism are not so much binaries or opposites (ideologically or pragmatically) but are instead resources that are used to argue for, legitimate, and implement one modernization strategy rather than another. In Maramureş, a diverse, seemingly divergent set of elite institutions, idioms and practices came to support (and validate) a single economic and modernization strategy – cultural tourism. What interests us is how one view, is a minority opinion regarding modernization and the future of the region, has become not just consensus but "reality" itself.

CONCLUSION

The material we collected in Romania shows the benefit "studying up" can have for both LIS researchers and the LIS research literature. If we are to understand how information and knowledge "work" in society, it is necessary to make explicit the links that exist between power, hierarchy, and knowledge. Furthermore, as the example of the Ecological Society of Maramureş shows, the best place to study this interaction is where it occurs most often and most obviously, and that is in elite institutions and among the upper class.

If the LIS research community does not add "studying up" to its agenda, LIS researchers will continue to neglect the role that hierarchy and class have in information behavior. This in turn will, however inadvertently, help perpetuate and legitimatize certain class agendas and interests. Perhaps it is time for the LIS research community to look at how the hierarchy defines how knowledge and information are acquired, disseminated, and used. Of particular interest here is how the role hierarchy plays in the production of knowledge and information in modern western societies has been both ignored and mystified.

ACKNOWLEDGMENTS

We wish to thank the audience at the 2006 Soyuz Symposium for their comments. We also thank Janine Golden, William Graves III, and Delmus Williams for their help on this manuscript.

REFERENCES

Allen, J. (2000). Power/economic knowledge: Symbolic and spatial formations. In: J. R. Bryson, P. W. Daniels, N. Henry & J. Pollard (Eds), *Knowledge, space, economy* (pp. 15–33). London and New York: Routledge.

Andrews, J., Pearce, K., Ireson, C., & Love, M. (2005). Information-seeking behaviors of practitioners in a primary care practice-based research network. *Journal of the Medical Library Association, 93*(2), 206–212.

Auster, E., & Choo, C. W. (1991). Environmental scanning: A conceptual framework for studying the information seeking behavior of executives. In: J. M. Griffiths (Ed.), *Proceedings of the 54th ASIS Annual Meeting (ASIS 1991)* (pp. 3–8). Medford, NJ: Learned Information.

Auster, E., & Choo, C. W. (1993). Environmental scanning by CEOs in two Canadian industries. *Journal of the American Society for Information Science, 44*(4), 194–203.

Auster, E., & Choo, C. W. (1994). How senior managers acquire and use information in environmental scanning. *Information Processing and Management, 30*(5), 607–618.

Baldwin, N. S., & Rice, R. E. (1997). Information-seeking behavior of securities analysts: Individual and institutional influences, information sources and channels, and outcomes. *Journal of the American Society for Information Science, 48*(8), 674–693.

Bates, M. J., Wilde, D. N., & Siegfried, S. L. (1993). An analysis of search terminology used by humanities scholars: The Getty Online Searching Project report number 1. *The Library Quarterly, 63*(January), 1–39.

Britz, J. (2004). To know or not to know: A moral reflection on information poverty. *Journal of Information Science, 30*(3), 192–204. Retrieved July 3, 2006, from EBSCO.

Chatman, E. A. (1987). The information world of low skilled workers. *LISR, 9*, 265–283.

Chatman, E. A. (1990). Alienation theory: Application of a conceptual framework to a study of information among janitors. *RQ, 29*(3), 355–369.

Chatman, E. A. (1991). Life in a small world: Applicability of gratification theory to information-seeking behavior. *JASIS, 42*(6), 438–449.

Chatman, E. A. (1992). *The information world of retired women.* Westport, CT: Greenwood Press.

Chatman, E. A. (1996). The impoverished life-world of outsiders. *JASIS, 47*(3), 193–206.

Chatman, E. A. (1999). A theory of life in the round. *JASIS, 50*(3), 207–217.

Choo, C. W., & Auster, E. (1991). Environmental scanning: Acquisition and use of information by managers. *Annual Review of Information Science and Technology, 28*, 279–314.

Cogburn, D. L. (2004). Elite decision making and epistemic communities: Implications for global information policy. In: S. Braman (Ed.), *The Emergent Global Information Policy Regime.* New York: Palgrave Macmillan.

Cole, C., & Kuhlthau, C. (2000). Information and information seeking of novice expert lawyers: How experts add value. *The New Review of Information Behavior Research*, *1*(December), 103–115.

Di Maggio, P., & Hargittai, E. (2001). From the 'digital divide' to 'digital inequality': Studying internet use as penetration increases. Available at http://www.webuse.umd.edu/webshop/resources/Dimaggio_Digital_Divide.pdf. Retrieved on May 31, 2006.

Dimitrov, R. S. (2003). Knowledge, power, and interests in environmental regime formation. *International Studies Quarterly*, *47*(1), 123–150.

Drucker, P. F. (1995). The information executives truly need. *Harvard Business Review*, *73*(1), 54–62.

Ellis, D., Allen, D., & Wilson, T. (1999). Information science and information systems: Conjunct subjects disjunct disciplines. *Journal of the American Society for Information Science*, *50*(12), 1095–1107.

Floridi, L. (2000). Information ethics: An environmental approach to the digital divide. *Philosophy in the Contemporary World*, *9*(1), 39–45. Available at http://www.wolfson.ox.ac.uk/~floridi/pdf/ieead. Retrieved on June 23, 2006.

Frohmann, B. (1994). Communication technologies and the politics of postmodern information-science. *Canadian Journal of Information and Library Science*, *19*(2), 1–22.

GEF. (2005). Strengthening Romania's protected area system by demonstrating government-NGO partnership in Romania's Maramures Park. Available at www.gefweb.org/Documents/Medium-Sized_Project_Proposals/MSP_Proposals /*Romania*_-_Maramure_Nature_*Park*.pdf. Retrieved on December 5, 2005.

Ginman, M. (1988). Information culture and business performance. *IATUL Quarterly: A Journal of Library Management and Technology*, *2*(2), 93–106.

Gorman, P. N. (1995). Information needs of physicians. *Journal of the American Society for Information Science*, *46*(10), 729–736.

Grefsheim, S. F., Franklin, J., & Cunningham, D. J. (1991). Biotechnology awareness study, Part 1: Where scientists get their information. *Bulletin of the Medical Library Association*, *79*(January), 36–44.

Guzelova, I., & Wright, R. (2000). Cyanide spill is felt on Danube: Romanian toxic incident, dead fish found as far south as Belgrade suburb. *Financial Times* (London edition), p. 10. Retrieved on December 21, 2005, from Lexis-Nexis Academic.

Hall, D. (2000). Tourism as sustainable development? The Albanian experience of 'transition'. *International Journal of Tourism Research*, *2*(4), 31–46.

Hall, D. (2004). Rural tourism development in Southeastern Europe: Transition and the search for sustainability. *International Journal of Tourism Research*, *6*(3), 165–176.

Hall, S. (1982). The rediscovery of ideology: Return of the repressed in media studies. In: M. Gurevitch, T. Bennett, J. Curran & J. Woollacott (Eds), *Culture, Society and the Media*. London: Methuen.

Harris, M. H. (1986). State, class, and cultural reproduction: Toward a theory of library service in the United States. In: W. Simonton (Ed.), *Advances in librarianship*, (Vol. 14, pp. 211–252).

Haruna, I., & Mabawonku, I. (2001). Information needs and seeking behaviour of legal practitioners and the challenges to law libraries in Lagos, Nigeria. *International Information and Library Review*, *33*(1), 69–87.

Haug, J. D. (1997). Physicians' preferences for information sources: A meta-analytic study. *Bulletin of the Medical Library Association*, *85*(3), 223–232.

Herman, E. (2004). Research in progress: some preliminary and key insights into the information needs of the contemporary academic researcher, Part 1. *Aslib Proceedings, 56*(1), 34–47.

Herzfeld, M. (2000). Uncanny success: Some closing remarks. In: J. de Pina-Cabral & A. P. de Lima (Eds), *Elites: Choice, Leadership and Succession*. Oxford: Berg.

Katzer, J., & Fletcher, P. T. (1992). The information environment of managers. *Annual Review of Information Science and Technology, 27*, 227–263.

Kligman, G. (1998). *The politics of duplicity: Controlling reproduction in Ceausescu's Romania*. Berkeley: University of California Press.

Kogan, M. (2005). Modes of knowledge and patterns of power. *Higher Education, 49*(1–2), 9–30.

Kuhlthau, C. (1999). The role of experience in the information search process of an early career information worker: Perceptions of uncertainty, complexity, construction, and sources. *Journal of the American Society for Information Science, 50*(5), 399–412.

Kuhlthau, C., & Tama, S. (2001). Information search process of lawyers: A call for 'just for me' information. *Journal of Documentation, 57*, 25–43.

Leckie, G., Pettigrew, K. E., & Sylvain, C. (1996). Modeling the information seeking of professionals: A general model derived from research on engineers, health care professionals, and lawyers. *Library Quarterly, 66*(2), 161–193.

Lonsdale, D. J. (1999). Information power: Strategy, geopolitics, and the fifth dimension. *Journal of Strategic Studies, 22*(2–3).

Mackenzie, M. L. (2004). The cultural influences of information flow at work: Manager information behavior documented. *Proceedings of the 67th ASISandT Annual Meeting, 41*, 184–190.

MacMullen, W. J., Vaughan, K. T. L., & Moore, M. E. (2004). Planning bioinformatics education and information services in an academic health sciences library. *College & Research Libraries, 65*(4), 320–333.

Marshall, N., & Brady, T. (2001). Knowledge management and the politics of knowledge: Illustrations from complex products and systems. *European Journal of Information Systems, 10*(2), 99–112.

Mick, C. K., Lindsey, G. N., & Callahan, D. (1980). Toward usable user studies. *Journal of the American Society for Information Science, 31*(5), 347–356.

Monbiot, G. (2000). The dead zone: With its cyanide lakes, toxic dust and arsenic-ridden soil, Baia Mare is the most polluted place in Europe. *The Guardian, 2*, 19 May. Retrieved on December 21, 2005, from Lexis-Nexis Academic.

Mosco, V. (1982). *Push button fantasies: Critical perspectives on videotext and information technology*. Norwood, NJ: Ablex.

Muica, N., Roberts, L., & Turnock, D. (1998). Transformation of a border region: Dispersed agricultural communities in Brasov County, Romania. *GeoJournal, 46*(3), 305–317.

Muica, N., & Turnock, D. (2000). Maramures: Expanding human resources on the Romanian periphery. *GeoJournal, 50*(2–3), 181–198.

Nader, L. (1969). Up the anthropologist-perspectives gained from studying up. In: D. Hymes (Ed.), *Reinventing anthropology*. New York: Pantheon Books.

Norris, P. (2001). *Digital divide: Civic engagement, information poverty, and the internet worldwide*. New York: Cambridge University.

NGO.ro. (2004). *Calendar evenimente: Festivalul traditiilor locale si conservarea biodiversitatii*. Available at http://ngo.ro/events/indexro.shtml?AA_SL_Session = 538a0e1c6cc77 e50828f97862fbf8737andx = 18380. Retrieved on December 22, 2005.

Otike, J. (1999). The information needs and seeking habits of lawyers in England: A pilot study. *International Information and Library Review, 31*(1), 19–39.

Owen, D. J., & Fang, M. E. (2003). Information-seeking behavior in complementary and alternative medicine (CAM): An online survey of faculty at a health sciences campus. *Journal of the Medical Library Association, 91*(3), 311–321.

Pawley, C. (1998). Hegemony's handmaid? The library and information studies curriculum from a class perspective. *Library Quarterly, 68*(2), 123–135.

Ploaie, G., & Turnock, D. (2001). Public perception of environment in the mountains of Vâlcea County. *GeoJournal, 55*(2–4), 683–701.

Primăria Municipiului Baia Mare. (2005). *Societatea Ecologista din Maramureş.* Available at http://baiamarecity.ro/catalogong/en/64%20Soc%20Ecologista%20prez-eng.htm and in Romanian from http://baiamarecity.ro/catalogong/ro/64%20%20Soc%20Ecologista%20 prez.htm. Retrieved on December 20, 2005.

Purvis, A. (2001). Triangle of death: Three factories pollute a Romanian town, stunting the health and lives of its children. *Time Europe, 157*(14). Available at http://www.time.com/ time/europe/eu/magazine/0,13716,104678,00.html. Retrieved on December 21, 2005.

Quigley, B. D., Church, G. M., & Peterson, A. (2001). Defining the need for information technology instruction among science faculty. *Science and Technology Libraries, 20*(1), 5–42.

Rasmussen, S. J. (2000). Parallel and divergent landscapes: Cultural encounters in the ethnographic space of Tuareg medicine. *Medical Anthropology Quarterly, 14*(2), 242–270.

Rockart, J. F. (1979). Chief executives define their own data needs. *Harvard Business Review, 57*(2), 81–92.

Rockart, J. F. (1982). The changing role of the information systems executive: A critical success factors perspective. *Sloan Management Review (pre-1986), 24*(1), 3–13.

Rogerson, S. (2004). The virtual world: A tension between global reach and local sensitivity. *International Journal of Information Ethics (renamed International Review of Information Ethics), 2.* Available at http://www.i-r-i-e.net/inhalt/002/ijie_002_22_rogerson.pdf

Radhika, S., & Wiedenbeck, S. (1993). Neither novice nor expert: The discretionary user of software. *International Journal of Man-Machine Studies, 38*(2), 201–229.

Sennett, R., & Cobb, J. (1972). *The hidden injuries of class.* New York: Vintage Books.

Shore, C. (2002). Introduction: Towards an anthropology of the elites. In: C. Shore & S. Nugent (Eds), *Elite cultures: Anthropological perspectives.* London: Routledge. ASAS Monograph 38.

Smith, M. (2001). Global information justice: Rights, responsibilities, and caring connections. *Library Trends, 49*(3), 519–537. Retrieved on June 15, 2006, from Infotrac.

Societatea Ecologista din Maramureş. (2003). *Prezentarea Societatii Ecologiste din Maramureş: ONG,* August. Available at http://www.arhimedes.ro/ecologymm/profile.htm. Retrieved on December 20, 2005.

Spies, M., Clayton, A. J., & Noormohammadian, M. (2005). Knowledge management in a decentralized global financial services provider: A case study with Allianz Group. *Knowledge Management Research and Practice, 3,* 24–36.

Stehr, N. (2003). The social and political control of knowledge in modern societies. *International Social Science Journal, 55*(178), 643–655.

Sturges, P. (1998). The political economy of information: Malawi under Kamuzu Banda, 1964–94. *International Information and Library Review, 30,* 185–201.

Sutton, S. A. (1994). The role of attorney mental models of law in case relevance determinations: An exploratory analysis. *JASIS, 45*(3), 186–200.

Turda, M. (2007a). The nation as object: Race, blood and biopolitics in Interwar Romania. *Slavic Review*, *66*(3), 413–441.

Turda, M. (2007b). From craniology to serology: Racial anthropology in interwar Hungary and Romania. *Journal of the History of Behavior Sciences*, *43*(3), 361–377.

Turnock, D. (2002). Prospects for sustainable rural cultural tourism in Maramureş, Romania. *Tourism Geographies*, *4*(1), 62–94.

UNEP. (2003). *Tourism and Local Agenda 21: The role of local authorities in sustainable tourism.* Available at http://www.uneptie.org/pc/tourism/library/local-agenda21.htm. Retrieved on October 15, 2006.

van den Hoven, J. (1995). Equal access and social justice: Information as a primary good. In: International Conference on the Ethical Issues of Using Information Technology (Eds.), *Proceedings of ETHICOMP 1995*. Leicester, UK: De Montfort University. Abstract available at http://www.ccsr.cse.dmu.ac.uk/conferences/ethicomp/ethicomp95/abstracts/vandenHoven.html

van der Linde, G. (1990). Knowledge, power and the academic library in postmodern society. *South African Journal of Library and Information Science*, *58*(September), 249–254.

Walder, A. G. (2003). Elite opportunity in transitional economies. *American Sociological Review*, *6*, 899–916.

Wales, T. (2000). Practice makes perfect? Vets' information seeking behaviour and information use explored. *Aslib Proceedings*, *52*(7), 235–246.

Warschauer, M. (2003). Dissecting the "digital Divide": A case study in Egypt. *The Information Society*, *19*(4), 297–304.

Wessel, C. B., Tannery, N. H., & Epstein, B. A. (2006). Information-seeking behaviour and use of information resources by clinical research coordinators. *Journal of the Medical Library Association*, *94*(1), 48–54.

Whipple, M., & Nyce, J. (2007). Community analysis needs ethnography: An example from Romania. *Library Review*, *56*(8), 694–706.

Wilkinson, M. (2001). Information sources used by lawyers in problem solving: An empirical exploration. *Library and Information Science Research*, *23*, 257–276.

Wolek, F. W. (1984). Managers and the distribution of scientific and technical information. *R and D Management*, *14*(4), 225–228.

Wolek, F. W. (1986). Managerial support and the use of information services. *Journal of the American Society for Information Science*, *37*(3), 153–157.

Zach, L. (2005). When is "enough" enough? Modeling the information-seeking and stopping behavior of senior arts administrators. *Journal of the American Society for Information Science*, *56*(1), 23–35.

ABOUT THE AUTHORS

Hermina G.B. Anghelescu is associate professor in the School of Library and Information Science, Wayne State University. She is also chair of the IFLA Library History Section and member of the editorial board of several professional journals. She earned her MA in Foreign Languages and Literatures from the University of Bucharest (Romania) and her MLIS and PhD from the School of Library and Information Science, University of Texas at Austin.

Aleksei S. Asvaturov has been head of the Department of Nationality Literatures (non-Slavic literatures) of the Russian National Library since 1998. Formerly, he is a research fellow in the Russian National Library and he is a graduate of the former Leningrad State University (now St. Petersburg State University). His research and professional interest is the preservation of the cultural heritages (especially, epistolary heritages) of religious, linguistic and cultural minorities of the former USSR.

Svetlana Breca is director of the Information Resource Center and Web Master at the US Embassy in Pristina, Kosovo. She received her BA in English Language and Literature from the Philological Faculty, University of Pristina and her MEd from Graduate Division of Educational Research, Faculty of Education, University of Calgary, Canada. Her experience includes research in response to complex reference requests about US culture, history and society, supervising English Language Programs and Library Programs throughout Kosovo and training Kosovo librarians in the use of online database EBSCO, use of HTML, website editors such as Dreamweaver, and Adobe PhotoShop for web design and photo editing.

Catherine Closet-Crane is a doctoral candidate at the School of Library and Information Management at Emporia State University. She comes to LIS having received international academic training in urbanism, architecture, and art history and has professional experience in the practice and teaching of architecture. Her research interests include the investigation of everyday information practices and behavior and the critical study of the library as place from the perspectives of environmental design and human behavior.

Susan Dopp is a doctoral student at the School of Library and Information Management, Emporia (Kansas) State University. Her research interests include information and knowledge processes in natural resource policy and services and public and private organizational partnerships.

Miroslaw Gorny is head of the Department of Information Systems and professor at the Institute of Linguistics, Adam Mickiewicz University of Poznan. He is also Vice-President of the Board for the Poznan Foundation of Scientific Libraries. His current research interests are information infrastructures in science, organization, technology and functions of information systems. He is cofounder of the first Polish digital library – Digital Library of Wielkopolska.

Maria Haigh is assistant professor at the School of Information Studies, University of Wisconsin-Milwaukee. She is a graduate of National Shevchenko University in Kyiv in applied mathematics and computer science and holds an MS in Information Science and a PhD in Information Systems from Drexel University. She researches information practices, policies and institutions in the former Soviet Bloc, and has published several articles exploring the social construction of Ukrainian libraries and library education and their co-evolution with Ukrainian national identity. In Spring 2007, she received a Fulbright award to spend six months teaching and conducting research in Ukraine.

Stanley Kalkus received his education in Library Studies at the University of Chicago. Following a long professional career, he retired as Librarian of the US Navy in 1992 and then accepted a teaching position in the Institute of Information Studies and Librarianship, School of Philosophy, Charles University, Prague. Since 1995, he has served as a member of the Committee for the Parliamentary Library of the Czech Republic. He has also served as a national representative for the Czech Republic to the SLA Europe Special Libraries Association.

Ellen M. Knutson is an associate of the Charles F. Kettering Foundation. She facilitates a workshop series for faculty wishing to incorporate civic engagement into their teaching and research. She received her PhD in Library and Information Science from University of Illinois at Urbana-Champaign.

Dmitry K. Ravinskiy is senior research fellow at the Russian National Library. He is a PhD in Pedagogical Sciences and is the author of more than 150 publications dealing with librarianship, sociology of the reader and the culture of Petersburg.

James Lukenbill is manager of Information Systems, Ingenix, Austin Office, Austin, Texas. He holds BA, MA and PhD degrees from the University of Texas at Austin. His career and research interests include health management systems.

W. Bernard Lukenbill is professor in the School of Information, University of Texas at Austin. He holds a BA from North Texas State University, MLS from University of Oklahoma and PhD from Indiana University. His research interests center on children and adolescent literature and media, communication theory, sociology of information and media-center administration and management.

Tatiana Nikolova-Houston earned a PhD in Information Studies from the University of Texas at Austin in 2008. She publishes prolifically about the digitization of Byzantine and Slavic medieval manuscripts and issues of preservation and access. Since 2001, she has been a consultant to different Bulgarian manuscript collections about assessment, preservation, cataloging and Web publishing. She collaborates with Bulgarian scholars from the fields of library and information science, Slavic history and Slavic linguistics and literature, pursuing her dream of uniting library communities of West and East through the electronic reunification of national patrimonies.

James M. Nyce is a cultural anthropologist at Ball State University and studies how information technologies emerge and are used in workplaces and organizations. He is a docent at Linkoping University, Sweden, and he is adjunct associate professor in the Department of Health and Environment, Faculty of Health Sciences. He is as well adjunct associate professor in the Department of Radiology, Indiana University School of Medicine, Indianapolis. Nyce has been visiting professor in Military Technology and War Science at the National Defence College, Stockholm, from 1998–2000 and 2005 to the present. He is also a visiting professor in Lund University's Master's Programme in Human Factors and System Safety and Lund University's Leonardo da Vinci Center for Complexity and Systems Thinking. He has edited three books and published more than 100 papers on culture, information/knowledge and technology.

Irene Owens is dean and professor, School of Library and Information Sciences at North Carolina Central University, the only Library and Information Sciences program in a Historically Black College or University (HBCU). She is the recipient of several awards, including the North Carolina Library Association REMCO Award for Library Education (2007), the Distinguished Alumni Award from the University of North

Carolina at Chapel Hill (2006), the Texas Excellence in Teaching Award (2000), and the Outstanding Service Award, Howard University (1987).

Mark Skogen is regional director of the USAID-funded, IREX administered, Internet Access and Training Program for Eurasia, having previously managed the Internet Access and Training Program in Central Asia and the Global Connections Program in Uzbekistan and Turkmenistan. He has been closely involved in efforts to bring ICT to communities throughout Eurasia, beginning with his work in a community center in a small, poor town in Kazakhstan as a US Peace Corps Volunteer in 2000. He also serves as a consultant and training specialist for the Bill and Melinda Gates Global Libraries Program in Romania, the Young Women's Leadership Program in Egypt, and the Iraq-based Building Bridges through Technology Program. He is a graduate of the University of Wisconsin-Madison with degrees in International Business and Marketing.

Myles G. Smith is regional director of the USAID-funded, IREX administered, Internet Access and Training Program for Eurasia and Program Manager of the US Department of State-funded, IREX administered, Supporting Technology in Education Program in Turkmenistan. He has been based at Ashgabat, Turkmenistan since 2007. He has written for several publications on education, international and security affairs. He received a BA in International Relations and Economics from Boston University in 2004.

Jacqueline Solis is humanities reference and instruction librarian at the University of North Carolina at Chapel Hill, having previously been outreach librarian at California State University, Northridge. Her research interests include information use and information literacy among undergraduate and graduate students, and information transfer and information policy in developing countries.

Zsuzsanna Toszegi is assistant professor at the University of Kaposvar and senior professional advisor to the President of the Hungarian Patent Office. Formerly, she was managing director of the John von Neumann Digital Library and Multimedia Centre (1997–2003), head of the National Database of Foreign Serials at the Hungarian National Széchényi Library (1987–1997), and director of the Library of the University of Applied Arts (1981–1987). She has published approximately 150 scientific papers and has received several prizes and awards.

AUTHOR INDEX

243